The Second Brain for Families

The Second Brain for Families

Organize Knowledge, Memories, and Plans

Arian Velkor

Mindful Pages

Published in 2026

ISBN: 9789376551866 (PB)
ISBN: 9789376552429 (eBook)

Publishcd by

Mindful Pages
Imprint of Alpha Editions LLC
312 W. 2nd St #1834
Casper, WY 82601, USA

Content

Introduction

In August 2005, in New Orleans, the air in a community centre off the higher ground carried a faint, sour smell of mould and damp timber. People queued with clear plastic folders, their papers softened at the edges, ink bled into pale halos. The Federal Emergency Management Agency was there, and so were volunteers with clipboards, trying to turn stories into forms and forms into help. Someone's birth certificate had survived; someone else had only a photograph of a passport, saved on a phone that now would not charge. A folding table in the corner had become a kind of household altar: receipts, medication lists, insurance numbers, a scribbled phone tree—everything that still proved a life had existed in the precise way bureaucracy requires. The kettle clicks off. Memory is a terrible filing system. In a crisis, the difference between "somewhere" and "here" is not philosophical; it is measured in hours, in calls returned, in whether a tired parent can answer a simple question without guessing.

Most families will never face floodwater in their living room, and yet the same basic physics governs the ordinary home: information falls, and it pools. It accumulates where friction is lowest and attention is thinnest—on a kitchen table, inside an inbox, at the bottom of a chat thread whose search function is optimistically called "search". Paper joins paper, screenshots join screenshots, and a household develops what looks like storage but behaves like sediment. No one intends this. No one wakes with the ambition to create a private museum of half-decisions. And yet, by the end of the week, important things are once again orbiting the same surfaces, pulled into the same gravity well.

The modern family's problem is not a lack of care. It is not even a lack of effort. It is a mismatch between the volume of incoming information and the capacity of human minds living under real constraints: tiredness, distraction, competing roles, different standards, different tolerances for mess. A child brings home a letter about swimming; a school portal posts a deadline; a grandparent texts a change of plan; an employer shifts a meeting; a prescription label needs repeating; a boiler service date arrives and vanishes. Each item, on its own, is small. Together they form a system of obligations that is invisible until it fails—until the morning goes wrong because a form cannot be found, until someone hears "I told you" and knows, with a cold certainty, that they did and that it did not matter.

A family is not a company, and it should not be managed like one. It is, however, a small civilisation: it runs on shared knowledge, shared plans, and shared memory. When those are scattered, the cost is paid in micro-frictions that add up to something more serious. You can measure it in the number of repeated questions—What time is pick-up? Which day is PE? Where is the login?—and in the gentle erosion of goodwill when one person becomes the default keeper of facts. You can hear it in the tone that appears when someone is asked, again, to locate a document that ought to have a home. You can see it in the habit of postponing decisions because gathering the relevant information feels like a chore in itself. What looks like forgetfulness is often search failure. What looks like laziness is often ambiguity.

The household "second brain" is a response to that structural mismatch: a trusted, shared, searchable home for what a family needs to know, remember, and carry forward. It is not the same as a calendar, which tells you when things happen but not what they mean. It is not the same as a group chat, which is excellent at chatter and terrible at retrieval. It is not the same as a photo gallery, which stores images while quietly discarding context. A second brain is closer to a family's collective memory and working notebook combined: the place where reference lives, where plans evolve without being endlessly re-made, where the right detail can be found without a dramatic performance of recall.

Consider how often families "re-decide" because their earlier decision cannot be reliably recovered. The child's packed lunch plan is agreed on Monday, forgotten by Wednesday. The rule about screen time is negotiated, then renegotiated, because no one can remember the edge cases and exceptions without arguing them afresh. A holiday is discussed in fragments across weeks, in car rides and hurried messages, until booking becomes a last-minute scramble. Each re-decision is a tax on attention. More subtly, it is a tax on trust: when decisions evaporate, promises begin to look optional, and people start to hedge, to keep contingency plans, to carry private reminders in their heads. The second brain is not about becoming impressively organised; it is about stabilising meaning. It gives decisions somewhere to live so they stop haunting the household as unfinished business.

A useful way to see the problem is to watch what happens when information arrives. In many homes, the arrival point is the same as the storage point. A school letter lands on the table and stays there because it is already "in the house", as if proximity were the same as accessibility. An email arrives and remains in a personal inbox because forwarding it feels like work, and because the sender has labelled it "important" with no additional structure. A message in a parents' chat contains a vital date, and everyone assumes they will remember it, until the day before when the same question appears twelve times: what time are we meeting? Show: the scrolling, the frantic thumb, the screen glare in a dim kitchen. Name: leakage. Explain: information leaks when its container is designed for conversation, not memory. Implication: families waste energy retrieving what they already received.

There is a second, more uncomfortable phenomenon: the silent designation of a "memory parent". The role is not always held by a parent, and it is not always consciously assigned, but most households know it. It is the person who can tell you the paediatrician's name, the Wi-Fi password, the deadline for the trip deposit, the shoe size, the friend's address, the allergy, the name of the teacher who must be emailed, the difference between the two nearly identical school logins. When that person is well and calm, the system can appear functional. It is a counter-example worth respecting: some families do have a single steward of information, and the household runs smoothly, at least on the surface. Still, the apparent efficiency hides fragility. If the steward is ill, travelling, overwhelmed, or simply not in the room, the family's capacity collapses into improvisation. The role also carries an emotional cost: being the one who remembers makes it hard to relax, because relaxation requires trusting that nothing urgent is being forgotten. The second brain does not eliminate responsibility, but it redistributes cognition. It turns private stress into shared clarity.

There is an ethical dimension to this redistribution. Organisation is often framed as a personal virtue, as if the organised person is morally superior to the messy one. In family life, that framing is not merely wrong; it is corrosive. When one person's habits become the household standard, every deviation is treated as negligence, and the system turns into a quiet battleground of shame and defensiveness. A shared second brain reframes the task as a form of care. It says: the point is not to prove competence; the point is to make life easier for the people you love, including your future self on a tired Wednesday. It is a kindness that happens in advance, when there is time to be deliberate.

The past few years have made the stakes of shared systems unusually visible. In March 2020, across the United Kingdom, schools closed to most pupils and the home became a classroom, an office, a canteen, and a counselling room at once. Families received instructions through email, portals, text messages, and hastily assembled websites; passwords proliferated; routines dissolved; "normal" shifted by the week. The point here is not to litigate policy, but to observe the informational consequence: households were forced to manage complex, changing guidance without the usual scaffolding of predictable school rhythms. Show: a parent at a laptop after bedtime, refreshing a page for updated timetables, copying a link into a message, then losing it in replies. Name: synchronisation strain. Explain: when external systems change rapidly, families need a stable internal place where decisions and references can be gathered and updated. Implication: without that place, each change becomes a fresh emergency.

A shared vault—call it that if the metaphor is helpful—is the simplest description of what the family second brain needs to be: one home for each item, designed for finding, not for impressing. It is not glamorous. It does not require perfect discipline. It requires something more achievable and more human: low friction, predictable habits, and enough structure that the household can trust it. Trust is not a feeling; it is behaviour. A family trusts a system when they stop asking, "Did you save that?" and start saying, "It'll be in the vault." Efficiency is not a buzzword; it is the quiet absence of repeated searching. Risk is not an abstract; it is whether, in a stressful moment, the right phone number can be surfaced in ten seconds.

This is why the system must be shared. A private set of notes maintained by one person is better than chaos, but it is still a single point of failure. A shared system changes the social shape of the household. Children learn, gradually, that questions have homes. Partners stop treating organisation as a personality trait and start treating it as a communal tool. Carers, grandparents, and trusted adults can be brought in thoughtfully, with boundaries, so help is possible without endless explanations. And because life is not only deadlines and documents, the same shared place can hold what makes a family feel like itself: the photograph that matters because it has a story attached, the voice note of a child describing a day they will later forget, the tiny tradition recorded so it can be repeated.

None of this should slide into technological evangelism. Digital tools can be fickle; companies change terms; devices break; logins get lost. There are families for whom the simplest answer is a paper binder and a magnetic whiteboard, and there are families for whom a digital vault is still the best choice because the household is already mediated through screens. There are also households where sharing has to be handled with particular care because privacy is not a nice-to-have; it is a boundary that protects dignity and autonomy. And yet, even with those caveats, the direction of travel is clear: the informational burden on families is not shrinking, and improvisation does not scale.

What makes a second brain viable is not the tool; it is the shape of attention it creates. It begins with capture: the tiny moment when a piece of information arrives and is given a home before it can vanish into the gravity well. That moment is where most systems fail because it feels like an extra step at the exact time the household is busiest. The paradox is that a few seconds of capture often saves an hour of hunting later, but the saving is invisible until the crisis arrives. A child's swimming letter is a perfect example—innocent, easily crumpled, essential on precisely the day it is missing. When capture becomes habitual, the vault starts to mirror reality rather than aspiration. It stops being a project and becomes an environment.

From there, structure needs to be modest, not ornate. Families do not need elaborate folder trees that look tidy but are impossible to remember. They need labels that match how they actually think: people, places, recurring themes, and the small time markers that turn vague intentions into something findable. Tags are powerful here because family life is multi-context by nature. A camp form belongs to a child, a term, an activity, and a health note all at once. Forcing it into a single folder is an argument disguised as filing. Tagging is a quiet agreement: we are allowed to see the same thing through different lenses, without duplication and without debate.

Templates and checklists are the next turn of the screw, and they are where calm becomes repeatable. A template is not bureaucracy; it is compassion for the future. If every trip begins with the same chaos—documents, packing, money, chargers, permissions—then the household is effectively choosing to re-live that chaos in exchange for the illusion of spontaneity. A short checklist before leaving the house is not infantilising; it is how aircraft leave the ground safely, not because pilots are forgetful, but because humans are human. The aim is not to automate family life into joyless procedure; it is to reserve attention for what deserves it, rather than spending it on the same preventable omissions.

The second brain becomes genuinely life-supporting in domains where stress amplifies the cost of missing information. School is one: a world of timetables, term dates, policies, portals, and shifting expectations, all of which arrive through multiple channels and assume immediate comprehension. Health is another: not in the sense of giving medical guidance, but in the sense of ensuring that the factual details a family already possesses—medications, allergies, appointment notes, key contacts—are reachable when anxiety makes thinking harder. In those moments, organisation is not aesthetic. It is relief. It turns the question "What did the doctor say last time?" from a memory test into a simple search.

Then there are the projects that quietly colonise family life: the holiday, the room that needs sorting, the new school application, the move, the purchase that requires research, the recurring event that always arrives sooner than expected. These are not chores; they are sequences with stages, dependencies, and decisions. When they live only in conversation, they create a low-grade feeling of unfinishedness, and the household becomes a place where everything is half-started. A simple visual board can change that not by making people work harder, but by making work visible. It reduces the need for status conversations that feel like nagging because everyone can see what "next" means.

Children can participate without being managed; adults can stop holding the whole plan in their heads.

And then there is memory, the part that makes organisation worth doing beyond mere survival. Families drown in photos precisely because the camera is always present and deletion feels like betrayal. The result is a hoard of images that no one revisits, a digital attic that is both too full and oddly empty because it lacks story. The second brain treats memory differently. It respects that not everything should be kept, and it also respects that what is kept should be findable, meaningful, and contextual. A single photograph with a sentence attached can outlast a thousand near-identical frames. A child's own words, captured casually, can become priceless. The question is not "How much can we store?" but "What do we want to remember, and why?"

A shared system only becomes shared when it is revisited. The weekly sync is not a corporate meeting in miniature; it is the household's way of keeping promises to itself. Without review, even the best vault becomes a graveyard of good intentions. With review, it becomes a living map that can be corrected gently, without blame, because the family is looking at the system together rather than accusing one another from inside it. Still, there is uncertainty here. Some weeks will be messy. Some seasons of life—new babies, exams, illness, bereavement—will make any system feel like too much. The measure of a second brain is not how it performs in an ideal week; it is how quickly it can be rebuilt after it collapses.

Resilience matters because digital life is not inherently durable. Accounts get locked. Devices are lost. Platforms change. A family's shared knowledge should not be hostage to a single app or a single person's password manager. There are pragmatic ways to make a vault sturdier without turning someone into an unpaid IT department: simple backup habits, clear permissions, and an honest approach to boundaries as children grow. Privacy is not a technical setting; it is a family agreement. A well-designed second brain can hold parents-only material, children's spaces, and shared reference without inviting surveillance or eroding trust. The goal is not transparency at any cost. The goal is clarity where it serves care.

The most interesting tension, once all the practicalities are acknowledged, is philosophical. A family second brain asks a quiet question about what it means to live well together: how much should be held in individual minds, and how much should be placed into a shared world that anyone can consult? Too much externalisation can feel sterile, as if love has been replaced by procedure. Too little externalisation turns love into strain, as if devotion must be proved by constant remembering. The sweet spot is different for each household, but the trade-off is universal. People do not resent each other because a system exists; they resent each other because a system does not, and the missing structure becomes a person's problem.

So the real decision is not whether to become "organised", whatever that caricature means. It is whether the home will continue to rely on heroic remembering—on the invisible labour of holding everything together inside one or two skulls—or whether it will build a shared place sturdy enough to carry the ordinary weight of modern life. The kitchen table will always exist, and things will always land there. The question is whether the table remains the gravity well, swallowing vital details into piles, or whether it becomes a mere transit point—an arrival surface on the way to a home that can be trusted.

A diagnostic question sits beneath all the tools and habits: when something matters, where does it go, and who can find it when the person who first received it is not available? The answer exposes a household's hidden architecture. It also suggests the possibility of changing it, not in pursuit of perfection, but in pursuit of a particular kind of calm: the calm that comes from knowing that what the family knows is not scattered across devices, drawers, and exhausted memories, but gathered, named, and within reach.

Chapter 1
Why Families Need Shared Systems

At 7:18 on a wet Wednesday, the kitchen becomes a small theatre of compressed time. A shoe is missing. A water bottle is half-full but somehow not clean. Someone is asking for a snack that must not be eaten before the snack that is apparently more appropriate. A phone vibrates with a message that begins, ominously, "Just a reminder..." and ends with a deadline that would have been harmless yesterday. Paper rustles. A printer refuses to cooperate with an error message as smug as it is unhelpful. In the background, a kettle rattles towards boiling, and the smell of toast—comforting, almost mocking—hangs in the air while a parent tries to remember where the form went. It was here. Everyone saw it. It has vanished with the peculiar talent that important documents possess: to be present until the moment they are needed.

This is not melodrama. It is the daily mathematics of family life, where small delays multiply into missed buses, strained voices, and apologies typed one-handed on a train. The paradox is that the family home is full of memory and yet routinely behaves as if it has none. Names of teachers, portal logins, appointment details, consent forms, packing lists, birthday plans, shoe sizes, medication instructions: all of it is known, somewhere, by someone, at some point. And still, the household acts as if it must re-learn itself every week. It is not that people forget. It is that knowledge is not living in a place where it can be found.

The modern family is surrounded by storage—phones, clouds, inboxes, chat histories—and still experiences scarcity: not of information, but of clarity. Clarity is a different substance. It is information that has been given a home, named, and made retrievable by the people who will actually need it. Without that, the household becomes a place where decisions are continuously remade from fragments: the same conversations repeated in different tones, the same searches performed at different times, the same "I thought you had it" said with different shades of disbelief. A family can survive like this for years. Many do. But it costs more than it seems.

A second brain, in family terms, is simply a shared place that remembers so the people do not have to. That definition is deliberately plain because the idea is not clever; it is practical. It is not a promise of a perfectly ordered life or a claim that domestic chaos can be engineered away. It is an answer to a specific problem: family life generates more information than any individual can carry reliably, and it generates it in too many places for informal memory to cope. The second brain does not compete with human memory. It supports it. It turns the household from a set of private brains attempting heroic recall into a small, collaborative system that can hold reference, decisions, and plans without constantly re-deciding.

It helps to be precise about what this is not. A calendar tells a family when something happens; it is an excellent instrument for time and a poor instrument for context. It rarely holds the "why" of an appointment, the documents that go with it, the message thread that changed it, the packing list that makes it workable, the phone number needed on the day. A group chat, meanwhile, is magnificent at immediacy and dreadful at memory. It is the place where meaning is created—and then buried. The information is technically still there, somewhere in the scroll, but it has been submerged beneath jokes, reactions, corrections, and unrelated updates. The effect is familiar: someone asks a question that was answered three days earlier, and the response contains a hint of irritation, as if asking were a moral failing. In reality, it is a structural mismatch. Conversation is not an archive.

A family second brain sits in the gap between those tools. It holds reference information—things that remain true for a while and need to be looked up—and it holds evolving plans—things that change, require decisions, and benefit from being tracked in one place. It is where the portal login lives, not because logins are spiritually important, but because the penalty for not finding them is disproportionate. It is where the school trip details are gathered, not because families enjoy documenting, but because the alternative is a frantic morning search and a child arriving without what they need. It is where "How we do mornings" can exist as a shared agreement rather than a recurring argument. It is, in other words, a household's memory made deliberate.

The difference becomes obvious in a small, mundane example. Imagine a family planning a weekend away. Someone has found a cottage link, someone else has checked the dates, someone has asked about the dog, someone has mentioned that the child's swimming lesson must be cancelled, and someone has said, "We'll sort it later." Over a few days, the plan exists as a cloud of half-remembered fragments scattered across a browser history, a text thread, an email confirmation, and a mental note that the car insurance needs checking. Then, on the day before departure, the family enters what looks like a flurry of productivity but is actually a re-creation of the plan: re-finding the booking, re-reading the address, re-checking what time check-in starts, re-deciding who packs what, re-searching for the cancellation policy. The household is busy, but it is not moving forward; it is spinning, converting time into rediscovery. When the same family has a shared second brain, the weekend away becomes something else: a single page or note where the booking lives, the address is pinned, the packing list exists, and the decisions are visible. The effort shifts from re-deciding to doing.

That shift matters because family life today is not merely busy. It is informationally saturated. The home used to be flooded primarily by objects: bags, shoes, letters, groceries, laundry. Those still arrive, of course, and they still create their own famous chaos. But now there is an additional flood that weighs nothing and still exhausts: notifications, app updates, portal messages, photos, and the persistent requirement to remember which channel holds which truth. A school might send reminders through an app, but forms through email and urgent changes through a text message. A club might post timetables in a private group, but invoice through a link. A healthcare appointment might be booked in one system and confirmed in another. A family can be diligent and still miss something simply because the information did not appear in the place the family expected it to.

The result is a particular kind of fatigue: the fatigue of carrying too many small obligations. It shows up in repeated questions because the household cannot afford to remember everything. It shows up in missed deadlines because each deadline is not a single date but a chain of actions: log in, find the form, sign the permission, pay the fee, pack the kit. It shows up in the simmering resentment that appears when one person is implicitly expected to be the human search engine for the family's life. "Just ask them," the household says—meaning one specific them—and that person becomes the point where scattered information is temporarily reconciled into an answer. This is not a character flaw. It is an architecture problem.

The lost-form morning illustrates it cleanly. The letter is given to a parent at pick-up. It is glanced at in the car. It is placed somewhere safe. That is the first lie of domestic life: "somewhere safe" is a location without coordinates. By the time the signature is needed, the household has moved. Bags have been unpacked. Other papers have arrived. A well-meaning child has "tidied". The letter, now vital, cannot be found, and its absence triggers a cascade: a rushed search, a sharp exchange, a message to a teacher, an apology, a plan to print a replacement, a late departure. The household pays not only in minutes but in atmosphere. Show: the scramble and the raised voice. Name: retrieval failure. Explain: information placed without a retrieval path becomes effectively lost.

Implication: the home becomes reactive, and reactivity breeds friction.

What makes this particularly insidious is that families interpret the symptoms as personal. The forgetful one is blamed for forgetting. The disorganised one is teased or scolded for mess. The anxious one is criticised for "making a big deal". The conscientious one is told to relax. Yet the deeper truth is that individual memory was never built to handle what modern households ask of it. Human memory is associative and emotional; it is excellent at stories and faces and patterns. It is mediocre at arbitrary details like "Tuesday is PE" and "the password has an exclamation mark". It is worse when stressed, and family life is a reliable stress generator. When the household treats memory as a moral test, it produces shame. When it treats memory as a limited resource to be supported, it produces systems.

Shared systems are not about imposing control. They are about reducing avoidable pain. Organisation, at its best, is not a domestic performance staged for visitors. It is a shared kindness extended across time. It says: we will not make tomorrow's version of ourselves suffer for today's inattention. It says: we will make it easier for one another to do what we already mean to do. It also says, quietly: we will stop pretending that love requires constant remembering. Love is not diminished when it is supported by structure. It is often freed.

The benefits of shared clarity are immediate, but they also deepen. At the surface, the household experiences fewer emergencies—fewer last-minute dashes for forgotten items, fewer frantic searches, fewer "I didn't know" moments that trigger a defensive spiral. Reliability improves: when decisions are recorded, follow-through becomes less dependent on mood and memory. Over time, children learn something subtle and empowering: that information can be found. Instead of asking by default, they can look. That is not a cold form of independence; it is confidence. It teaches a child that the household is navigable, that they can orient themselves, that adult life is not merely a series of mysteries solved by grown-ups behind closed doors.

A calm pre-trip check is a good example because travel distils family dynamics. The frantic version is familiar: the night before, bags open on the floor, chargers hunted, passports questioned, bookings rechecked, medicines counted, and someone saying "I thought you packed that" with a tight voice. It is exhausting because it compresses many decisions into a short window, and it feels like failure because the chaos arrives precisely when the family wants to begin with excitement. The calmer version does not require a saintly household. It requires that the trip has had a home for weeks: a shared place where the booking confirmation sits, where the packing list is already built, where the child's swim cancellation has been noted, where the pet arrangements are clear. The family still packs, still forgets something small, still improvises. But the texture changes. The kettle clicks off, and the kitchen is not a crime scene of paper. It is just a kitchen.

There is a deeper payoff, too: fewer arguments about reality. Families fight about facts more than they realise. Did the school say it was Friday? Did we agree on 7 p.m.? Was the deadline moved? Was the payment made? When information is scattered, each person's recollection becomes a competing narrative, and the household burns energy adjudicating truth. A shared system does not eliminate disagreement, but it gives the family a common reference point. It turns "I remember it this way" into "Let's check." That small shift is civilisational. It replaces rhetorical combat with verification, and it gives everyone permission to be wrong without losing face.

Still, it is essential to resist fantasy. Shared systems do not remove all chaos, and the attempt to make them do so is a common reason they fail. A family is not a controlled environment. Children grow, schedules change, energy fluctuates, unexpected illnesses arrive, and entire seasons can be swallowed by events no system can tame. The point of a second brain is not to sterilise family life into a series of checkboxes. The point is to reduce preventable chaos so that the inevitable chaos is easier to carry. There is also a myth that good systems require perfect discipline, as if one missed day means the whole thing collapses. In practice, the most durable family systems are forgiving. They are built to survive lapses. They assume that some weeks will be messy and that the system must be easy to return to without shame.

Another myth is that the right app will solve the problem. Tools matter, but not in the way marketing suggests. The best tool is the one a tired adult will actually use at 10:45 p.m. and a child can navigate without asking. The danger of tool obsession is that it postpones the harder, more valuable work: deciding what belongs in the shared vault, what stays private, and what habits make information land where it can be found. Many families already have the raw ingredients—devices, email, a shared calendar, a cloud folder—without having the structure that turns them into a coherent second brain. The miracle, such as it is, lies in making the household's existing resources behave like a single memory rather than a set of disconnected piles.

A "good enough" standard is the antidote to perfectionism. Good enough means the important things can be found quickly by more than one person. Good enough means the system reduces repeated questions and prevents avoidable scrambles. Good enough means the vault is trusted often enough that people stop performing heroic remembering and start placing information where it belongs. The before-and-after is rarely cinematic; it is domestic and quietly profound. Before: a parent hunting for a portal link while the child waits, anxious, and the evening slips away. After: the link is where it always is, labelled and findable, and the evening becomes available again for what it was meant to contain.

The chapter that follows is concerned with this pivot: from individual coping to shared systems. It begins by clarifying what a second brain is in the daily language of family life, and why it is distinct from the familiar tools that already crowd the home. It then names the overload for what it is, not as a personal weakness but as a structural condition of modern parenting, caring, and partnership. It holds up the benefits not as productivity theatre but as a way of treating one another with gentleness across the week. And it insists on realism, because the household that aims for perfection often abandons the project entirely the first time life becomes difficult—which is to say, almost immediately.

The motif worth keeping in mind is simple: gravity. Information will fall. It will pool. It will accumulate wherever it is easiest for it to land. A shared second brain is not a denial of gravity; it is an attempt to shape the landscape so that what falls does not disappear into a swamp of "somewhere". The question is whether the family will continue to live at the mercy of these hidden forces, or whether it will build a few quiet structures—small dams, gentle channels, named places—that let daily life flow with less friction.

There is a particular kind of relief that comes when a household stops treating memory as the only storage. It is not the relief of a perfectly tidy home. It is the relief of knowing that the family's knowledge has a home outside any single person's mind, and that the home can be reached even on days when everyone is tired. That relief is not trivial. It changes how people speak to one another. It changes how children learn responsibility. It changes how partners share labour. It is, in the end, a decision about what kind of household this is going to be: one that runs on last-minute heroics, or one that invests, quietly and repeatedly, in shared clarity that can be trusted.

Turn the page, and the household's chaos will not be mocked or romanticised. It will be examined. Not to judge it, but to understand it well enough to stop being surprised by it. The first step is not technology. It is recognition: of what families are being asked to hold, and of how much kinder life becomes when the load is shared by a system designed to remember.

What Second Brains Are

In July 1945, in the United States, Vannevar Bush published an essay in *The Atlantic* with an unusually domestic ambition for a man best known, at the time, for wartime science. From his office life in Washington, D.C., he described the "memex"· a desk-like device that would store books, records, and communications, and—crucially—allow a person to create trails through them, linking one thought to the next. Bush was writing at the hinge of an era, when the volume of technical knowledge had become too large for any single mind to hold neatly. His wager was not that humans should remember more, but that they should be able to *find* what they had already encountered, and return to it fast enough to think well with it. The problem was retrieval. The proposed solution was an external memory built for use, not display. It worked, for a while.

That old, half-imagined desk still matters because families now live inside Bush's problem, but with fewer assistants and less sleep. The family home is a factory of small facts: names, dates, codes, decisions, preferences, policies, routines. The difficulty is not that the information is unavailable; it is that it is scattered across containers designed for other purposes. School apps publish updates in fragments. Messaging threads bury decisions under jokes and emojis. Email dutifully timestamps everything while making it strangely hard to assemble into a coherent plan. Photos multiply without context. The mind, asked to act as a filing cabinet, becomes brittle.

A second brain, in the sense used here, is a deliberately chosen place—usually digital—where family knowledge is stored so that family members do not have to hold it all in working memory. It is less a tool than an agreement. The agreement is simple: important information gets a home outside any one person's head, and that home is structured so the household can retrieve it under pressure. The system becomes an *anchor*: something you can return to when the day is noisy, when someone is stressed, when recollection turns argumentative. Without an anchor, families drift into improvisation. With one, they can navigate.

The easiest way to understand what a second brain is, is to watch a household without one perform the same mental labour repeatedly. A form arrives about a school trip, and the details are read in the car, half discussed, then placed "somewhere safe". A message appears in a parents' group chat about a change of pick-up time; a parent sees it while queuing in a supermarket and tells themselves they will remember. A calendar event is created for the trip date, but the packing requirements, the medical note, the payment confirmation, and the teacher's contact details remain elsewhere. Days later, another parent asks, "What time is it again?" Someone scrolls. Someone guesses. Someone is wrong. Show: the thumb flicking through a thread while a kettle rattles. Name: re-deciding. Explain: when decisions are not stored where they can be found, the household is forced to recreate them from fragments. Implication: family time is converted into search, and search into friction.

This is why a second brain is not "just a calendar". Calendars are superb at representing time. They are poor at representing meaning. A calendar entry can tell a family that the trip is on Thursday; it rarely tells them what needs doing because of it, where the consent form is, what the policy says about packed lunches, or where the payment receipt lives. In practice, the calendar becomes a trigger for another hunt. The hunt might be quick on a quiet day. It becomes punishing on a busy one. The abstraction is efficiency; the visible behaviour is the number of separate places a person must check to complete one task without guessing.

Nor is a second brain "just a group chat". Messaging is designed for immediacy and social glue: it is a river, not a reservoir. Rivers are excellent at moving things along. They are terrible at holding them still. In a busy family thread, yesterday's crucial detail is submerged beneath today's memes and tomorrow's logistics. The outcome is predictable: repeated questions, repeated answers, and a subtle shift in tone. A household begins to treat asking as incompetence, when the true culprit is the medium. Show: "Was it 3.15 or 3.30?" appearing again. Name: retrieval mismatch. Explain: conversational tools optimise for flow, not recall. Implication: families spend emotional energy policing one another's attention instead of improving the container.

A second brain sits in a different category. It is built for reference and for evolving plans. Reference is the stable stuff that must be reachable: logins, contacts, term dates, allergy notes, insurance numbers, the "how we do this" knowledge that otherwise sits in one person's head. Evolving plans are the not-yet-finished things: the holiday that is half booked, the birthday party that is still an idea, the school application that will require documents and deadlines, the home project that keeps resurfacing as guilt. These plans change over time. They need a home where the latest version is visible, and where the household can return to the same shared truth rather than generating competing recollections.

The notion that groups can share memory is not new. In 1995, the cognitive scientist Edwin Hutchins published *Cognition in the Wild*, describing how navigation on a U.S. Navy ship depended not on a single brilliant navigator, but on distributed cognition: instruments, procedures, and people together performing the task of knowing where the ship was. The point was not that individuals became less capable; it was that complex tasks required systems that carried cognition across people and artefacts. Families are smaller than naval crews, but the principle transfers cleanly. Show: one parent "just knows" every login and timetable. Name: single-point cognition. Explain: when family knowledge is concentrated, the household becomes dependent on one person's availability and mental bandwidth. Implication: stress becomes personal, and resilience collapses when that person is tired, ill, or absent.

There is also a sharp empirical edge to this. In 2011, Betsy Sparrow, Jenny Liu, and Daniel Wegner published research in *Science* on what is often summarised as the "Google effect": when people expect information to be available externally, they remember the information itself less well, but remember better where to find it. The study's nuance is frequently lost in casual conversation, yet its relevance here is practical rather than moral. The second brain does not aim to make people forget; it aims to shift effort from rote storage to reliable retrieval. The metric is not how much a parent can recall on demand, but how quickly the household can locate the right detail without conflict.

This shift changes the emotional climate of a home because it changes the default questions families ask each other. Without a second brain, the question is often "Do you remember...?" which is really a demand for performance. With one, the question becomes "Where is...?" and eventually "Is it in the vault?" which is a demand for process. Trust, in this context, is not a vague sentiment. It is the behaviour of checking the shared system first, and the relief of knowing that the answer is likely to be there. The same principle that makes a lab notebook valuable—writing down what matters so the work can continue—makes a family second brain valuable. The household becomes less dependent on mood and more dependent on a shared record.

A second brain also clarifies what "being organised" actually means. Organisation is often imagined as tidiness, a visual aesthetic. The second brain reframes it as retrieval speed under constraint. How many seconds does it take to find the school's absence policy when a child wakes with a fever? How many taps to reach the address of the party? How reliably can a teenager locate the Wi-Fi password without asking? These are not abstract questions. They are small tests of whether the household's knowledge has a home. The aim is not perfection; it is reduced friction in moments that are already tense.

The architectural decision at the heart of a second brain is to give each important item one primary home. Families suffer when documents exist in multiple versions: the same form photographed, then emailed, then saved by two people in two different places, then updated by one person without the other knowing. Duplication feels safe. It often breeds confusion. A second brain treats the "home" as the canonical version, and everything else as a pointer. A photo of a letter becomes a captured record that is stored in one place; a message thread becomes a source that is distilled into a reference note. Show: two parents arguing about which screenshot is "the right one". Name: version drift. Explain: multiple copies create competing realities. Implication: families waste attention reconciling the past instead of acting in the present.

This is where the concept becomes foundational. If the household cannot trust that the second brain contains the latest version of something important, it will not use it. Trust is earned through consistent capture and predictable structure, not through clever features. The second brain is therefore less like a gadget and more like a household habit made visible. It relies on a repeated decision: when new information arrives, it is placed into the shared home rather than left in the gravitational field of the kitchen table, the inbox, or the chat scroll. The anchor must be returned to, or it stops being an anchor.

The history of personal computing offers a useful analogue for why this works. On 9 December 1968, at the Fall Joint Computer Conference in San Francisco, Douglas Engelbart gave what is now known as the "Mother of All Demos", showing a system that combined text editing, linking, collaborative work, and the mouse. Engelbart's deeper point was not about hardware. It was about augmenting human intellect: reducing the friction between thought and record, making it easier to build on prior work rather than repeatedly reconstructing it. Families are not research labs, but they are continuously building on prior work—yesterday's routines, last term's policies, last year's holiday checklist. When the record is hard to access, the household's intellectual life is forced into short-term memory. When the record is easy to access, the household can accumulate wisdom.

A family second brain, then, is a mechanism for cumulative learning. It allows a household to remember what worked last time, not as folklore ("We always forget chargers") but as a concrete artefact (a packing checklist that already includes chargers). It allows routines to mature. It allows the family's "how we do things" to be written down once and reused, rather than re-taught and re-argued. The visible behaviour here is repetition: how often the household repeats the same conversation, solves the same problem, or re-locates the same information. The implication is subtle but profound: fewer repeated negotiations frees attention for actual relationships.

And yet there is a credible limitation that must be faced honestly. Externalising memory can become an excuse for indiscriminate capture, producing a digital attic rather than a second brain. The tools make it easy to save everything; the result can be an archive so swollen that retrieval becomes no easier than scrolling through a chat. The household feels busy saving, but remains stuck searching. This is not a failure of discipline; it is a failure of boundaries. A second brain is not a promise to preserve every scrap. It is a commitment to preserve what will be useful, meaningful, or protective—what will change a future decision or reduce a future emergency.

There is a second limitation, sharper still: digital fragility. In May 2017, the WannaCry ransomware attack disrupted parts of the UK's National Health Service, leading to cancelled appointments and locked systems across numerous sites. The lesson is not that families should fear technology as such, but that dependence on a single digital point can carry risk if access fails. A family second brain must therefore be designed with resilience in mind: not as a paranoid project, but as a recognition that devices can be lost, accounts can be locked, and platforms can change. The implication is practical: the value of a second brain increases when it can survive disruptions without becoming unusable.

These limitations do not refute the idea; they refine it. The antidote to the digital attic is selectivity and structure that reflects real questions a family asks. The antidote to fragility is modest redundancy and thoughtful access, so that the shared knowledge does not vanish with one broken phone or one forgotten password. The anchor must be sturdy enough to hold against routine turbulence. It must also be simple enough to be used when people are tired. Complexity is a tax. Families already pay enough.

The most revealing test of whether something qualifies as second-brain material is whether its absence would force the household to improvise under pressure. A child's medical summary does. A school's contact information does. The method for resetting the router does. The location of passport scans does. The thread of decisions for an upcoming trip does. A casual joke does not. A stream of reactions does not. The second brain is not where life happens; it is where life is made legible.

When a second brain is in place, the household stops treating knowledge as personal property. That shift matters ethically. If one person holds all the important details, they become the gatekeeper by accident, and the family becomes dependent. Shared systems distribute not only labour but agency. A child who can find their timetable is a child less at the mercy of adult attention. A partner who can locate the boiler manual does not need to interrupt the other's work. A carer who can access an "in case of" note can act without panic. These are not productivity wins; they are autonomy gains.

The underlying question is not whether families should store information outside their heads. They already do. The question is whether they will do it deliberately, in a shared place designed for retrieval, or accidentally, in a set of scattered containers that punish them at exactly the wrong moment. The second brain is the deliberate choice. It is an anchor against drift. It replaces heroic remembering with reliable finding. It trades a small, repeated act of capture for a large reduction in last-minute search.

There is, finally, a tension that remains unresolved—and should. How much should a family formalise? Too little structure, and the household repeats itself endlessly. Too much structure, and the system becomes a bureaucratic artefact no one loves, maintained out of guilt and abandoned at the first busy week. The second brain lives in that narrow band between chaos and rigidity, and it will always require judgement. The forward test is diagnostic: when something important arrives, does it fall into a shared home that the household trusts, or does it disappear into the familiar gravity well of "somewhere", to be rediscovered later at a cost?

Family Life Information Overload

On 9 January 2007, at the Moscone Center in San Francisco, Apple put a small slab of glass and metal on a stage and persuaded the world that it could live inside a pocket. Steve Jobs called it an iPhone and, in doing so, helped collapse several previously separate channels—phone calls, email, photographs, web browsing—into one always-on conduit. The cultural consequence was not merely convenience. It was a new default: information could arrive anywhere, at any time, with a vibration. Homes did not become quieter as a result. They became more permeable. Messages, updates, reminders, permissions, photos, and notifications began seeping through the day like water through a roof you have not yet noticed is leaking.

Now place that permeability into a kitchen at 7:18 on a wet weekday. A child needs a signed form. Another needs a specific piece of kit. Someone's school app has posted a late change. A work calendar has shifted. The smell of toast competes with the sharp tang of cold coffee. The phone screen glows. The form is missing again. Not lost in any dramatic sense—no thief, no fire—just absorbed into the ordinary churn of surfaces, bags, piles, and half-read messages. The household is not careless. It is saturated.

Information overload in family life is often described as if it were a personal weakness, a failure to "stay on top of things". That framing is both inaccurate and cruel. The modern home is a junction where institutions offload administrative work onto individuals: schools, clubs, healthcare systems, employers, service providers. Each has its own portals, its own conventions, its own expectations about response. The household becomes a switching station, converting incoming fragments into decisions and actions. Show the reality: a parent toggling between a school app, an email thread, a messaging group, and a photo album to answer a simple question. Name it plainly: channel sprawl. Explain why it bites: the more places information can land, the harder it is to be confident you have seen it, captured it, and can retrieve it later. The implication is not merely missed items. It is a constant low-grade vigilance that makes rest feel irresponsible.

The channels are not neutral. Each one shapes behaviour. School apps deliver information in bursts and badges, rewarding immediate attention while making retrieval awkward once the moment has passed. Messaging groups deliver social context and urgency at the same time; a date arrives wrapped in opinion, emotion, and a dozen unrelated replies. Email is orderly in theory and chaotic in practice: it preserves everything yet buries meaning among threads, forwards, and attachments named "Document(4).pdf". Paper letters are still astonishingly common, and they arrive with the special talent of paper to become invisible the moment they are placed down. Photos and screenshots add another layer: families now "capture" information by photographing it, which preserves the surface while often losing the structure that would make it findable later. The scroll becomes the household's unofficial archive, a long ribbon of "somewhere" that feels searchable until it suddenly is not.

This is not simply about volume. It is about the kind of mental work families are asked to do. Herbert A. Simon, writing in 1971, observed that "a wealth of information creates a poverty of attention". The home experiences this as a practical constraint. Attention is finite, and family life spends it in small coins: a glance at a message while stirring pasta, a quick reply during a meeting break, a half-read notification while tying shoelaces. Show the mechanism: fragments arriving in the gaps between tasks, never given the dignity of full focus. Name it: fragmented intake. Explain the effect: when information is received in partial attention, it is less likely to be encoded into memory and more likely to be misfiled mentally as "handled" when it has merely been seen. The implication is the most familiar sentence in busy households: "I thought I'd done that."

Cognitive science does not need to be invoked to scold the brain into behaving better; it is more useful as a permission slip to stop expecting the impossible. In 1956, George A. Miller's paper "The Magical Number Seven, Plus or Minus Two" helped popularise the idea that working memory—the mental space where we hold information in the moment—is sharply limited. Later work refined the numbers and the details, but the lived point remains stable: people cannot juggle many arbitrary items reliably, especially under stress. Show the everyday consequence: a parent trying to hold in mind three separate pick-up times, a forgotten login, and a deadline while also making breakfast and negotiating a sibling dispute. Name it: working-memory overload. Explain why it fails: the brain prioritises what feels urgent and emotionally charged; administrative detail is easily displaced. The implication is predictable: the household offloads the load onto whoever seems most reliable, and a "memory person" emerges by accident.

That accidental role is one of the hidden costs of information overload. Families rarely announce, "You will be our human database." It happens quietly, through reinforcement. One person is quicker at finding things. Another has a lower tolerance for chaos. Someone cares more about not missing deadlines. Soon, the household routes questions to them, and their attention becomes communal property. Show the behaviour: "Ask Mum" or "Ask them, they'll know," said as casually as passing the salt. Name it: cognitive centralisation. Explain what it does: it concentrates not only information but also anxiety, because the person who holds the facts also feels responsible for the consequences of missing them. The implication surfaces as resentment—not necessarily loud, often simmering—because carrying everyone's administrative load is labour even when it is invisible.

Resentment is rarely about one missing form. It is about patterns. Repeated questions are one of those patterns, and they are easy to misread. A repeated question sounds like laziness or inattentiveness. More often it is a symptom of an unreliable system for retrieval. Show: the same question about PE kit asked every week, answered every week, and still returning. Name: retrieval debt. Explain: when information has no trusted home, it must be "paid for" each time through interruption, explanation, and emotional regulation. The implication is not merely inefficiency; it is a subtle degradation of kindness. The person being asked feels pestered. The person asking feels foolish. The household pays twice.

Deadlines add sharper edges. A missed payment window for a school trip is not just a missed task; it can trigger a chain of consequences: frantic emails, embarrassed children, a scramble to borrow equipment, an awkward conversation at the gate. The visible metric is not abstract "stress" but the number of last-minute recoveries a household must perform in a month. Show: late-night printing, emergency shopping, apologetic messaging. Name: reactive recovery. Explain why it proliferates: when information arrives across many channels and is stored nowhere canonical, families discover requirements late, when there is no slack. The implication is that family time becomes increasingly consumed by damage control, and the home begins to feel like a place where everything is urgent.

Photos and screenshots deserve special attention because they are the modern household's improvised filing system. A parent photographs a letter because paper feels fragile. Another screenshots an appointment confirmation because the portal is annoying. A teenager saves a timetable image because it is quicker than logging in again. This looks like capture, and it is—partly. Show: a camera roll full of documents and the mild panic of searching it. Name: image hoarding. Explain what's missing: images preserve content but not context; without naming, tagging, or a shared location, they remain trapped in personal devices, effectively private and often forgotten. The implication is a strange kind of loss: the information exists, but not where the family can use it.

The scroll returns here as motif and mechanism. The scroll is seductive because it offers the illusion of permanence: everything is "still there". Yet permanence without structure is simply a long corridor of closed doors. Families scroll to find the address, scroll to find the date, scroll to find the link, and often stop when they see something that looks close enough. That "close enough" is where errors breed. Show: a parent copying the wrong time from a similar message. Name: approximate retrieval. Explain why it happens: under time pressure, people trade accuracy for speed, and the scroll encourages that trade by making everything look equally plausible. The implication is risk in the most domestic sense—mistakes that cost time, money, goodwill, or a child's sense of being cared for.

Not all households experience this equally, and it matters to acknowledge the counter-example without romanticising it. Some families have fewer moving parts: one child, a stable work schedule, a school that communicates through a single channel, a strong culture of paper noticeboards. Some households also have a high-tolerance information steward who genuinely enjoys maintaining order, and the system feels smooth. These cases are real. They show that overload is not destiny. But even these families are not immune to structural change. Schools adopt new platforms. Clubs migrate to social-media groups. Health systems shift to portals. Employers add scheduling tools. The baseline is not static. The reconciliation is therefore simple: the presence of a calm household does not disprove overload as a structural condition; it shows that structure can be managed when channel sprawl is limited or when a household has built its own reliable anchor points.

The structural nature of the problem becomes easier to see when you trace the flow of information into a home over a single week. A school sends an update through an app; a teacher posts homework in a portal; a parents' association shares an event through a messaging group; a club sends a late cancellation by text; a service provider emails a renewal notice; a relative shares travel plans in a chat; a child brings home paper. None of these channels is malicious. Each is rational from the sender's perspective. Together they create what can be measured as context-switching: the number of times a person must change tools and mental frames to maintain basic household functioning. Show: switching from an app to an email to a calendar to a photo album in five minutes. Name: administrative thrash. Explain: every switch carries a cognitive cost—reorientation, searching, reconciling versions. The implication is fatigue that feels like laziness because it does not look like "work", yet it drains as surely as work does.

There is also a moral hazard in how information is delivered to families. Many institutions assume a responsive adult with time, focus, and a stable digital identity. That assumption is baked into interfaces and expectations. A portal assumes you will remember the password you last used three months ago. A school app assumes you will see notifications promptly and interpret them correctly. A letter assumes it will reach the right adult intact. A group chat assumes you will scroll back and find the key detail. These assumptions are not tailored to real homes, where adults have fragmented attention, children carry papers, and devices are shared, lost, silenced, or simply ignored during busy hours. Show: a notification arriving mid-meeting, then vanishing under subsequent alerts. Name: unrealistic user model. Explain: systems designed for ideal users produce predictable failure in real households. The implication is misplaced blame: families internalise the failure as personal incompetence when it is a design mismatch.

Naming the overload is therefore not an act of complaint. It is an act of accuracy. When a family says, "We are overwhelmed," the important part is not the emotion; it is the diagnosis. Overwhelm is often the feeling of too many open loops—unfinished tasks, pending decisions, vague obligations—each tugging at attention. The second brain concept introduced earlier matters precisely because it offers a way to close loops reliably by giving information a retrievable home. But before any tool or structure can help, the household has to stop treating its current state as a character verdict. The problem is not that people do not care. The problem is that they are living inside a system that produces scatter.

Return, briefly, to the lost form. The form arrived. Someone saw it. Someone intended to deal with it. The household did not fail to receive information. It failed to create a retrieval path. That distinction is liberating. It shifts the question from

"Who messed up?" to "Where did it land, and why?" It makes room for structural solutions rather than personal scolding. It also reveals why overload feels so demoralising: it repeatedly converts good intentions into visible failures, and visible failures into self-judgement. A family can begin to repair its administrative life only when it stops confusing moral worth with memory performance.

The scroll, the inbox, the pile—these are not merely clutter. They are symptoms of gravity: information will always fall into the lowest-friction places. A modern home cannot stop information arriving, and it cannot force human brains to become infinite. It can, however, choose whether the default landing zones remain accidental, personal, and opaque, or become shared, named, and searchable. That choice is not about becoming a different kind of family. It is about reducing the number of mornings derailed by preventable search.

The forward test is blunt and slightly uncomfortable: when the next important detail arrives—an update, a deadline, a form—does it enter a system that more than one person can trust, or does it join the scroll, waiting to be rediscovered later in a moment of panic?

Benefits of Shared Clarity

On 30 October 1935, at Wright Field in Dayton, Ohio, the U.S. Army Air Corps watched a prototype bomber, the Boeing Model 299, lift off, pitch upward, stall, and crash, killing two of the five crew. The aircraft was not a fragile machine; it was, by the standards of the day, startlingly advanced. The investigation did not end in a melodrama about reckless pilots or defective engineering. It ended in something quieter and more unsettling: the pilots had forgotten to release a set of control locks. The aeroplane had become too complex to be flown safely by memory alone. Out of that shock came a shift that would spread far beyond aviation: the use of checklists as a normal part of competent work, not as a confession of incompetence. A handrail stops the fall.

Family life is not a runway, but it shares the same predicament in miniature. Complexity has crept in while the expectations of flawless performance have remained stubbornly high. Families are asked to remember the right detail at the right moment across multiple channels—school apps, portals, emails, text messages, paper letters, photo rolls—often while tired, often while rushed, sometimes while managing conflict, illness, or work demands. When something goes wrong, it is tempting to blame character: forgetful, disorganised, careless. The deeper explanation is structural. A home without shared clarity is like an aircraft without a checklist: it may fly on good days, but it becomes fragile when conditions turn.

The phrase "shared clarity" can sound abstract until it is tethered to what it replaces. It replaces the minor emergencies that fill a household's week: the last-minute dash for kit, the frantic hunt for a form, the late-night printing session, the apologetic message sent while walking to the station. It replaces the repeated questions that interrupt thought and sour the tone of perfectly ordinary conversations. It replaces the subtle but corrosive inequality where one person becomes the household's unofficial database and everyone else becomes a customer of their attention. Shared clarity is not tidiness. It is not aesthetic order. It is the practical condition in which the family's knowledge and plans can be found quickly by more than one person, even when the day is noisy.

The first benefit is the one families feel in their shoulders: fewer emergencies. Emergencies, in this domestic sense, are often manufactured by poor retrieval rather than by genuinely unpredictable events. Show the mechanism in a familiar scene. A child needs a permission slip signed "today". The slip existed all week. Someone read it in the car. Someone placed it somewhere safe. Now, at 7:18, it cannot be found. The kitchen smells faintly of toast and wet coats. The phone screen is bright in a dim room. Voices tighten. The morning tips. Name what is happening: time is being converted into search, and search into stress. Explain why shared clarity helps: when key items have a trusted home, the household does not need to recreate the past in order to act in the present. The implication is not merely punctuality. It is emotional margin—less of the day consumed by self-inflicted urgency.

The second benefit is reliability, and reliability is a moral force in family life. A household is, among other things, a web of small promises. Some are spoken: "I'll pay that fee tonight." "I'll book the dentist." "I'll email the teacher." Others are implied: children assume that adults will remember what matters; partners assume that commitments will not be quietly dropped. When information is scattered, follow-through becomes erratic for reasons that look personal but are often logistical. Show: the fee reminder arrives in an app, the payment link is in an email, the deadline is mentioned in a chat, and the card details are stored elsewhere. Name: fragmented execution. Explain: when a single task requires stitching together multiple sources, completion depends on unusually good timing and attention. The implication is that the household begins to experience itself as unreliable, which breeds defensive habits—nagging, double-checking, private reminders, silent resentment.

Shared clarity changes the texture of reliability because it changes the shape of remembering. In a household with a shared second brain, follow-through is less a test of individual memory and more a function of the environment. This is not wishful thinking; it mirrors what high-stakes systems have learned. In 2009, the surgeon Atul Gawande published *The Checklist Manifesto*, drawing on work including the World Health Organization's Surgical Safety Checklist (introduced in 2008) to argue that complex domains fail not only from ignorance but from missed steps, and that simple, shared prompts can prevent avoidable errors. The family analogue is not surgery, and no medical claims are needed to grasp the principle. Families miss steps because the steps live in heads and messages rather than in a shared place. Reliability improves when the household stops relying on perfect recall and starts relying on shared prompts and shared records.

The third benefit is developmental: children learn to orient themselves. In many homes, the "information economy" trains children into dependence. They ask because it is faster. They ask because adults have historically been the only place answers live. They ask because searching the scroll is miserable. When information has a consistent home, something changes. The child still asks, of course, because children are human and because conversation is part of family life. But they also begin to look. That act—looking before asking—is a kind of apprenticeship into adulthood. It teaches that the household is legible, that systems exist, that one can find one's way. Trust becomes visible behaviour: a teenager checks the shared place for the Wi-Fi password rather than interrupting; a child finds the sports schedule and packs without a parental monologue; siblings consult a shared list instead of negotiating the same argument twice.

That shift is not merely convenient. It alters power. When only one adult holds the household's knowledge, that adult becomes a gatekeeper by accident. Others become dependent. Shared clarity distributes agency. Show: a co-parent travelling for work and still able to answer a question because the answer is not trapped in their head; a grandparent stepping in and finding the school contact details without a frantic call; a child locating the plan for the day without a cascade of questions. Name: distributed cognition, to borrow Edwin Hutchins's term from *Cognition in the Wild* (1995), where he described how teams coordinate knowledge through shared artefacts and routines. Explain: shared records and shared structures allow groups to think together without one person carrying everything. The implication in family life is resilience: the household can function without requiring any single individual to be perpetually available.

The benefits become especially obvious in the arena that reliably exposes household weaknesses: travel. Consider two versions of the same pre-trip evening. In the first, a family has agreed, vaguely, to leave early. The booking confirmation is somewhere in someone's email. The address was sent in a message that is now buried. The packing is improvised from memory, which means it is shaped by anxiety rather than reality: three pairs of socks and no chargers, a raincoat forgotten because it was assumed, medication not checked because nobody wants to think about it until it becomes urgent. The atmosphere is tense not because anyone is malicious, but because uncertainty is contagious. The household does not know what it knows. The result is a flurry of re-deciding: re-finding the booking, re-checking the route, re-arguing who packs what, re-remembering that the child's swimming lesson needs cancelling, re-asking whether passports are required for this particular trip. The family is active. It is not coherent.

In the second version, the same family reaches for a shared list. The list is not a monument to discipline; it is a record of prior learning. The booking details are there. The address is there. The packing list exists because it existed last time and was adjusted, rather than re-created. The cancellation note is recorded. The documents are gathered in one place. None of this removes the normal chaos of children and suitcases. It does, however, convert the evening from improvisation to execution. The kettle boils. Bags are packed. Someone still forgets something small, because families are alive, not automated. But the forgotten thing is no longer the expensive or embarrassing thing. The difference is not personality. It is structure.

This is where organisation reveals itself as kindness. Kindness is often imagined as spontaneous: a hug, a compliment, a small gift. Shared clarity is a different category of kindness—kindness that travels forward in time. It is the kindness of saving a future self from a predictable scramble. It is the kindness of making it easier for a partner to carry their share of the load without mind-reading. It is the kindness of making expectations explicit so they stop being weapons. It is also, quietly, self-respect: refusing to treat one's exhausted brain as the only place a family can store its life.

There is a further benefit that is rarely discussed because it sounds too grand for domestic life, yet it is real: shared clarity reduces conflict about reality. Families argue about facts more than they notice. What time did we agree? Which day is it? Did the school say trainers or shoes? Was the fee paid? When information is scattered, each person's recollection becomes a competing narrative, and the argument takes on a moral flavour: you didn't listen, you don't care, you always forget. Shared clarity shifts the argument from rhetoric to verification. The visible behaviour is simple: instead of debating, someone checks. The implication is profound: being wrong becomes less shameful because the household has a shared reference point, and shame is one of the fuels of domestic conflict.

This does not mean shared clarity is always easy or universally welcome. A credible limitation must be admitted: systems can become instruments of control. In some homes, "shared" can slide into "monitored". The second brain can become a place where one person's standards are enforced and everyone else's autonomy is narrowed. Children can experience shared plans as surveillance rather than support. Partners can experience shared checklists as a veiled accusation: *If it's written down, you have no excuse.* That is a real risk, and it explains why some people recoil from organisation talk; they have lived through systems used as weapons.

The reconciliation is not to abandon shared clarity. It is to understand that the value comes from reducing friction, not from increasing compliance. The second brain is meant to be an anchor, not a courtroom. Its moral centre is mutual aid: making the household easier to navigate for everyone, not creating a ledger of failures. The distinction becomes visible in how the system behaves when something is missed. In a punitive system, a missed item becomes evidence. In a supportive system, it becomes feedback: the environment did not make the right action easy enough, or the information did not land where it could be found. The household learns. The handrail is adjusted, not used to blame the person who slipped.

A second limitation is more mundane and more common: over-ambition. Families often abandon systems not because they dislike clarity, but because they attempt an unliveable version of it. They build structures too complex to maintain, or they demand perfect capture, or they insist that every detail be recorded immediately. The household then experiences the system itself as another obligation. Show: a carefully built set of folders no one can remember, or a tagging scheme so intricate it requires explanation at the very moment when time is scarce. Name: maintenance burden. Explain: when the cost of using a system is high, people revert to the lowest-friction habits—piles, scrolls, "I'll remember". The implication is disillusionment, and disillusionment is dangerous because it convinces families that clarity is for other people.

Shared clarity, at its best, is the opposite of that. It is modest. It is designed around the household's real questions, not around an ideal of order. It is judged by outcomes a family can actually feel: fewer last-minute panics, fewer repeated interruptions, more even distribution of the "knowing" work, more calm in transitions that used to trigger conflict. "Efficiency" here is not a slogan; it is the number of times the household has to re-find the same information. "Risk" is not theoretical; it is the likelihood of missing something with real consequences. "Trust" is not sentimental; it is the moment when someone says, without sarcasm, "It'll be in the vault," and the other person believes it.

There is a quiet philosophical gain as well: shared clarity makes room for attention. Families often think they need more time. They may, but time is not the only scarce resource. Attention is scarcer, and it is what makes time usable. When a household spends its attention on finding, re-deciding, and policing memory, it has less attention for the parts of life that justify the whole enterprise: conversation, play, rest, learning, tenderness, even boredom. A shared second brain does not create extra hours. It can, however, stop hours leaking away into searches that feel inevitable only because they have become habitual.

The motif returns, because it deserves to: the handrail. A good handrail is not a sign that the staircase is dangerous; it is a sign that someone anticipated ordinary human frailty—wet shoes, tired legs, a hurried step—and built a small piece of support into the environment. Shared clarity is that kind of architecture. It does not assume perfect people. It assumes people who are carrying bags, managing feelings, switching contexts, and making a hundred small decisions. It offers a stable thing to hold, not to restrict movement, but to prevent unnecessary falls.

The forward test is therefore not whether a family *likes* organisation, or whether they admire a particular app, or whether they can keep a spotless digital cupboard. The test is sharper and more human: when the next stressful moment arrives—and it will—does the household have an anchor that turns panic into a quick check, or will it default to improvisation, searching, and blame? The answer does not flatter. It informs. It reveals whether clarity is being treated as a shared kindness, or left to chance.

Setting Realistic Expectations

In October 1985, at Carnegie Mellon University in Pittsburgh, researchers began releasing a deceptively modest piece of software called *Andrew*—a file system and computing environment designed to make digital work easier to store, share, and find. The ambition was practical: let people access their files anywhere on campus, without the brittle chaos of floppy discs and local storage. The system worked, and the ideas behind it influenced later networked computing. Yet even in that controlled environment—trained users, institutional support, predictable infrastructure—order did not arrive as a permanent state. Files still went missing. Naming conventions drifted. People saved documents in the wrong place. The real achievement was not perfection; it was resilience: the ability to recover, re-index, and continue without collapsing into disorder.

Families need that same expectation from a second brain, but the home is a far harsher laboratory. Unlike a university campus, the household runs on interruption. It runs on fatigue. It runs on emotion. Children spill juice on keyboards. Grandparents text last-minute changes. School portals demand passwords at the precise moment the Wi-Fi is sulking. A family that expects its shared system to eliminate chaos will eventually experience chaos as betrayal. That is the fastest route to abandonment. Perfection breaks fast.

The point is not to lower standards until nothing changes. The point is to set the right kind of standard: one that is measurable in real household outcomes and forgiving of human variance. A second brain is a tool for reducing avoidable friction, not for purifying life. The right expectation is not "no more mess", but "less repeated pain". That sentence matters because it re-assigns what success looks like. Success is not a spotless vault. Success is fewer derailed mornings, fewer missed deadlines, fewer arguments about who said what, fewer moments where one person becomes the only functioning memory in the house.

The first myth worth dismantling is that a system succeeds only when everyone is perfectly disciplined. Show the fantasy in the wild: a family sets up an immaculate structure on a quiet

Sunday afternoon, creates categories, writes templates, announces new rules, and feels briefly triumphant. Then Monday arrives. A school app posts a late update while someone is commuting. A child comes home with a letter crumpled into a pocket. A work call runs long. Dinner happens. Bedtime happens. The capture step that felt effortless on Sunday feels like climbing a hill in mud on Monday night. The system is not used. The guilt arrives. Name the myth: discipline-as-engine. Explain why it fails: discipline is a limited resource, and families spend it on behaviour, care, and survival; a system that demands constant discipline competes with life itself. The implication is predictable: the system becomes a monument to good intentions rather than an instrument of daily relief.

A more accurate engine is design. Design is what makes the right action easy when willpower is low. The visible metric is friction: how many steps it takes to capture something, how hard it is to file it, how quickly it can be retrieved. A second brain that requires elaborate sorting at the moment of capture is asking for heroics. A second brain that allows fast capture and later organisation is asking for something human. That difference is the difference between persistence and abandonment. Families do not fail because they are lazy; they fail because the system does not fit the conditions under which it must operate.

The second myth is that advanced tools are necessary. This one is especially seductive for intelligent people, because tool research can feel like progress. It has the pleasant texture of competence. Show: a parent comparing apps late at night, reading reviews, watching demonstrations, making a shortlist, seeking the "best" system. Name: tool-chasing. Explain what is happening: the household is substituting optimisation for adoption, and confusing feature richness with reliability. The implication is delay, followed by disappointment when the chosen tool does not magically produce habits. Most systems fail not because the tool is inadequate, but because the household did not agree on what "home" means for important information.

A third myth is more subtle: that the system must be comprehensive. The comprehensive dream says that every important thing should be captured, perfectly tagged, perfectly filed, always up to date. It is appealing because it promises control. It is also, for most families, a lie. Show: the avalanche of photos, messages, letters, and micro-decisions arriving each week. Name: completeness bias. Explain: when the standard is total capture, every lapse feels like failure, and failure becomes a reason to quit. The implication is brittle ambition. A robust second brain accepts that some things will be missed, and it is built to recover quickly when they are.

Here the "good enough" standard becomes not a compromise but a strategy. Good enough means the household can retrieve the handful of categories that matter most, with enough speed and confidence to change behaviour. It means the system is trusted for the things that cause disproportionate pain when they go missing: school logistics, health reference, travel documents, key contacts, household how-to notes, and the few recurring routines that repeatedly cause friction. It means the structure is light enough to use when tired and clear enough for more than one person to navigate. Good enough can be tested. Can a second adult find the school absence policy without asking? Can a teenager locate the Wi-Fi password? Can the family locate the trip booking confirmation in under thirty seconds? These are not abstract questions. They are diagnostic.

The motif that supports realistic expectations is the handrail again, because it captures the right kind of modesty. A handrail does not prevent every stumble. It does not abolish gravity. It simply reduces the consequences of ordinary human weakness. A family second brain is an architectural intervention of that kind. It is not a moral project. It is a practical one. The ambition is not to turn the home into a machine; it is to stop the home demanding machine-like performance from humans.

A before-and-after story shows what "good enough" looks like when it is real rather than aspirational. Before: a family keeps school information in a mixture of places. One parent has emails. The other has screenshots. The child has a timetable image somewhere in their camera roll. On a Tuesday morning, the child appears in the kitchen wearing the wrong kit for PE because nobody remembered it was PE day. The parent tries to check the school app. The app demands a login. The password is wrong. The reset email is sent to an account that is not currently open. The child is anxious. The parent is irritated. A message is sent to the teacher. The morning leaves a residue.

After: the family's school information has a shared home. Not everything. Just the essentials. The timetable is stored there. The weekly kit days are written in one place, with the child's name clearly attached. The relevant portal links are recorded. When the child asks, "Is it PE today?" the parent does not gamble on memory. They check. The check takes seconds. The child changes. The morning proceeds. No angels sing. The house is still noisy. But the particular panic does not occur. That is progress without perfection, and it is precisely the kind of progress that survives a busy month.

To understand why "good enough" works, it helps to look at how systems survive in other domains. In 2018, the UK's National Cyber Security Centre published guidance on "Cyber Security for Small Businesses" that emphasised basic controls and sensible hygiene rather than exotic technical measures. The philosophy matters more than the specific domain: resilience often comes from a few well-chosen, consistently applied practices, not from maximal sophistication. Translate that into household terms and the implication is clear. A family system should prioritise the simple practices that prevent the most painful failures, not the elaborate practices that look impressive while remaining unused.

This is also where realistic expectations protect relationships. When a system is treated as a perfection project, it becomes a new arena for judgement. One person becomes the enforcer. Another becomes the rebel. Children learn that organisation is a test they can fail. Partners learn that mistakes will be recorded. The second brain turns from handrail to weapon. The visible behaviour is the sigh when someone forgets to capture something; the sharp tone when a note is filed "wrong"; the passive aggression of "Well, if you'd put it in the vault..." The implication is that the system, meant to reduce friction, increases it.

A healthy expectation avoids that trap by treating lapses as data. When something goes missing, the question is not "Who failed?" but "Where did the process allow it to fall?" This is not managerial language; it is kindness in analytical form. It protects dignity. It also improves the system. If paper letters consistently derail mornings, the household learns that paper needs a dedicated capture ritual. If messages in a group chat repeatedly contain key dates, the household learns that those dates need extraction to the shared home. If the vault is not used under stress, the household learns that retrieval is too hard or that the system is not trusted. Each failure becomes a measurement. The handrail is adjusted.

A credible limitation still remains. Some families, for reasons of temperament or circumstance, will not tolerate even modest system maintenance during certain seasons. A new baby, a demanding job change, a caregiving crisis, exam periods—these can consume all discretionary attention. The honest response is not to pretend otherwise. It is to recognise that the system must be able to hibernate and then revive. A second brain that collapses permanently after two chaotic weeks is not a family system; it is a hobby. The reconciliation is to define success as recoverability. Can the family return to the vault after a hard fortnight without feeling defeated? Can the system be reset quickly—by capturing the most urgent items and letting the rest wait—without needing a complete rebuild? These are design questions disguised as emotional ones.

There is also the uncomfortable truth that families differ in what they consider tolerable chaos. Some people feel safe in a little mess; others feel attacked by it. A shared system cannot erase those differences. It can, however, prevent them from becoming constant conflict by creating a common ground. The system becomes a negotiated artefact. It carries agreements in a neutral form. It reduces the need for one person to interpret another's behaviour as disrespect. That is not sentimental. It is observable: fewer "I told you" moments, fewer last-minute scrambles that become accusations, fewer interruptions routed to one person.

Realistic expectations also require one more shift: from "set up" to "iterate". Setup is a moment. Iteration is a posture. Families often attempt to build the final system immediately, and when reality exposes flaws, they judge the system as a failure rather than a prototype. Yet the home changes constantly—children grow, schools change platforms, routines evolve, new commitments appear. A second brain should be expected to change with the family. The visible behaviour is small adjustment: a note renamed because people search differently than expected; a template simplified because it was never used; a folder reduced because it created debate. The implication is longevity. A living system is not the one that never changes; it is the one that changes without drama.

The handrail returns here for the last time because it holds the right ethic: modest, pragmatic, forgiving. Nobody expects a staircase to be safe because everyone is careful all the time. They expect the environment to support ordinary human movement. A family second brain should be expected to do the same. It should support the household's real rhythms, not its fantasies about itself. It should be stable enough to trust, simple enough to use, and forgiving enough to survive.

The forward test, then, is not whether the family can build the perfect vault. It is whether the family can choose a standard that keeps them honest without making them brittle: will the second brain be treated as a handrail—used when needed, adjusted when it fails—or as a showcase that must remain pristine to count as real? The answer will decide whether the system becomes part of the household's life, or another abandoned attempt at becoming someone else.

Chapter 2
Designing Your Shared Vault

In 1854, in Soho, London, a doctor named John Snow walked the streets with a notebook and a stubborn idea. Cholera, he suspected, was not a moral failing or a miasma of bad air, but a pattern that could be traced—if only the right information could be gathered and kept in one place. He marked deaths on a map and, by doing so, made something visible that had previously been experienced only as panic and grief. The now-famous Broad Street pump was not discovered by genius alone; it was discovered by organisation. A scattered set of tragedies became a coherent story because the data had a home. Once the story was visible, action became possible.

Families rarely face anything as stark as an epidemic, and yet the domestic version of Snow's problem is constant: crucial information is real, but it is dispersed; plans exist, but they are fragmented; memory holds the pieces, but it cannot reliably assemble them on demand. The result is not only inconvenience. It is a form of chronic uncertainty. People do not merely forget; they hesitate, they re-check, they re-ask, they re-decide, because they cannot see the whole shape of what they already know. A shared vault is the household's answer to that: not more information, but a place where information becomes legible.

The phrase "shared vault" can sound grander than it is. It is, at heart, a single trusted home for the family's reference and evolving plans—the point where knowledge stops floating and starts belonging. The emphasis is on *shared*, because the household is not a solo enterprise. The emphasis is on *vault*, not because it must be mysterious or locked away, but because it must be dependable. A vault is something you do not rebuild every week. You return to it. You trust it. You stop asking whether the important thing is "somewhere" and start assuming it has a proper home.

The most persuasive argument for a shared vault is not a slogan about productivity; it is the simple physics of retrieval. In the absence of a deliberate home, information falls into the nearest container—an inbox, a camera roll, a chat scroll, a kitchen pile—and every future use becomes a search problem. Search problems expand to fill the time available, and then they expand further, because they produce social friction. "Where is it?" becomes "Why didn't you do it?" and, on a bad day, "Why do I always have to do everything?" The vault does not fix character. It changes architecture. It turns the household's most frequent question from a scavenger hunt into a quick look-up.

For that to happen, the vault has to be designed with a few principles that are less glamorous than they are decisive. The first is the idea of one home for each important item. This does not mean there is only one copy in existence—families will always take photos of letters and share links—but it does mean there is a single place that counts as the authoritative version. Without that, the household will drift into version confusion: two similar documents, two partial notes, three screenshots, each slightly different, each defensible. A vault that cannot answer "Which one is the right one?" is a vault that will be ignored under stress.

The second principle is easy search. It is astonishing how many organisational efforts forget that the point is not to file beautifully but to *find quickly*. The vault should behave like a well-labelled cupboard: not a museum, not a complex taxonomy, just a place where the most-used items are easy to reach and the rarer items still have a reliable home. The test is not whether the structure looks neat on a screen. The test is whether someone can locate what they need in the moment they need it, without knowing how the system was built. A parent half awake. A teenager in a hurry. A partner juggling work calls. A grandparent helping at short notice. If the vault makes sense only to its architect, it will collapse into being another private stash.

The third principle is low friction. Families live on thin margins of attention. Any system that demands lengthy decisions at the point of capture—Where should this go? Which category? Which tag?—will be bypassed when the day is busy, which is to say most days. Low friction does not mean sloppy; it means forgiving. It means the vault allows quick capture now and refinement later, because the family's reality is that "later" may never come, and the system must still remain usable. The vault should accept imperfect input and still produce reliable retrieval. That is not a feature; it is a philosophy.

Designing the vault, then, is not primarily about the tool. It is about boundaries. Without boundaries, the vault becomes what every attic becomes: a repository for things that might be useful, saved without decision, later impossible to navigate. Digital spaces are particularly prone to this because storage feels infinite and deletion feels emotionally charged. The vault must therefore draw a line between what belongs and what does not. School information belongs because it is time-sensitive and consequential. Health reference belongs because it is stressful to reconstruct when needed. Money basics—practical household documents, renewal dates, key account details—belong because their absence triggers disproportionate panic. Home reference belongs because it reduces dependence on one person's memory. Trips belong because travel magnifies the cost of missing information. Memories belong, selectively, because meaning without structure becomes a pile rather than an archive. What does not belong is the endless social chatter that produced the decision. The vault is not the place to preserve every message, only the distilled outcome that future-you will need.

This distillation is where many families stumble, because it feels like an extra task layered onto life. Yet it is also where the vault earns its keep. The household does not need another channel to read. It needs a place where the noise has been translated into clarity. A message thread can remain where it is; the vault holds the key details extracted from it. The vault does not compete with conversation; it protects conversation from becoming the only storehouse of truth.

Once boundaries are clear, the most delicate design problem appears: privacy. A shared vault that ignores privacy will either be rejected outright or quietly undermine trust. Families contain different roles, different ages, and different rightful degrees of autonomy. Partners may share most household information but still need private space for thoughts that are not ready to be communal. Teenagers need a sense that not everything they write or save is open to adult inspection. Even younger children benefit from having a space that feels like theirs—safe, respected, not treated as a public noticeboard. The vault's design must therefore hold a paradox: be shared enough to reduce dependence and confusion, private enough to protect dignity.

This is not merely a technical issue of permissions, though permissions matter. It is also a cultural agreement. A family that treats the vault as a place to spy on one another will destroy it. A family that treats it as a place to support one another can use privacy boundaries as a form of care: parents-only areas for adult administration, children's spaces for their own plans and projects, shared spaces for shared reality. The vault becomes not a panopticon but a household commons with private rooms. That architecture, done well, makes it possible to invite children into the system without making them feel managed. It also makes it possible to share responsibility without demanding total transparency.

The risk here is to overthink. Some families, thrilled by the idea of a vault, build elaborate structures and then discover that nobody can remember where anything lives. The temptation is understandable: a complex life seems to demand a complex organisational scheme. Yet complexity is a tax paid repeatedly. A family system must serve the questions the household actually asks, not the questions an imaginary administrator might ask. "What is happening this week?" is a real question. "Where are the trip documents?" is a real question. "What do we need for school on Tuesday?" is a real question. "Where is the boiler manual?" is a real question. A structure that answers those quickly is more sophisticated than one with a beautiful hierarchy nobody uses.

This is why the chapter's focus is minimum viable structure. Not minimalism for its own sake, but the smallest set of containers and labels that makes the vault trustworthy. Sections that match household domains. A handful of tags that map to people, places, and recurring themes. Names that are obvious to tired eyes. A top level that can be memorised without effort. The goal is not to create a perfect taxonomy; it is to create a map that can be navigated under pressure. When the vault is designed around real questions, it becomes a tool of calm rather than an object of maintenance.

Modern relevance makes this design work urgent. The home is now a point where institutions deliver obligations by default, often through systems that assume uninterrupted attention. Families cannot control the number of inputs, but they can control where those inputs land. A vault is, in that sense, an act of sovereignty. It says: we will not allow every platform to dictate our household's attention. We will decide what counts, where it goes, and how we will retrieve it. That is not technophobia. It is adult governance of a domestic ecosystem that otherwise runs on platform rules.

The motif from the beginning returns as a quiet reminder of what is at stake: visibility. John Snow's map did not eliminate cholera by itself. It made the pattern visible enough to act upon. A shared vault does something similar for family life. It takes scattered details and turns them into a coherent picture that can be checked, updated, and trusted. It does not remove the messiness of people. It reduces the messiness of information. That distinction matters because it prevents a common disappointment: expecting a system to solve human unpredictability. The vault does not make children stop forgetting. It makes forgetting less catastrophic. It does not make schedules stop changing. It makes change easier to track. It does not remove disagreement. It gives disagreement a shared reference point.

There is also an emotional payoff that deserves to be named without sentimentality. When the household's knowledge has a home, people can stop carrying so much in their heads. That mental space does not automatically become bliss. It becomes availability. Availability for attention, for patience, for noticing. The home feels less like a place of constant reactivity and more like a place where life can be lived deliberately, even in small ways. The vault, done well, is not a tyrant of order. It is a support beam.

The page that follows asks for a particular kind of courage: the courage to design for real life rather than for fantasy. To choose boundaries rather than hoarding. To choose simplicity rather than elegance. To choose privacy with clarity rather than privacy through secrecy. To choose a structure that answers the household's real questions rather than one that flatters the organiser. The trade-off is unavoidable and therefore worth facing directly: how much friction is the family willing to accept at the moment information arrives in order to save far more friction later, when that information is needed quickly? The answer will determine whether the vault becomes a trusted home or another digital attic with a nicer label.

Core Principles of a Vault

In 1876, in Amherst, Massachusetts, a young librarian named Melvil Dewey published a slim book that did not look like a revolution. It proposed a numbering system for arranging knowledge on shelves so that a stranger could walk into a building, locate a subject, and find a specific volume without pleading for help. The Dewey Decimal Classification did not make libraries quieter, nor did it reduce the number of books arriving at the door. It did something more foundational: it gave information a stable address. Retrieval stopped depending on whoever happened to be on duty. Order became a property of the system rather than the memory of a person. Every item needs an address.

Families do not run libraries, but they do live amid a comparable problem: a growing stock of information, arriving through too many channels, with too many opportunities for misplacement and duplication. A shared vault is a family's attempt to create what Dewey was creating—an environment where the right thing can be found by the right person at the right moment, even when nobody feels especially capable. The vault is not a decorative idea. It is a response to the limits of attention and the social cost of relying on heroic remembering. Its value is measured in retrieval speed under stress: how quickly the household can surface the absence policy, the booking confirmation, the medication list, the school contact, the instructions for the boiler, the pack list that prevents a ruined morning.

The first principle is deceptively simple: one home for each important item. Not one copy in existence, but one canonical location that counts as "where it lives". Show the opposite and the harm appears immediately. A school letter is photographed by one parent, saved as a screenshot by another, forwarded in an email thread, and then mentioned in a chat. When the deadline arrives, there are four artefacts and no certainty. Name the failure precisely: version drift. Explain how it forms: duplication is created for convenience, but convenience fragments authority; each copy becomes a competing reality. The implication is not merely wasted time. It is a household argument about which copy is true, and arguments about truth corrode trust far faster than arguments about preference.

Systems engineering has a phrase for the cure: "single source of truth", a practice common in software, manufacturing, and operations because it prevents teams from building decisions on mismatched data. The family translation is blunt. When an item matters, the household needs to know where the authoritative version lives, and the system needs to reward that knowledge by making the authoritative version easy to reach. If the vault does not hold the canonical version, it becomes a polite fiction—nice to have, rarely used, quietly ignored when things become urgent.

The second principle is retrievability before tidiness. A vault is not an art project. It should be judged like a tool. Can someone find what they need quickly, without knowing how the organiser thinks? Show the lived test: a partner, mid-call, tries to locate the holiday booking address; a teenager, already late, needs the timetable; a grandparent, helping for one afternoon, needs school pick-up instructions. Name what is being measured: time-to-find. Explain why it matters: under pressure, people default to the path of least resistance; if the vault is slower than asking a person, the vault will be bypassed. The implication is social as much as practical—interruption becomes the household's default interface, and the same person is interrupted repeatedly.

Search sits at the heart of retrievability. Not because search is magical, but because family information is naturally cross-cutting. The same document can belong to a child, a term, an activity, and a trip. When retrieval depends on browsing a perfect folder tree, the household is forced into guessing where the organiser "meant" the item to go. That guessing produces friction and, eventually, avoidance. Search changes the game: it allows families to retrieve by the word that comes to mind, which is usually the word spoken aloud in a moment of need—the child's name, the school's name, "passport", "dentist", "swimming", "Wi-Fi". A vault that cannot be searched reliably is not a vault; it is storage with better marketing.

Libraries learned this long ago. Dewey's system was a shelving scheme, but libraries did not stop at shelves. They built catalogues, subject headings, cross-references—methods of retrieval that did not require a patron to understand internal storage decisions. The family analogue is straightforward: a vault should behave like a labelled cupboard, not a puzzle box. The labelled cupboard comparison is useful precisely because it is not mystical. A cupboard works when the most used items are easy to reach, labels match common language, and nobody needs a tutorial to put the mug back. A vault should aspire to that same ordinary competence.

The third principle is low friction. This is not a slogan about laziness; it is a recognition of conditions. Families encounter information when they are already occupied—walking out of the door, stirring a pan, commuting, supervising homework. If capture requires a long sequence of steps, it will not happen consistently, and a vault that is not consistently populated cannot be trusted. Show the familiar failure: a parent intends to "sort it later" and later never arrives; a screenshot sits in a camera roll until it is swallowed by hundreds more; an email remains personal because forwarding feels fiddly. Name the pattern: deferred capture. Explain why it is lethal: delayed handling increases the probability of loss and multiplies future search time; the item's context fades, and with it the ability to file it sensibly. The implication is that the vault becomes thin and unreliable, which invites more reliance on memory, which increases stress, which further reduces capture. A loop closes around the household.

Low friction has a particular shape. It favours quick capture now, and optional refinement later. That is not sloppiness. It is a practical concession to the way attention behaves. Research on prospective memory—the ability to remember to perform a future action—has repeatedly found that people miss intended actions when cues are weak and attention is divided; a classic overview is Mark A. McDaniel and Gilles O. Einstein's work on prospective memory (including their 2007 book *Prospective Memory: An Overview and Synthesis*). The household version is unromantic: "I'll do it later" is a weak cue. The vault should therefore be designed so "later" is not required for the item to become findable. If a letter is captured quickly with a sensible name, it can already be retrieved, even if it is not beautifully organised.

The fourth principle is predictability of location and language. A vault only becomes shared when people can anticipate where things belong. Show the alternative: one adult files by topic, another by person, a teenager by whatever word is funniest in the moment. The vault fills with idiosyncratic naming, and the household's search terms stop matching what was saved. Name the failure: semantic mismatch. Explain the cause: people search using their own mental models; if naming conventions are private, retrieval becomes a translation problem. The implication is quiet: the vault remains technically available while socially unusable, and the household returns to interruption as the fastest path.

Predictability is created by small, stable conventions. It is created by names that reflect how families speak, not how they aspire to speak. "School – Term dates" is a better anchor than "Academic Calendar 2026" because it matches the words likely to be typed at speed. "Boiler manual" is better than "Domestic heating documentation" because nobody searches for the latter while standing in a cold kitchen. The metric here is behavioural: what do people actually type when they are stressed? A vault succeeds when its labels meet the household's instinctive language.

The fifth principle is selective scope. Without selectivity, the vault becomes the digital attic it was meant to replace. This is not a moral failure; it is a predictable outcome of cheap storage and sentimental reluctance to delete. Show the bloat: hundreds of screenshots, duplicates of documents, half-finished notes, a stack of "important" emails with no further categorisation. Name what has happened: retrieval dilution.

Explain why it bites: as the ratio of useful-to-noisy items falls, search results become crowded and confidence erodes; people stop trusting that the first thing they find is the right thing. The implication is severe: the vault stops reducing friction and starts adding it.

A useful counter-example comes from personal and organisational information management research that has observed "piling" as a common human strategy—people cluster items without strict filing because classification carries a cost. Richard H. R. Harper's ethnographic work on office life and paper, including *The Myth of the Paperless Office* (with Abigail Sellen, 2002), describes how people keep piles because they are cognitively cheap and context-rich. Families do the same digitally. The lesson is not that filing is bad; it is that classification effort must pay for itself. A vault that demands too much classification will be avoided. A vault that permits light clustering while maintaining findability can endure.

Selectivity also clarifies what the vault is for. It is for reference and evolving plans, not for preserving every fragment of conversation. Chat threads are often valuable, but their value lies in social warmth and immediate coordination. The vault's value lies in distilled outcomes: the decision, the date, the link, the document, the contact details, the checklist that will be used again. The vault is where meaning is extracted from noise. That extraction is not an act of superiority over conversation; it is a way of ensuring conversation does not become the sole archive of the family's life.

The sixth principle is shared access with deliberate boundaries. Although privacy design becomes its own topic later, the core principle belongs here because it affects trust from day one. A vault that is technically shared but socially unsafe will not be used honestly. People will withhold, create private stashes, and the system will fracture. Show: a teenager refuses to engage because they assume their notes will be read; a partner avoids logging something sensitive because it feels exposed; an adult keeps a parallel system "just in case". Name the failure: trust bypass. Explain the mechanism: when sharing lacks boundaries, people protect themselves by routing information elsewhere. The implication is fragmentation, which reinstates the very overload the vault was meant to relieve.

Trust, here, is not sentimental. It is operational. It is the behaviour of putting important things into the vault because one believes the vault will not be misused and will remain accessible. Trust grows when the system behaves consistently: items placed there can be found; boundaries are respected; the vault is not used as a device for surveillance or blame. A vault is an object, but it sits inside a relationship. The principles are therefore not only technical. They are ethical.

Two checkable moments from outside family life sharpen what is at stake. One is the aviation disaster already discussed earlier in the book's arc: the Boeing Model 299 crash at Wright Field in 1935, which helped normalise checklists because complexity outpaced memory. The other is a digital-age reminder of fragility: the WannaCry ransomware attack in May 2017, which disrupted parts of the UK's National Health Service and made systems temporarily unusable. Neither example is invoked for drama. Each is a demonstration of a principle. Complexity demands external supports. Digital dependence introduces failure modes. The family vault sits at the intersection: it externalises memory to reduce cognitive load, and it must therefore be designed to remain usable when life is messy and when technology misbehaves.

This brings the principles into a single, practical synthesis. One home for each important item reduces version drift. Easy search and predictable naming reduce time-to-find and semantic mismatch. Low friction capture reduces deferred capture, which keeps the vault trustworthy. Selective scope prevents retrieval dilution, preserving confidence. Shared access with boundaries prevents trust bypass, preserving participation. Each principle can be observed in behaviour. Do people check the vault first? Can someone else find the thing? Does capture happen in the moment? Do search results feel reliable? Does the vault feel safe enough to use honestly? These are not abstract virtues. They are system properties experienced through daily acts.

A vault designed by these principles resembles a labelled cupboard not because families should be reduced to domestic management, but because the cupboard is a triumph of modest engineering. It makes daily life work without demanding constant attention. It allows multiple people to participate without central control. It tolerates imperfection: someone puts the mug back slightly wonky and the cupboard still functions. The cupboard does not get offended. The vault should share that temperament. It should be a place the family can rely on when nobody has the energy to be impressive.

The unresolved tension is unavoidable and worth facing directly, because it will shape every later design choice: the vault must ask for some effort at the point information arrives, but it must not ask for so much effort that people stop using it. Too little friction and the vault becomes a heap; too much friction and it becomes a museum. The diagnostic question is therefore sharp: when the next important item appears, will the household give it a clear address in the shared vault, or will it leave it to gravity and hope memory will do the rest?

What Belongs in It

On 13 April 1970, NASA's Apollo 13 suffered an explosion en route to the Moon, and Mission Control in Houston was forced into a ruthless discipline: decide what mattered, surface it fast, and ignore everything else. The crew did not survive because someone had a beautifully annotated archive of every prior thought, message, and memento. They survived because the right procedures, readings, and constraints could be retrieved under pressure, shared across a team, and acted upon. Only the essentials mattered then. That moment is extreme, but it illuminates a domestic truth that is easy to miss: when life demands clarity, the problem is rarely a lack of information. It is the presence of too much, in the wrong places, without a reliable way to separate signal from noise.

A family vault is not an ambition to store everything. It is an ambition to store what changes outcomes. That is the boundary line that prevents a shared vault becoming a digital attic: the vault holds the items whose absence would force the household to improvise, argue, or scramble. It holds what deserves an address. The rest—however emotionally tempting—either belongs elsewhere or belongs nowhere at all.

The difficulty is that "important" is a poor sorting criterion. Everything feels important when it arrives, especially when it arrives with a deadline, a notification badge, or another adult's tone of urgency. Yet importance is often situational. A school newsletter may be broadly informative and mostly skimmable until it contains the one sentence about a change to pick-up arrangements. A group chat may be ninety per cent social glue until it contains the one instruction about what to bring tomorrow. A photograph may be one of fifty near-identical frames until it becomes the single image that will matter to the family in ten years. The vault needs a sharper filter than "important". It needs a filter anchored in consequence and retrieval.

Show the familiar failure. A parent remembers seeing the trip letter. They remember thinking, "I'll do that later." Later becomes bedtime. Bedtime becomes tomorrow. Then, at 7.18, the child is in the kitchen, the toast is burning slightly at the edges, and the form cannot be found. Name what went wrong: the household failed to give the form an address. Explain why this matters: an item without an address becomes a scavenger hunt, and scavenger hunts are expensive when time is tight. The implication is immediate: stress rises, voices sharpen, and the morning starts with a sense of deficiency that has nothing to do with love and everything to do with retrieval.

The vault exists to reduce those costs, so the first question is not "What could we store?" but "What repeatedly hurts when it is missing?" Families can measure this without spreadsheets. Count how often the household has to ask the same question twice. Count how often something triggers a last-minute dash, an apology, or a panicked search. Count how often the same person is interrupted to provide a fact. These are behavioural metrics, not moral judgements. They reveal what belongs in the vault because they reveal where the household is currently paying retrieval debt.

School information almost always qualifies because it has the perfect combination of complexity and consequence. Schools are multi-channel institutions: they use apps, portals, emails, paper letters, and human beings at the gate who assume you have seen the message. The family's risk is not theoretical; it is whether a child arrives without what they need, whether a deadline is missed, whether an absence is handled smoothly, whether a payment is confirmed. The vault should therefore hold the parts of school life that are repeatedly needed and repeatedly hard to reconstruct: key contacts, term dates, timetables, uniform and kit requirements, portal links, and the small policies that become urgent precisely when you cannot find them. Show the difference: instead of scrolling through a chat to remember which day is PE, a parent searches the child's name and "PE" and gets a single, stable note. Name the benefit: time-to-find collapses from minutes to seconds. The implication is less interruption and fewer friction-filled mornings.

Health reference also belongs, handled with appropriate care and boundaries, because stress makes memory unreliable. This is not about offering medical guidance; it is about storing the factual details a family already has and may need to present quickly: allergy information, current medications, appointment notes, key numbers, and summaries that avoid re-telling the same story under pressure. A household that has ever sat in a waiting room trying to remember dates, names, or prior instructions knows that recall is not a virtue in those moments. It is an obstacle. Show: someone searching for a medication name while a child fidgets and the clock ticks. Name: cognitive squeeze. Explain: anxiety narrows attention and degrades recall, even for intelligent people. The implication is that a concise, retrievable record reduces stress and reduces the chance of error in what is communicated.

Money basics belong for a similar reason: not because families should become amateur accountants, but because administrative life is full of renewals, reference numbers, and documents that are painful to reconstruct when missing. The vault should hold the household's own practical artefacts—policy documents, warranty details, renewal dates, key account references, and any family-level documents that are repeatedly requested by institutions. The benefit is not abstract "control". It is fewer moments of rummaging through email for "that PDF" while someone waits on the phone. Show: a service provider asks for an account reference and the household produces it calmly. Name: reduced latency. Explain: the vault turns "I'll have to find it" into "Here it is". The implication is not merely speed; it is a different feeling of adulthood—less improvisation, more steadiness.

Home reference belongs because homes are machines disguised as rooms. Boilers, routers, washing machines, and meters all come with instructions, schedules, and service histories that are usually held in one person's head until they are suddenly needed by someone else. Households repeatedly rediscover the same facts: which filter needs changing, which number to call, where the stopcock is, what the make and model is for a replacement part. Show: a partner away from home receives a message asking how to reset the router; they can answer by pointing to the shared note rather than typing from memory. Name: dependency reduction. Explain: when procedural knowledge is written down, the household stops depending on one person's presence. The implication is resilience—especially useful when the person who "usually knows" is exhausted, ill, or simply not available.

Trips and travel plans belong because they compress complexity into short time windows. A holiday is not one decision; it is a chain: dates, bookings, addresses, tickets, documents, packing, cancellations, contingencies. When those are scattered, the household repeatedly re-decides, often late at night, often with rising tension. A vault can hold the evolving plan in one place: a record of what has been booked, what remains, what the household agreed, what to bring, and what documents matter. Show: the night before departure, instead of searching through three inboxes, the family checks one shared page and packs. Name: coherence. Explain: a single shared record prevents re-creation of the plan. The implication is emotional: travel begins with anticipation rather than panic.

Memories belong too, but selectively, and this is where many vaults fail by kindness. Digital storage has made it effortless to keep everything, and yet "everything" is the fastest route to losing meaning. A family vault is not a camera roll. It is a place for chosen artefacts and their context: the handful of photographs that represent an event, the short story that explains why a picture matters, the small milestone note that future-you will treasure precisely because it is brief and specific. Show: a child's first day at a new school captured not only in an image but in a sentence of their own words. Name: contextual preservation. Explain: without context, images become anonymous; with a small annotation, they remain alive. The implication is that the family's archive becomes usable rather than merely large.

If those are the core "yes" categories, the most important "no" is equally clarifying: the vault should not become the family's chat transcript. Conversation is valuable. It is also noisy by design. A group chat is a social space where meaning is created in motion, and the motion is the point. Trying to store the whole motion in the vault is how digital attics are born. What belongs is the distilled outcome: the decision, the date, the link, the final address, the agreed checklist. Show: a parents' group thread with forty messages about a meeting point; the vault holds a single line: "Saturday, 10.00, entrance by the library." Name: distillation. Explain: distillation preserves what will be needed later without preserving all the noise that made it hard to find. The implication is that the vault stays lean enough to trust.

This distillation is not only about reducing clutter; it is about protecting relationships. When the only archive is a scroll, families end up policing each other's attention: "It was in the chat, you should have read it." That is a design failure masquerading as moral instruction. The vault offers an alternative: the household can keep chat for chat, and use the vault for what must be retrievable. The behaviour changes. People stop arguing about whether someone saw a message. They check the shared address instead.

A second "no" is the impulse to treat the vault as a dumping ground for raw inputs: every screenshot, every forwarded email, every unprocessed photo of a letter. It feels safe to save everything, and it often begins as self-protection: "At least we have it." The hidden cost is retrieval dilution. As the vault fills with unlabelled, uncurated fragments, search results become crowded, confidence drops, and people revert to asking the human memory person because it is faster. Show: searching "trip" produces twenty near-identical screenshots and no clear answer. Name: dilution. Explain: when signal-to-noise falls, a repository becomes slower than the problem it was meant to solve. The implication is abandonment—not dramatic, just gradual, as the household quietly stops checking first.

At this point, the boundary question becomes sharper: what is the smallest piece of information that will prevent future pain? Often it is not "the entire email thread". It is the booking reference and the address. Not "every message about the school play". It is the date, time, costume note, and ticket link. Not "all the photos from the party". It is three photographs and a sentence about what made the day special. This is how a vault stays alive: it stores what changes outcomes, not what merely passed through the family's hands.

A useful counter-example—and a caution—comes from the history of digital "paperless" dreams. In 2002, Abigail Sellen and Richard Harper published *The Myth of the Paperless Office*, showing that paper persisted not because people were irrational, but because paper is frictionless in certain ways: it is easy to annotate, easy to glance at, easy to pile, rich in context. Families replicate paper behaviour digitally: they create piles of screenshots and PDFs because classification feels expensive. The lesson is not that families should file like librarians. The lesson is that the vault must respect human tendencies. If it demands perfect filing at the point of capture, people will pile. If it allows simple capture and still produces findability, people will use it. The vault should be designed to work with human behaviour rather than to shame it.

There is also a credible limitation that must be faced: not everything should be shared. Families contain privacy, adolescence, vulnerability, and rightful secrecy. A vault that tries to hold every thought becomes invasive. A vault that refuses to hold anything sensitive becomes useless in exactly the moments when stress is highest. The reconciliation is to decide not only what belongs, but where it belongs within the vault's architecture: shared commons for shared reality, parents-only areas for adult administration, personal spaces for teenagers and children where boundaries are honoured. The key is that the vault's usefulness depends on trust, and trust depends on respected limits. Show: a teenager contributes willingly when they know their space is not a public noticeboard. Name: participation through safety. Explain: people share more honestly when they are not exposed. The implication is a richer, more reliable system rather than a brittle one built on avoidance.

The motif of the address returns because it carries the whole argument in a single idea. The vault is not "storage". It is a place where family knowledge receives an address that others can use. When everything is saved without an address—unnamed screenshots, vague notes, piles of PDFs—the vault becomes the very attic it was meant to prevent. When the right items are given clear addresses—school essentials, health reference, household how-to, key documents, trip plans, selected memories—the vault becomes a working environment rather than a graveyard of good intentions.

The question that remains, and should remain, is not whether a family can list what belongs. It is whether the family can commit to boundaries strongly enough to resist digital hoarding. Every input will tempt the household with the same lie: "Save it; decide later." Later is rarely kind. The forward test is therefore practical and slightly uncomfortable: when the next piece of information arrives, will it be given a clear address in the vault because it will matter later, or will it be saved "somewhere" and allowed to swell the attic, making the next urgent search a little harder than the last?

Shared Versus Private Spaces

In April 2018, Facebook's Mark Zuckerberg sat in Washington, D.C. and answered questions before the United States Congress after revelations about Cambridge Analytica had forced a public reckoning with how personal data could travel far beyond its intended audience. The spectacle was political theatre, but the underlying lesson was domestic: information shared without clear boundaries has a habit of escaping. People do not become cautious because they enjoy caution.

They become cautious because they have seen what happens when privacy is treated as optional. A family building a shared vault is not facing Congress, but it is facing the same structural problem at a smaller scale: if the system feels unsafe, people will not use it honestly.

Privacy is often spoken of as a right, and it is, but it is also a condition for participation. A household second brain requires contributions: capture, updates, notes, small records of decisions. Contributions do not arrive when people feel watched. They arrive when people feel respected. A shared vault that collapses all family life into one open room will produce the opposite of what it intends: secrecy, parallel systems, and a return to the old pattern where one person quietly carries the real information alone. Boundaries are not a complication. They are the mechanism by which the system becomes truly shared.

The difficulty begins with a confusion that feels innocent. Many families treat "shared" as a technical setting rather than a social agreement. They create a shared folder or notebook, invite everyone in, and assume that clarity will follow. Then someone hesitates. A teenager refuses to add anything because they assume it will be read. A partner does not record a sensitive reminder because they fear misinterpretation. A parent begins to keep certain things in private notes, "just for now", and those private notes gradually become the real system. Show: the vault exists, but people tiptoe around it. Name: trust bypass. Explain: when a shared system does not feel safe, people route information elsewhere; the vault becomes a display shelf rather than a working environment. The implication is fragmentation, which reintroduces the very overload the vault was meant to reduce.

To design shared versus private spaces well, the family has to accept an uncomfortable truth: privacy is not the enemy of clarity. It is one of its prerequisites. Without privacy, people protect themselves by withholding; with privacy, people can contribute without fear. The goal is not maximal transparency. The goal is dependable shared reality where shared reality is needed, and protected personal space where personal space is deserved. This is the architecture of any healthy commons: there is a public square, but there are also homes with doors.

The most useful way to think about this is to separate three kinds of information by function, not by moral weight. Some information is communal by nature. School schedules, trip plans, household routines, shared contacts, emergency details—these are not intimate diaries. They are the scaffolding that allows a family to coordinate. Keeping them private does not protect dignity; it creates dependence. Show: one adult alone can find the school portal link, so every question routes to them. Name: cognitive gatekeeping. Explain: when coordination knowledge is held privately, the household cannot distribute labour. The implication is predictable: one person becomes the bottleneck and the default memory-holder.

Other information is personal by nature. Thoughts, worries, reflections, private projects, drafts of difficult conversations—these do not belong in the communal square. They require room to be unfinished without becoming communal property. Teenagers, especially, need this. Developmental psychologists have long emphasised adolescence as a period of identity formation and increased desire for autonomy; classic work in this area includes Laurence Steinberg's synthesis in *Adolescence* (multiple editions across decades). The point does not require jargon. Teenagers test ideas by writing them down, by changing their minds, by being inconsistent as they become themselves. A vault that treats their drafts as public text will either silence them or push them into hidden corners of the digital world. The implication is not only a poorer vault. It is a poorer relationship to writing, to planning, to selfhood.

A third category sits between: sensitive household information that needs to exist but not in full view. Money basics, certain health reference, and adult administration often fall here. These are real and sometimes urgent, but they are not always appropriate for every family member to browse casually. The answer is not to hide them entirely. The answer is to place them in a parents-only area or a restricted space that is still part of the vault's overall architecture. Show: an "Adult admin" section with key documents and references, accessible to those who need it. Name: scoped sharing. Explain: scoped sharing keeps the system coherent while preventing accidental exposure. The implication is trust: people can rely on the vault without fearing it will become an indiscriminate broadcast.

A vault designed with these distinctions does not become complicated; it becomes legible. The shared space is the default for coordination. The private spaces are the default for personal reflection and autonomy. The restricted spaces are the default for adult administration and sensitive records. The family does not need to treat this as a philosophical debate every time something is saved. It needs a few stable norms. When norms are clear, capture becomes easier because decisions about where things go are no longer loaded with anxiety.

The tension, of course, is that families are not static. Children grow. Roles change. What is appropriate for a nine-year-old is not appropriate for a fourteen-year-old. What is private for a teenager may become shareable later, by choice, and should remain theirs to share. The vault must therefore be designed as an environment that can evolve without betrayal. Betrayal is the right word, because privacy violations in families do not feel like mere technical errors. They feel like a breach of respect. A system that creates even one such breach will be avoided thereafter, no matter how elegant its structure.

Visible behaviours reveal whether the vault's privacy architecture is working. Do children add to their own spaces? Do they check shared notes before asking? Do partners record decisions in the shared area rather than hoarding them privately? Does the "memory person" role begin to soften? These behaviours are metrics. They show whether the vault feels safe enough to use. They also reveal whether the vault is being used as a tool of support or a tool of control.

Control is the credible counter-example that must be handled honestly. It is possible to build a second brain and use it badly. A family can use shared lists as an instrument of nagging. A partner can treat a system as evidence in arguments. A parent can treat the vault as a surveillance mechanism, checking what a teenager writes, who they contact, what they plan, under the banner of "organisation". Some of this is motivated by genuine concern. Some of it is motivated by anxiety. All of it corrodes the vault. The show is painful: a teenager discovers an adult has read private notes and stops participating. Name: surveillance drift. Explain: when shared tools become monitoring tools, trust collapses; people stop recording honestly, or they move to hidden channels. The implication is not only a failed system. It is a damaged relationship.

The reconciliation is not to pretend this risk does not exist. It is to design against it, culturally and structurally. Culturally, the family must treat the vault as a commons whose purpose is coordination and support, not judgement. Structurally, the vault should separate spaces in a way that makes casual browsing of private areas less likely, and makes the "shared" part genuinely shared rather than cluttered with personal material. The point is to remove temptation and ambiguity. Most privacy breaches in families are not planned crimes; they are opportunistic peeks justified in the moment by stress. A good design prevents those moments from arising.

The motif worth threading here is the door. A door is not an insult. It is a form of respect. It marks a space as someone's. It makes asking possible: you knock. It makes consent visible. A family vault needs doors—private spaces with clear boundaries—not because families should become secretive, but because shared systems without doors become coercive. The door is also a practical device. It reduces noise. It prevents a shared space from becoming psychologically crowded, where people hesitate to add anything because it will be seen by everyone, interpreted by everyone, perhaps used by everyone. Doors create freedom by limiting exposure.

There is also a subtler benefit to privacy-aware design: it protects the meaning of "shared". When everything is shared, nothing feels shared. The shared area becomes a swamp of personal reminders, half-thoughts, and unfinished drafts, and then the household can no longer find the coordination items that matter. The very act of carving out private spaces keeps the shared commons clean. It makes the shared space feel like a place where the family's collective truth is kept: the schedule, the plans, the references, the checklists. Show: a shared area that answers real questions quickly. Name: commons hygiene. Explain: keeping the shared space focused reduces retrieval time and increases trust. The implication is adoption: people return because the system rewards them.

Two named examples from outside the family sharpen the argument without overloading it. One is the principle embedded in the European Union's General Data Protection Regulation, which took effect in May 2018: data should be processed with purpose limitation and access control. The household translation is simple: information should be shared for a reason, and access should match that reason. The other is the long-standing practice of compartmentalisation in secure environments, where access to information is restricted to those who need it to perform a role. The point is not paranoia. It is clarity: different roles require different visibility. Families have roles too—parents, carers, teenagers, younger children—and pretending otherwise produces either overexposure or brittle secrecy.

A family vault that honours privacy does not eliminate difficult judgement calls. There will be grey areas. A teenager may have a project plan they want to keep private until they are ready to share. A parent may need to record something sensitive for practical reasons and may struggle to decide whether it belongs in the restricted space or elsewhere. A couple may have different instincts about what "shared" should mean. These tensions are not design flaws. They are part of being a household composed of distinct persons. The vault's job is not to resolve every moral question. It is to reduce the number of moments when the household is forced into improvisation, and to prevent the system itself becoming a source of conflict.

The most effective privacy architecture therefore begins with an explicit boundary: the shared vault is not the family's total internal life. It is the family's coordination layer and reference memory. Personal spaces exist alongside it, respected as such. Parents-only spaces exist alongside it, used for adult administration and sensitive records. Children's spaces exist within it, not as performance arenas but as places where they can practise organising, planning, and remembering without being watched. The household can then invite participation without demanding exposure. That is a profound shift. It turns "shared" from a demand into an offer.

The forward test is a question about behaviour, not about feelings. When a child or teenager considers adding something to the vault, do they believe the door will be honoured? When a partner records a sensitive household detail, do they believe it will be seen only by those who need it? When the household checks the shared space for the week's reality, does it find coordination rather than private debris? The vault succeeds here not by maximising visibility, but by designing visibility with restraint. The decision is unavoidable: will the family build a commons with doors, or will it build an open-plan archive and then wonder why everyone starts keeping secrets?

Setting Simple Structure

In 1976, in Atlanta, Georgia, the architect John Portman opened the Hyatt Regency, a hotel built around a vast interior atrium that made orientation oddly effortless. Visitors did not need a map to understand where they were. They stepped inside, looked up, and the building announced its logic: corridors ringed the open space; lifts ran visibly; the centre held the whole. The design did not remove complexity—there were hundreds of rooms—but it reduced *lostness*. People could recover their bearings quickly because the structure served the questions they were actually asking: Where am I? How do I get back? Where does everything connect?

A shared vault needs that same quality. Not grandeur, but recoverability. Families do not fail at organisation because they lack intelligence; they fail because they cannot maintain orientation when information is arriving through too many channels and life is moving too fast. The most damaging experience is not "mess". It is the moment of pause before searching, when no one is sure where to begin. You forget the name. You forget the folder. You scroll. You ask. The system, in that moment, has no centre. Keep it small.

Simple structure begins with a refusal: a refusal to build a perfect taxonomy. The perfect taxonomy is the enemy of the working vault because it confuses the pleasures of design with the reality of use. A family's structure must answer lived questions, not hypothetical ones. "What is happening this week?" "Where are the trip documents?" "What does school need tomorrow?" "Where is the boiler manual?" These questions are asked under time pressure, often one-handed, often with a child waiting. The structure that serves them is not necessarily elegant. It is navigable.

The first move is to choose a small set of top-level areas that match how families actually think, and to keep them stable. Stability matters more than cleverness. Show what instability does: one week, school information sits under "Kids"; the next, it sits under "Education"; someone else creates "Term" and "School Year" and then forgets which is which. Name the failure: orientation drift. Explain the mechanism: when the top-level map changes, people stop trusting their instincts; every retrieval becomes a guess. The implication is that the vault becomes slower than asking another human, and asking becomes the default again.

A minimum viable structure keeps the top level almost boring. It might include a shared space for coordination, a school space, a health space, a home space, a money basics space, a trips space, and a memories space, with private and parents-only areas running alongside. The exact labels matter less than the fact that they are few, consistent, and written in ordinary household language. A vault should sound like a home, not like a filing cabinet in a law firm. The metric here is recall: can a tired adult name the top-level areas without opening the app? If not, the structure is already too complex.

Within each top-level area, the next principle is shallow structure: avoid deep nesting. Deep nesting feels tidy but punishes retrieval because it forces people to remember a path. Families do not search by path; they search by cues. They remember a child's name, a place, a month, a keyword like "uniform" or "passport". They do not remember whether "Uniform" sits under "School > Policies > Clothing > Requirements" or "Kids > School > Admin". When a system requires path memory, it recreates the very burden it was meant to remove. Show: someone tapping through three levels of folders while a child asks, "Are we going now?" Name: path dependence. Explain: deep hierarchies require precise recall of classification decisions made long ago. The implication is predictable: people give up and revert to search through chat threads and inboxes.

This does not mean folders are useless. It means folders should serve broad domains, not fine-grained distinctions. Fine-grained distinctions belong in tags, titles, and search, because those match how humans retrieve under pressure. Here, a handful of tags can do more work than a hundred folders. Tags are not decoration. They are cross-cutting handles. A single note about a school trip can carry the child's name tag, the school tag, and a "Trip" tag, making it retrievable through multiple routes without duplication. The visible behaviour is quick filtering: type a name, see everything relevant. The implication is speed and confidence—two things families rarely have enough of.

The strongest argument for simple structure is that families do not maintain complex systems consistently. This is not laziness; it is a property of life. The ethnographic work of Abigail Sellen and Richard Harper on information management, including *The Myth of the Paperless Office* (2002), helps explain why: people prefer low-effort "piling" when classification effort feels too high, because piles preserve context and reduce decision fatigue. Families pile digitally as well: screenshots, forwarded emails, half-notes. A structure that demands constant micro-classification will be bypassed, and the bypass will fill the vault with unprocessed debris. The reconciliation is not to fight the human tendency to pile. It is to design the system so a little piling is safe: capture quickly into the right broad area, then rely on titles and tags to make retrieval workable even when refinement lags.

A worked example makes this concrete without turning it into a tutorial. Imagine a household setting up a shared vault on a Sunday evening. They decide, in advance, that the vault's centre will be a shared "Dashboard" space: a place for the present tense. This is where the family looks first. It holds the week's plan, current projects, and the few lists that genuinely govern daily life. The centre matters because it reduces the distance between need and retrieval. When someone asks, "What is happening this week?" the household does not browse a category tree; it opens the centre.

Around that centre sit the stable domains. "School" holds term dates, timetables, portal links, key contacts, and anything that needs to be referenced repeatedly. "Health" holds factual references and notes that the household may need under stress, stored with care. "Home" holds manuals, service details, and household how-to notes. "Money basics" holds key documents and references the household repeatedly needs, without becoming a full accounting system. "Trips" holds travel plans, bookings, and packing templates. "Memories" holds curated artefacts with context, not raw photo dumps. Alongside, a "Parents-only" space holds adult administration, and individual private spaces exist for partners and for children, especially teenagers, so participation does not require exposure. The system is not a maze. It is a map.

Now watch what happens when information arrives. A school email contains a date change. The family captures the outcome as a note in "School" with a title that uses the words they will later search: "School trip – Year 6 – 12 March – payment link". They tag it with the child's name, the school, and "Trip". If they do nothing else, retrieval still works. Later, during the weekly check, they can pull the date into the "Dashboard" week view. The design allows imperfect capture without losing the plot. The metric is retrieval time: can someone else find it in under thirty seconds? If yes, the structure is already doing its job.

The crucial part of this example is not the labels. It is the logic: centre for the present, domains for stable reference, tags for cross-cutting retrieval, and minimal depth to prevent path dependence. Each choice serves a real household question. "What's happening this week?" is served by the centre. "Where are the trip documents?" is served by the "Trips" domain plus a "Trip" tag. "What does school need tomorrow?" is served by "School" plus child tags. "How do I reset the router?" is served by "Home" plus a search term. The vault becomes a place where the household's questions have predictable landing zones.

A credible counter-example is the temptation to make the structure mirror institutional categories: "Education",

"Healthcare", "Finance", "Facilities", "Operations". It is neat. It is also alien. Families do not speak like institutions, and they do not retrieve like them. Show: a household builds professional-sounding categories, then forgets where anything belongs because the categories do not match their lived language. Name: category alienation. Explain: when labels do not match how people think, the system becomes cognitively expensive; people hesitate, misfile, or avoid filing entirely. The implication is that the vault becomes a private project maintained by one person, which defeats the purpose of shared clarity.

The reconciliation is to treat the vault's structure as a design for cognition, not a reflection of reality. The vault does not need to represent the world perfectly. It needs to be searchable and usable by the people in it. That means using names that feel obvious. It means resisting the urge to create a separate folder for every subtopic. It means accepting that some items will land in the "wrong" place and still be retrievable because titles and tags compensate. It also means revisiting structure with humility. A family might discover that "Kids" is too broad, or that "Home" needs a sub-area for "Services", or that "Memories" works better when split by year. Those adjustments are not failures. They are iterations. The only structural failure is to keep a system that consistently confuses its users.

Simple structure also protects privacy in a practical way. When shared and private spaces are separated at the top level, the household reduces accidental exposure. People know where to put what. They can contribute without anxiety. A teenager can add a homework plan in their own space and optionally link or share parts of it with the family. Parents can store adult administration without making it the background texture of the shared commons. The shared "Dashboard" stays focused on coordination rather than on private debris. The vault's commons remains legible because doors exist elsewhere. This is not merely ethical; it is operational. The vault is easier to use because the shared space is not cluttered with material that others should not browse.

The motif of the building returns, because good structure is about wayfinding. A family vault should allow quick recovery from disorientation. Nobody should have to remember the architect's intent. If someone forgets where an item lives, search should rescue them. If they forget what the note was called, tags should help. If they forget both, the top-level domains should still narrow the field. The goal is graceful failure: when memory fails, the system catches the fall. That is what "simple" really means here—not fewer features, but fewer points of confusion.

The most honest test of the structure is behavioural and slightly ruthless. When the household is tired, do they still use it? When something urgent appears, does it go into the vault or into the scroll? When someone else needs information, do they ask a person or do they check the system? These are not personality tests. They are design tests. A structure that works only on calm Sundays is not a family structure. A structure that still works on wet Wednesdays has earned its place.

The forward tension sits in a trade-off that no system can avoid: every additional category can make filing feel precise, and every additional category can make retrieval feel uncertain. Precision flatters the organiser. Recoverability serves the family. The diagnostic question is therefore simple enough to repeat: when someone in the household asks, "Where would I look for that?", does the answer arrive immediately, or does it require a discussion about where it *ought* to be? The vault will be built from many small decisions, but this is the one that decides whether the structure becomes a map or a maze.

Chapter 3
Choosing Tools and Setting Up

In December 2010, in the United States, Netflix's engineers published a post describing a tool they called Chaos Monkey, designed to deliberately break parts of their own system in order to prove it could survive failure. The point was not masochism. It was realism. Complex digital life does not fail politely; it fails at inconvenient moments, and the only systems worth trusting are those built to endure imperfect conditions. That logic has quietly crept into the home. Families now depend on networks, logins, apps, devices, and sync without ever consenting to the complexity. A school portal assumes stable access. A group chat assumes you will scroll back and find the key detail. A calendar assumes it will appear on every device at the right time. These assumptions hold—until they do not.

The household second brain is already a countermeasure against one kind of failure: the failure of human memory under load. Yet it introduces a new question with its own risks: what should the family build the vault in? Families do not lack tools. They drown in them. A phone already contains notes, reminders, a cloud drive, a camera roll, messaging, and email; the problem is not absence, it is coherence. Choosing tools is therefore not a shopping trip for features. It is a decision about what kind of friction the family is willing to tolerate, and what kind of reliability it needs when things become messy.

This is where many well-intentioned households stumble. They treat tool choice as a referendum on their seriousness. They assume the "best" app will produce the best behaviour. They begin an anxious hunt, comparing features late at night, watching demonstrations, reading reviews, promising themselves that once the right system is selected everything will finally click. In reality, tool obsession often masks a more human anxiety: the fear of committing to a system that will expose imperfect habits. A tool can always be changed later. A habit, once chosen, must be lived. The irony is that the most sophisticated tool in the world will fail in a family if it feels fiddly when someone is tired.

Tools matter because they shape behaviour. A notes space invites capture. A task manager invites commitment and follow-through. A cloud drive invites storing documents, but often resists quick, casual retrieval. A visual board invites shared progress by making work visible rather than remembered. Each tool type embodies a different bias about what "work" is. The home, however, does not care about philosophical purity. It cares about whether a parent can add a school deadline in ten seconds, whether a partner can find a booking confirmation without asking, whether a teenager can check a plan without feeling supervised, whether a grandparent can step in and locate the right instructions when needed.

The chapter's task is to move tool choice out of the realm of ideology and into the realm of household physics. Notes apps are generous surfaces; they are excellent for reference, for evolving plans, for the written "how we do things" that otherwise lives in one person's head. Their weakness is that they can become a graveyard of good intentions unless the vault's structure is kept simple. Task managers excel at taking intentions and turning them into commitments; they are good for repeatable routines and for reducing "I meant to" into something trackable. Their weakness is that they can invite guilt if overused, turning family life into a dashboard of unfinished tasks. Cloud drives are reliable for documents and attachments; they keep the PDFs, scans, and manuals together, and they tend to persist over time. Their weakness is that they can be slow to navigate and hostile to quick capture unless paired with a more fluid notes layer. Visual boards—kanban boards in particular—shine when a family has projects: travel planning, home improvements, applications, events. Their weakness is that they can become performative if they drift into being a display rather than a working board. None of these tools is a total solution. That is the point. Families need a small stack of tools that complement one another, not a single app that promises to be everything and becomes, inevitably, another place where information can vanish.

The most useful comparison is not technical; it is experiential. Imagine the same parent across one ordinary day. At 7.18, they need to know whether it is PE day and what kit is required. At midday, they remember they need to pay for a trip and cannot recall where the link lives. At 5.30, a message arrives about a change to tomorrow's pick-up time. At 9.45, they finally have quiet enough to review the week and coordinate with their partner. A good tool choice makes each moment slightly easier without demanding new rituals at each turn. A bad tool choice adds micro-friction—extra taps, confusing sharing settings, awkward searching—that accumulates into abandonment.

That is why the criteria here are intentionally unromantic. Ease of use beats power. Sharing beats personal customisation. Availability across devices beats clever interface tricks. Long-term reliability beats novelty. A family second brain is not an enthusiast's playground; it is infrastructure. Infrastructure should not require constant attention. It should work while people live. Children, especially, are honest users: they will not tolerate an interface that feels like homework. Adults, under fatigue, are not much different. The criterion of "fun to tap" is not frivolous. It is shorthand for low friction and high likelihood of adoption. If a tool feels pleasant and straightforward, the household will use it more often. If it feels like a chore, it will become another abandoned system with a ghostly skeleton of notes and folders.

Tool choice also intersects with privacy and trust. A tool that makes it difficult to separate shared and private spaces will push families into awkward compromises: either oversharing that feels invasive or hiding that fractures the vault. A tool that has clumsy permissions will tempt the household into shared passwords and informal workarounds that may later become brittle. A tool that changes frequently or disappears creates risk—not in the dramatic sense of catastrophe, but in the steady erosion of confidence that the vault will remain there next year. The family is investing attention into building shared clarity; it deserves a reasonable expectation of continuity.

Yet the most important criterion is rarely spoken aloud: the tool must match the family's existing habits. Families already have a rhythm. They already check certain apps. They already use certain accounts. The best setup is often the one that makes the smallest behavioural demand while producing a noticeable improvement. Starting from scratch can feel virtuous. It often fails because it ignores inertia. In the home, inertia is not laziness; it is the stabilising force that keeps life moving when there is no energy for reinvention. A second brain that begins by replacing everything at once is declaring war on inertia. The wiser move is to recruit inertia: take what the family already uses and give it a clearer purpose.

This is where concrete patterns become more helpful than abstract principles. A simple setup might consist of a shared notes space for the vault, paired with a shared calendar for time. A slightly richer setup might add a visual board for projects, keeping plans visible without constant conversation. A document-heavy household might keep scans and PDFs in a shared drive while keeping the "front door" of the system in a notes space, so retrieval remains fast and human. The point of these setups is not to prescribe a single correct arrangement; it is to demonstrate that tool stacks can be modest and still powerful when each tool has a clear job and a clear boundary.

The chapter's emotional centre is also worth naming. Many families feel shame about their current state: piles on the table, chaos in the inbox, screenshots everywhere, repeated forgetting. Tool choice can become another theatre for that shame—another opportunity to feel behind, to feel technologically incompetent, to feel that other households have mastered something you have not. The truth is more forgiving. Most systems fail not because families choose the wrong app, but because they choose too much change at once, or because they choose a tool that demands more attention than their life can give. The path to shared clarity is not a leap into a new digital identity. It is a small set of decisions that make the household's existing digital life behave like a coherent vault.

There is also a philosophical question hiding beneath the practical one. Tools are not neutral. They shape what a family values. A tool that foregrounds tasks can make life feel like a to-do list. A tool that foregrounds notes can make life feel like a record. A tool that foregrounds boards can make life feel like projects. The household must choose what it wants to *see* when it looks at itself. That choice is not permanent. It should not be treated as destiny. But it is worth making consciously, because families become what they repeatedly attend to.

The motif here is the switchboard: the home as a place where signals arrive from schools, employers, clubs, services, relatives, and devices, and where those signals must be routed into shared clarity rather than left buzzing in the background. Tool choice is not about acquiring more signals. It is about choosing a cleaner switchboard—one that routes a school update into the vault, a task into a reliable list, a document into a stable home, a project into a visible board. When the switchboard is well designed, the household stops acting like an emergency response unit and starts acting like a place where life can be planned without drama.

The page ahead turns tool choice into a set of questions that can be answered without falling into endless comparison. It treats tools as a family environment rather than a personal preference, and it treats setup as an act of gentle engineering rather than a makeover. The trade-off will remain, because it always does: do you prioritise simplicity and adoption, or flexibility and feature depth? The forward test is equally blunt: when the next important detail arrives while everyone is tired, will the family have tools that make capture and retrieval feel almost automatic, or will the detail fall back into the scroll, waiting to be rediscovered later at a cost?

Understanding Tool Types

On 4 April 1973, in New York City, Martin Cooper of Motorola walked along Sixth Avenue and made a call on a handheld mobile phone prototype. The technical feat is easy to admire. The social consequence is more interesting: communication stopped being tied to a place. Messages could arrive anywhere, which meant decisions could be made anywhere, which meant the administrative life of a family could now be distributed across pockets and minutes. That distribution is convenient until it becomes unmanageable. A child's school message, a calendar change, a photo of a letter, a payment link, a reminder about dinner—all of it can land on the same glowing rectangle, and then vanish into different apps, different scrolls, different private memories. The question is not whether families have tools. They do. The question is whether the tools behave like a system or like a swarm.

A family second brain becomes practical only when it has a shape, and that shape is determined less by philosophy than by tool types. Tool types are not brands. They are behavioural containers: each type nudges information into a particular form and makes certain actions easy while making others awkward. If a family mistakes a tool's bias for a personal failure—"I can't stay organised", "I never stick to lists"—they will keep blaming themselves for what the interface is quietly encouraging. When a family understands tool types, it can choose containers that match the household's needs and stop demanding that one app behave like four different instruments.

The four tool types that matter most for a family vault are notes spaces, task managers, cloud drives, and visual boards. Each is good at one thing and bad at another, not because developers are incompetent but because design involves trade-offs. The family's work is not to find perfection; it is to assemble a small kit in which each tool has a clear job, and the jobs align with how the household actually moves through the week. The motif worth keeping in mind is the switchboard: information arrives as signals, and the household must route those signals into places that can hold them without distorting them. When the switchboard is messy, the household keeps re-deciding. When the switchboard is clear, decisions become durable.

Start with notes spaces, because they are the most forgiving container and the closest thing to a general-purpose room in the vault. Notes spaces are good at holding reference and evolving plans in human language. They can contain a school contact list, a packed-lunch routine, a travel plan, a "how to reset the router" guide, a family emergency sheet, a curated memory note with a photograph and a line of context. Show: a parent searching a child's name and finding the trip details, the kit list, and the teacher's email in one place. Name: narrative storage. Explain: notes can hold context, not just data; they accommodate the messy reality that family information is often best understood as a story with fragments attached. The implication is trust: people return because the vault answers questions quickly without requiring a precise path.

Notes spaces have a failure mode, and it is common. They become a graveyard of fragments. A note is created in a rush, never titled well, never revisited, then buried beneath dozens more. Search begins to return too many results. Confidence drops. The vault starts to feel like another scroll. Name the failure: note sprawl. Explain: when capture is easy but organisation is optional, accumulation outpaces curation; the system becomes noisy. The implication is behavioural: under pressure, the household stops checking first and starts asking a person. A notes space needs light structure—clear naming, a few stable areas, minimal tagging—so it stays retrievable without becoming bureaucratic.

Task managers are different. They are not primarily for storing knowledge. They are for committing to action. Their central promise is not memory but follow-through. Show: a recurring task for "send PE kit on Tuesdays" or "put bins out" that surfaces at the right time. Name: temporal prompting. Explain:

task managers excel at turning intentions into scheduled prompts, especially for routines and time-bound tasks. The implication is reduced cognitive load: fewer "I meant to" moments, fewer late-night realisations. In a family context, task managers also make shared commitments visible, which can reduce the quiet resentment that grows when one person feels they are doing everything.

Task managers also have a failure mode: they can become a guilt engine. Families add too many tasks, the list becomes endless, completion becomes demoralising, and the tool begins to feel like a scoreboard of inadequacy rather than a support. Name: obligation inflation. Explain: task managers encourage enumeration; families are tempted to capture everything, including tasks that are too vague or too large to be meaningful. The implication is abandonment, often sudden: the tool is ignored for a week, then two, and then it becomes another place where truth might be outdated. Task managers work best in family life when used for what is genuinely actionable and time-sensitive, not for every diffuse aspiration.

Cloud drives occupy a third role: they are built for files. They are good at storing documents that should remain stable and shareable over time: PDFs, scans, manuals, policies, certificates, booking confirmations, warranties. The family advantage is durability. A well-chosen cloud drive behaves like a filing cabinet that does not burn down when a laptop is replaced. Show: a scanned school form filed once, then retrieved months later without hunting through old emails. Name: durable storage. Explain: files systems are designed for persistence, versioning, and sharing; they hold artefacts in their original form. The implication is risk reduction in a practical sense: key documents are less likely to be lost when devices change and accounts shift.

Cloud drives, however, are rarely good at daily use. They can be slow to navigate on phones. They can hide context. They can encourage deep folder trees that feel tidy but are difficult to remember. The family ends up with "Documents" folders inside "Documents" folders, and then with multiple copies because it is faster to upload again than to find the original. Name: folder labyrinth. Explain: file systems reward hierarchical thinking; families retrieve by cues and search terms, not by path memory. The implication is friction at the moment of need, which pushes people back to screenshots and inboxes. Cloud drives work best as the back-room archive for stable files, with a more human front door—often a notes space—that links to the right documents and adds context.

Visual boards, especially kanban-style boards, form the fourth type. Their power is not storage but visibility. A board is a way of representing work-in-progress as a set of items moving through stages—ideas, next actions, done—so that people can see what is happening without a meeting. Show: a family planning a weekend away with cards for booking, packing, pet care, and cancellations, each moved across columns as decisions are made. Name: visible workflow. Explain: boards externalise progress; they reduce the need for status conversations that can feel like nagging, because the state of the project is visible. The implication is collaboration: children can participate by moving their own cards; partners can coordinate without constant checking-in.

Boards also have a failure mode: they can become performative. A board can look satisfying while hiding the fact that nothing moves. Cards accumulate. Columns become crowded. The board becomes a museum of intentions. Name: stalled board. Explain: boards require a rhythm of review; without it, they accumulate as static display. The implication is cynicism: people stop believing that the system reflects reality, and then they stop using it. Used well, boards do not need constant attention, but they do need a periodic moment where the family checks what is "next" and closes what is "done". Otherwise the board becomes another kind of scroll.

These tool types can be compared through a family lens without reducing them to slogans. Notes spaces are strong at *explanation* and *reference*; they answer "What is this?" and "Where is the information?" Task managers are strong at *commitment* and *prompting*; they answer "What must happen next?" Cloud drives are strong at *preservation* and *sharing files*; they answer "Where is the document?" Visual boards are strong at *coordination* and *progress visibility*; they answer "What stage are we at?" Each tool has a weakness that maps to a predictable family pain. Notes can become noisy. Tasks can become oppressive. Drives can become labyrinthine. Boards can become static. Tool choice, then, is about matching strengths to needs and limiting each weakness through boundaries.

A worked scene shows how these types interact in real household motion. A school trip email arrives with a PDF attachment, a payment link, and kit requirements. A notes space can hold a single trip note with the date, the summary, and a link to the PDF. A cloud drive can store the PDF itself in a stable place. A task manager can hold the payment action with a deadline. A visual board can represent the trip as a project card that moves from "planned" to "booked" to "packed". The household does not need to use all four tools for every event, but seeing the division of labour clarifies why one tool alone often disappoints. If you use a task manager to store reference, it feels clumsy. If you use a notes space to manage recurring prompts, it feels unreliable. If you use a cloud drive as your daily front door, it feels slow. If you use a board as an archive, it feels absurd. The tool types are not interchangeable. They are complementary.

Two named, checkable examples from wider digital life illuminate why these categories exist. One is the development of kanban itself, associated with Toyota's production system in the mid-twentieth century, where visualising work helped control flow and limit overload. The family point is not to mimic manufacturing; it is to note that visibility reduces the need for constant verbal coordination. Another is the way personal computing evolved to separate documents from reminders from communication: email did not replace file systems, and calendars did not replace notebooks, because different tasks require different representations. The household's mistake is often to ask one tool to carry all representations at once.

A credible counter-example deserves respect: some families succeed with almost no tooling. They keep a paper calendar on the fridge, a labelled folder for school papers, and a small set of routines held in habit rather than in apps. This works, especially when the household's channels are limited and the family's rhythm is stable. The reconciliation is not to dismiss this. It is to recognise what makes it work: clarity of "where things go", shared visibility, and low friction. Those are tool-type properties, even when the tool is paper. Digital tools become helpful when the household's information arrives digitally and when sharing across devices and people becomes necessary. The underlying principles remain the same. The switchboard just changes material.

Understanding tool types therefore has a liberating effect. It stops the family expecting a notes app to behave like a calendar, or a chat thread to behave like a vault, or a cloud drive to behave like a dashboard. It also stops the family from misreading tool friction as personal weakness. If a task manager makes someone feel guilty, the answer may not be "try harder"; it may be "use tasks more sparingly, and store reference elsewhere". If a notes space feels messy, the answer may not be "be more disciplined"; it may be "reduce capture noise and improve titles". If a drive feels unusable, the answer may not be "learn folders"; it may be "use search and keep hierarchy shallow, with notes as the front door". Tool types turn moralised frustration into solvable design.

The unresolved tension remains, because it is the real decision families must make: do you prioritise a single, simple tool that everyone can use, accepting its limits, or do you combine a small set of specialised tools, accepting the overhead of integration? Both can work. Both can fail. The diagnostic question is sharp enough to guide the choice: when the next urgent piece of information arrives—late at night, mid-commute, in the middle of dinner—will the household know which container it belongs in, and will that container make retrieval easier than asking a person?

Criteria for Family Tools

In January 2012, in Washington, D.C., the National Transportation Safety Board issued its report on the 2010 "Miracle on the Hudson", the US Airways Flight 1549 ditching in the Hudson River after bird strikes disabled both engines. The story is remembered for calm heroism, and that is fair. It is also a story about equipment and procedure working under strain. The aircraft's design, the crew's training, and the checklists did not make the day easy; they made it survivable. Families are not flying airliners, but they do depend on systems functioning when minds are crowded. A second brain tool that works only when everyone is fresh and polite is the wrong tool. The household needs tools that behave reliably when the day is noisy, devices are low on battery, and attention is torn.

Tool choice, then, is not an exercise in taste. It is a decision about what the family can trust. Trust, here, is not a warm feeling; it is a habit: the habit of putting information into the system because you believe you will find it later, and the habit of checking the system before you interrupt another person. A tool earns that habit when it is easy enough to use under fatigue, shareable enough to distribute cognition, available enough to reach from wherever life happens, and durable enough not to collapse the moment a device is replaced or a company changes direction. Those criteria sound banal. They are decisive.

Begin with ease of use, because families do not fail because they lack sophistication. They fail because the cost of using the tool competes with the cost of living. Show the moment when ease matters. A parent receives a school message while carrying bags. They have seven seconds of attention. They need to capture the key detail before it vanishes into the scroll. If the tool requires choosing a folder, selecting a category, deciding among multiple templates, then waiting for sync, capture will not happen. Name the principle: friction threshold. Explain why it rules: under time pressure, people choose the lowest-friction path; if capture feels like work, "I'll do it later" wins. The implication is a predictable drift back to piles and private memory.

Ease of use is not the same as minimal features. It is the experience of moving through the interface without hesitation. It is the feeling that the tool expects human imperfection. This is where "fun to tap" matters. It is an inelegant phrase for a profound behavioural truth: tools that feel pleasant and straightforward get used, and tools that feel fussy get abandoned. Children are honest about this because they are not invested in being seen as competent; if an interface feels like paperwork, they will avoid it. Adults, under fatigue, behave similarly. A tool can be brilliantly powerful and still fail in a home because it produces micro-hesitations—little moments of "Where is that?" that add up to avoidance.

Psychology offers a useful lens without turning this into a lecture. In 2004, the researcher BJ Fogg began formalising what is often called the behaviour model: behaviour happens when motivation, ability, and a prompt converge. The family translation is simple. Motivation is fragile in domestic life; it fluctuates with tiredness and stress. Prompts are plentiful; notifications are everywhere. Ability—how easy the action is—becomes the lever families can actually control. Tools that increase ability by reducing steps make capture and retrieval more likely. Tools that reduce ability by adding complexity demand motivation the household cannot reliably supply.

Sharing options are the second criterion, and they are where many personal productivity tools fail a family. A family second brain is not a solo notebook. It is a shared environment. Show the consequence of poor sharing. One adult can see the notes. The other cannot. A teenager cannot access the relevant list without borrowing a phone. A grandparent helping at short notice is outside the system. The household immediately falls back into the old pattern: one person becomes the memory hub, and everyone else becomes dependent. Name the failure: cognitive centralisation. Explain: when access is uneven, cognition concentrates, and the system becomes a private hoard with a polite label. The implication is resentment and fragility—if the memory hub is unavailable, the family's ability to function drops.

Sharing, however, is not merely about inviting everyone into one room. It also requires control of boundaries, because a family is not a group of identical users with identical rights to see everything. A tool with clumsy permissions forces families into awkward compromises: either oversharing that feels invasive or hiding that fractures the vault. The behaviour to watch is avoidance. If people refuse to contribute because they fear exposure, the tool is not "shared" in any meaningful sense. Sharing options must therefore include the ability to separate communal areas, parents-only areas, and personal spaces without turning the system into a maze. When this works, it produces a visible effect: participation. Children add to their own spaces. Partners record decisions in the shared space. The vault stops being one person's hobby.

Availability across devices is the third criterion, and it is more than convenience. The household does not live in one place. Information arrives at the school gate, on trains, in supermarkets, in waiting rooms, in cars. If the tool works only on one device, it will miss the moments when capture matters most. Show the everyday friction. A parent sees an email on a phone, but the only way to file it properly is on a laptop, and the laptop will not be opened until late. The detail is forgotten. Or the parent keeps a private note on a personal phone because the shared tool is not available there. Name: capture displacement. Explain: when the capture tool is not present at the moment of intake, the household delays capture; delayed capture increases loss and reduces trust. The implication is that the system fills with gaps, and gaps invite reversion to memory.

Cross-device availability also protects retrieval. A partner at work needs the address for the plumber. A grandparent on a different device needs pick-up instructions. A teenager needs their timetable on their own phone, not on a parent's. Retrieval should not depend on being in the right room with the right device. When it does, families will continue to experience "somewhere" as the dominant location of important things. The metric is blunt: can two adults access the same vault within ten seconds from wherever they are? If not, the system is a partial solution at best.

Long-term reliability is the fourth criterion, and it is easy to underestimate because novelty feels like progress. Many tools are delightful in the first week. They are colourful. They promise to organise life. Then the company changes pricing, removes features, loses interest, or disappears. Or the tool works well but does not export cleanly, turning the family's knowledge into a hostage. In May 2017, the WannaCry ransomware attack disrupted parts of the UK's National Health Service, reminding everyone that digital dependence introduces failure modes. Families do not need to live in fear of catastrophe to respect the principle: if the family is investing attention into building a vault, the vault should not be fragile.

Reliability has several visible components. Does the tool sync consistently, or does it produce duplicates and conflicts that erode confidence? Does it work offline or in poor connectivity, or does it become inaccessible at exactly the wrong time? Does it allow sensible exporting, so the family is not trapped? Does it have a track record, or is it a fashionable experiment? These questions can be answered without technical expertise by watching the tool's behaviour over a week. If a tool produces repeated small failures—notes not appearing across devices, sharing links breaking, permissions behaving unpredictably—it will not be trusted. Trust, remember, is habit. Habit collapses when the system feels unreliable.

A short scenario makes the criteria tangible because families do not choose tools on paper; they choose them in motion. Imagine a parent trying two tools during one day. Tool A is powerful, dense with features, and demands deliberate organisation. In the morning, the parent tries to capture a school update while making breakfast. Tool A asks them to pick a workspace, choose a template, decide whether the note is a task or a document, and then prompts them to tag it properly. The parent closes the app. They tell themselves they will do it later. Later never arrives. In the afternoon, the parent tries to find yesterday's homework note. Tool A has it somewhere, but the parent cannot remember the path, and search returns too many results with similar names. They ask the child again. The child shrugs. Tension rises. Tool A is impressive. It is not adopted.

Tool B is simpler. In the morning, the parent taps a single button and captures the key detail as a short note with a title that matches how they will search later. It automatically lands in the shared school area. In the afternoon, the parent searches the child's name and a keyword and finds it. In the evening, the partner checks the same note from another device without asking. The tool does not have all the features Tool A offers. It has something better for a family: low friction and consistent retrieval. The day is still busy. The administrative edges are less sharp.

This scenario is not a manifesto against sophisticated tools. Sophisticated tools can work well for families with high tolerance for maintenance, stable routines, and a keen organiser who enjoys the craft. That is the credible counter-example, and it matters. Some households genuinely benefit from richer feature sets: advanced automation, complex linking, fine-grained permissions. The reconciliation is to recognise that the household is not choosing a tool for its abstract excellence; it is choosing a tool for its behavioural fit. A tool should match the family's lowest-energy user, not its most enthusiastic. The family system will be maintained at the pace of the most tired adult and the most distracted child, because those are the conditions under which life actually happens.

These criteria also protect families from a particular modern trap: endless app hunting. App hunting feels productive because it is measurable—you can compare features, read reviews, create a shortlist. It is also infinite. There will always be a tool with a cleaner interface, a new feature, a cleverer approach. The household can lose months in a perpetual audition process while the real need—shared clarity—remains unmet. The way out is to treat tool choice as a commitment to *behaviour*, not as a bet on perfection. Choose tools that make the desired behaviour easy: capture, retrieval, sharing, and review. Reject tools that make the behaviour feel like a chore. That is not anti-intellectual. It is design literacy.

The motif of the switchboard returns because it captures the practical point. A tool is not a trophy. It is a switch. It routes information. If the switch is fiddly, people stop flicking it. If the switch is reliable, people use it without thinking. Families do not need a switchboard with a thousand options; they need one that routes the most important signals into the shared vault consistently, across devices, and with boundaries that protect trust.

The forward test is therefore a question about lived moments rather than features. When the next key detail arrives—mid-commute, mid-dinner, mid-tantrum—can it be captured in under ten seconds, shared without fuss, and retrieved later by another person without a tutorial? If not, no amount of cleverness will compensate. If yes, the family can stop hunting for the perfect tool and start building the only thing that matters: a system that survives real life.

Example Tool Setups

In October 1962, at Cape Canaveral in Florida, NASA launched Mercury-Atlas 8, sending astronaut Wally Schirra into orbit. The craft was not a single magical machine. It was a stack: capsule, guidance systems, tracking, communications, mission control. Each component did a narrow job well, and the mission succeeded because the boundaries between those jobs were clear. That is the quiet lesson families need when they assemble a second brain. The household does not require a super-app that claims to do everything. It requires a small kit in which each tool has a defined role and the handoffs between roles are frictionless enough to survive real life.

The danger of tool talk is that it becomes abstract. Families imagine themselves trapped between two unpleasant futures: either they keep their current sprawl of apps and piles, or they commit to a complex system that demands constant attention. Example setups make a third possibility visible. A family can build a second brain with surprisingly few moving parts if those parts are chosen for how the household behaves under stress: capture quickly, retrieve without debate, share without begging for access, and review without turning the process into a second job. Tools are not identity. They are containers. Use the ones you already touch.

A useful motif here is the switchboard. Information arrives as signals—school updates, appointment details, documents, decisions—and the household's task is to route each signal into the right place so it can be retrieved later. A good setup reduces the number of switches you must flick and the number of places you must search. A bad setup adds channels. The following three patterns scale from minimal to richer, and they are written deliberately without brand names because the underlying logic matters more than the logo on the icon.

Consider first the simplest viable setup: a shared notes space paired with a shared calendar. This is the "two-tool" arrangement. The notes space serves as the vault's front door: reference information, evolving plans, and the distilled outcomes extracted from noisy channels. The calendar serves as the family's time layer: events, deadlines, and appointments that must appear on everyone's devices. Show it in action. A school app posts that PE day has shifted. The household records the new pattern in the shared notes space under a "School" area, tagged with the child's name, and then adjusts the relevant calendar reminder. Name the pattern: reference-plus-time. Explain why it works: families need a place to store context and a place to store time, and these are distinct representations; trying to force one tool to behave like both creates friction. The implication is immediate: the family stops hunting through messages for the "real" schedule because the vault holds the current truth and the calendar holds the prompt to act on it.

In this two-tool setup, school information lives primarily in the notes space, because school life is not merely dates; it is policies, contacts, kit lists, portal links, and a stream of decisions that benefit from being captured in human language. Health reference also lives in the notes space, stored with care in a restricted section when appropriate, because what matters is quick retrieval of factual details and a shared place for appointment summaries that reduce repeated retelling. Projects—such as a holiday, a room redecoration, or a school application—begin as notes: a single page that holds the evolving plan, with links to any relevant documents and a few key decisions written down so they are not remade weekly. The calendar's role is not to become an archive. It is to keep the family oriented in time. When someone asks, "What is happening this week?", the calendar answers. When someone asks, "Where is the information about that?", the notes space answers.

The most common failure in this arrangement is to treat the notes space as a dumping ground. If everything is captured without titles that match future searches, the vault becomes noisy. The remedy is not more complexity. It is better naming and a small, stable structure: a "Dashboard" note for the current week, and a handful of domains underneath. The behavioural metric is simple: can a second adult find the PE day information in under thirty seconds? If yes, the setup is working. If not, the problem is not that the family needs a new app; the problem is that the capture and naming conventions need tightening.

Now consider the next level: the "three-tool" setup, which adds a task layer to the shared notes space and calendar. This pattern suits families whose pain points include recurring obligations and missed follow-through—bin night, payments, forms, routine reminders—where remembering "to do" is the bottleneck rather than remembering "what is true". In this arrangement, the notes space still holds reference and context. The calendar still holds time-specific events. The task tool holds commitments: actions with deadlines, recurring routines, and the small steps that make plans real. Show it in a day. At 8.10, the parent sees a school message: trip payment due by Friday. They capture the details in the school trip note in the vault, then create a task "Pay Year 6 trip fee" with a due date, shared with the other parent. Name: commitment externalisation. Explain: tasks are a different cognitive object from notes; a task is meant to disappear through completion, whereas a note is meant to persist. The implication is fewer late-night scrambles, because the obligation is now tracked as an action rather than existing as a half-remembered worry.

In this three-tool setup, school still lives in the notes space, but school actions—pay fees, sign forms, submit replies—live in the task layer when they have deadlines and consequences. Health reference remains in the notes space, while appointment follow-ups—booking, collecting documents, preparing questions—can live as tasks when appropriate. Projects take on a slightly clearer structure: the plan note holds the context, and tasks capture next actions. The family stops debating what to do next because "next" is visible as a set of commitments that can be shared and reassigned. The danger here is obligation inflation: the task list becomes an endless ledger and starts to feel accusatory. The measure is emotional as much as practical. If opening the task list causes immediate dread, the household has put too much into it. The reconciliation is to keep tasks for what is truly actionable and time-bound, and keep the rest as notes or as ideas.

The three-tool arrangement also has a subtle benefit for fairness. One of the most corrosive patterns in family life is invisible labour: one person privately tracks everything and then becomes irritated when others do not "just know". Shared tasks make the load visible without requiring a dramatic conversation. The work is there, written down. It can be claimed, reassigned, or deferred deliberately rather than by neglect. The tool is not morally superior; it simply exposes reality, which can be the beginning of a more equitable household.

The third pattern is for families who have genuine projects—multiple moving parts, shared responsibilities, and a desire to see progress at a glance. This is the "project-visible" setup: shared notes space, calendar, and a visual board, sometimes with tasks folded into the board depending on the tool, sometimes kept separate. The board is not for everything. It is for work that benefits from visibility: travel planning, home improvements, major school applications, parties, seasonal preparations. The notes space remains the vault for reference and context, the board becomes the project cockpit. Show a concrete scenario. A family plans a weekend away. The notes space holds the trip page: booking reference, address, check-in details, a link to tickets, a packing list, and a line about the dog arrangements. The board holds cards: "Book accommodation", "Confirm transport", "Pack chargers", "Cancel swimming", "Print tickets", "Leave house". As each card moves across columns, everyone can see progress without asking. Name: progress visibility. Explain: boards reduce status conversations because the state of work is visible; they also reduce overwhelm by limiting attention to what is "next" rather than to everything at once. The implication is calmer coordination and less nagging, because the system itself answers "Are we done with that?"

In this project-visible arrangement, school still lives in notes and calendar, but major school projects—applications, trips, exam seasons—can have their own board card or mini-board, making complex sequences manageable. Health remains in notes for reference, with relevant projects—such as managing a series of appointments—optionally represented on the board if it helps coordination. The board's danger is stall. A board can become a museum of cards. The remedy is rhythm: a brief weekly review where cards move or are archived. If nothing moves for weeks, the board becomes demoralising.

The vault must reflect reality, not aspiration. The metric is blunt: does the board reduce questions, or does it create another place to check?

A credible counter-example helps keep this grounded. Some families attempt the richest setup immediately—a notes vault, a drive, tasks, boards, automations—and then they discover that integration itself becomes the work. They spend more time maintaining the system than benefiting from it. This is not a failure of character; it is a mismatch between complexity and bandwidth. The reconciliation is to see these patterns as modular. Start with the smallest kit that produces a noticeable reduction in friction, then add a layer only when the household repeatedly hits a limit. If the family constantly forgets actions, add tasks. If the family constantly argues about project status, add a board. If the family constantly loses documents, add a stable document store. Growth should follow pain, not fashion.

Across all three patterns, one principle stays constant: the notes space is usually the front door. Families need a place that can hold context in human language, where a plan can be explained, where decisions can be recorded, and where a child's name can retrieve everything relevant. Documents can live in a drive behind the scenes. Tasks can live in a separate layer. Boards can make projects visible. But the front door must remain simple. People must know where to begin. That is why the switchboard motif matters. A household second brain is a routing system. When the routing is clear, the number of times the family re-decides drops sharply.

These setups also demonstrate that "using what you already have" is not second-best; it is often best. Many families already have a calendar that everyone checks. Many already have a notes tool on every phone. Many already have some form of shared storage through existing accounts. The work is not to replace these with something more fashionable. The work is to assign each a role and a boundary, so the household stops using a chat thread as an archive and stops using a calendar as a filing system. When the roles are clear, the system begins to behave like one coherent vault rather than a swarm of unrelated apps.

The forward test, then, is not "Which setup is ideal?" It is "Which setup will the family actually inhabit?" Choose the pattern that the most tired adult can maintain and the least interested child can tolerate. Then watch the week. Do people capture and retrieve, or do they revert to "somewhere"? Do questions reduce, or do they continue unchanged? The answer will reveal whether the switchboard is routing signals into shared clarity—or whether the household is still living in the swarm, hoping the right detail will surface when it is needed.

Starting With What You Have

On 6 August 1991, from CERN in Geneva, Tim Berners-Lee posted a short message to the alt.hypertext newsgroup announcing the World Wide Web. The decisive detail was not a dazzling new machine or a sealed proprietary platform. It was a modest architecture layered on what already existed: the internet's plumbing, the culture of open protocols, the habit of sharing documents across networks. The outcome is visible in hindsight precisely because it was not theatrical. The web spread because it did not demand that the world rebuild itself first. It offered a new organising layer over familiar infrastructure, and it asked for a small behavioural change—link, publish, retrieve—rather than a total reinvention.

Families building a shared vault face the same choice, minus the academic glory. They can treat the second brain as a clean-slate project, a ceremonial migration into a new digital identity, or they can treat it as a retrofit: a way of giving clearer jobs to devices and accounts already in their pockets. Small systems beat grand overhauls. That sentence is not cynical. It is a practical acknowledgement of inertia, the most underestimated force in domestic life. Inertia is not laziness; it is the tendency of a household to keep moving by repeating familiar actions, even when those actions are imperfect. A system that fights inertia must win every day. A system that recruits inertia can win once and then coast.

The seduction of starting from scratch is that it promises purity. No clutter. No messy legacy. No awkward shared email address with an embarrassing username created in 2014. The trouble is that purity is an expensive fantasy. Starting from scratch often requires a cascade of decisions—new accounts, new permissions, new habits, new app installs, new learning curves—and families rarely have the surplus attention to sustain that cascade past the first enthusiastic evening. When the cascade stalls, the household is left with two partial systems: the old sprawl and the new vault that is not yet trusted. That is a recipe for more confusion, not less.

Starting with what you have does not mean accepting mediocrity. It means choosing the smallest set of changes that produces a noticeable reduction in search, re-deciding, and interruption. The criterion is not elegance. The criterion is adoption under fatigue. A second brain earns its place when it is used on wet Wednesdays, not only on calm Sundays. That is why repurposing existing tools is so powerful: the family already knows how to open them, tap them, and live alongside them without resentment. The system can begin immediately, and immediacy matters because it builds trust through experience rather than through promises.

A useful way to see what you already have is to follow the household's information as it arrives. Messages arrive through email and chat. Documents arrive as attachments, PDFs, photos, and paper captured on phones. Plans arrive as calendar events, reminders, and half-made commitments. Memories arrive as photos and short videos. The household already has containers for each of these streams. The problem is that the containers have not been given clear roles, so information lands wherever gravity pulls it, and retrieval becomes a scavenger hunt. Starting with what you have means assigning roles and boundaries to existing containers so that the family's switchboard becomes legible.

The most common "existing asset" is a shared email address, whether explicitly shared or effectively shared through forwarding. Families often already receive school and club communications by email because institutions like email's permanence and because attachments travel well that way. This is not glamorous, but it is useful. A shared inbox can act as an intake funnel: a place where incoming obligations are visible to more than one adult, where forwarding rules can reduce the chance that one person becomes the sole memory-holder, and where the household can treat email as a source rather than as an archive. The vault's job is not to turn the inbox into a filing cabinet. The vault's job is to extract the durable parts—dates, decisions, documents—and give them an address elsewhere, while leaving the conversational noise where it belongs.

A second existing asset is a shared cloud folder. Many households already have some form of shared storage, even if it is chaotic: a folder where someone once dropped a scan of a passport, a PDF of a boiler manual, a school policy, a warranty. The folder may currently resemble a junk drawer. That does not make it worthless. It makes it under-specified. The simplest move is not to reorganise the entire folder tree. It is to designate one folder as "Family Documents" and treat it as the canonical home for stable files, while using the vault's front door—typically a notes space—to point to those files with context. This reduces duplication and avoids the common failure where families re-upload the same document repeatedly because it is faster than finding the original. The behaviour to aim for is boring: one file, one home, and a reliable way to reach it.

A third asset is the messaging app the family already uses. Messaging is not a vault. It is a river. Still, it can be repurposed as a capture channel rather than an archive. Families already forward screenshots and links to one another; the shift is to treat those forwards as temporary signals that must be distilled. A household can decide that when a key detail appears in chat—an address, a date change, a requirement—it triggers a single action: record the distilled outcome in the shared vault. The chat remains social glue and rapid coordination; the vault becomes the record. This single boundary prevents a great deal of domestic conflict, because it stops "You should have seen the message" from masquerading as a reasonable expectation.

Starting with what you have also means making peace with the fact that families rarely have a single shared device ecosystem. One person might use a phone and laptop from one manufacturer; another might use different hardware entirely. Children might have tablets. Grandparents might have older devices. Tool choices that depend on everyone living inside one company's walled garden often fail at the moment someone changes phones or someone outside the immediate household needs access. Cross-device availability is therefore not a luxury; it is a practical test of whether the vault will remain shared as life shifts. The family is building infrastructure, not a personal dashboard.

A named, checkable example from outside the home shows how consolidation can succeed without requiring a clean slate. On 17 October 2012, the UK Government launched GOV.UK in London, consolidating a large number of departmental websites into a single domain. The project was not perfect, and it did not erase every legacy system overnight, but it made something crucially different: it gave citizens one front door. The lesson for families is not political; it is architectural. You do not have to rebuild every back-end system to gain clarity. You can create a clear front door that points to what exists, and then improve the back rooms over time. The front door creates immediate benefit. Benefit builds adoption. Adoption creates the capacity for deeper changes later.

There is, however, a credible limitation to starting with what you have, and it must be faced rather than waved away. Legacy tools can carry legacy risks. Shared passwords, informal access, and ad hoc workarounds may be tolerable when the system is small and the stakes are low, but they can become dangerous when the vault becomes the home of sensitive documents and critical references. There is also the risk of inheriting a cluttered structure that teaches the family to accept noise as normal. Starting with what you have is not a permanent commitment to the past. It is a strategy for momentum. The reconciliation is to treat the initial setup as a working prototype: use existing tools to build shared habits, then migrate only what truly needs migrating, once the household can see which parts of the system are carrying real weight.

The difference between momentum and stagnation is often visible within one evening. A "first evening" setup does not require a weekend. It requires a single hour of focused, cooperative attention and a willingness to prioritise usefulness over completeness. It begins with a small decision: choose one existing tool to act as the vault's front door, the place everyone agrees to check first. In many homes, the most sensible choice is a shared notes space that already exists on phones and laptops, because it is fast, searchable, and flexible enough to hold reference and evolving plans. If the household does not have a shared notes space, it can still begin with a shared folder and a shared email; the front door can be a single "Family Index" document stored where everyone can reach it. The point is not the brand. The point is the agreement.

Picture the hour. At 7.30 pm, two adults sit down, not to redesign their lives, but to make the next week less brittle. They decide on the top-level areas, keeping them few and obvious: a shared dashboard for the present, and broad domains for school, health, home, money basics, trips, and memories, with parents-only and personal spaces alongside. They do not build subfolders for every nuance. They write the labels in the words the family actually uses. They create a single "This Week" note in the dashboard and a single "In Case Of" note for emergency essentials, even if those notes are initially sparse. The system now has a centre.

At 7.40, they connect the intake channels they already have. If there is a shared email address, they ensure both adults can access it and that school communications are directed there, either by using that address for school contacts or by setting up forwarding. If they do not use a shared email, they decide on a rule: any school email containing a deadline is forwarded to the other adult and distilled into the vault within twenty-four hours. The rule is simple enough to survive fatigue. The goal is not perfect inbox hygiene. The goal is shared visibility.

At 7.50, they choose one shared place for stable files. If a shared folder already exists, they designate a "Family Documents" folder within it and place a small handful of anchors there: scans of key documents if they already have them, or at least placeholders created as empty notes that say what should be stored later. They add links or references to those documents inside the vault's relevant notes, so that the front door points to the back room. This reduces future hunting. It also reduces duplication, because the family now knows where the canonical file lives.

At 8.00, they add three items that will pay for themselves quickly. They create a school contacts note with the school's main phone number, key email addresses, and portal links. They create a simple routines note for the two or three recurring friction points—PE days, bin night, or morning essentials—captured in plain language without sermonising. They create a trips template note with headings ready to be filled: bookings, documents, packing, cancellations. None of this is comprehensive. It is enough to be useful next week. Usefulness builds trust.

At 8.10, they test retrieval. They do not philosophise. They perform a simple drill: one adult asks the other to find one item—say, the school's main contact number or the current PE day—and times how long it takes. If it takes more than thirty seconds, they adjust names and placement until it does not. This is not obsessive. It is engineering. Families are designing for speed under stress, and speed can be measured without drama.

At 8.20, they agree on the smallest capture habit. Not a manifesto. A single behavioural rule: when a key detail arrives, it gets a home in the vault, preferably immediately, and at worst by the next quiet moment. The rule is anchored in a cue the family can recognise. "If it has a date or a requirement, capture it." That cue is not perfect, but it is better than "Remember it." They decide who will do the capture when, not as a permanent assignment, but as a starting point. Shared systems fail when "someone" is responsible. They succeed when responsibility is visible and light enough to share.

At 8.30, the hour ends. The vault is not finished. It is not even tidy. It is, however, real. It has a front door, a few stable domains, an intake pathway, and a retrieval test it can pass. The family can now start using it tomorrow, which is the only moment that counts.

This approach prevents the most common trap: endless app hunting in the hope that the right tool will supply motivation. Motivation is unreliable in family life. Design is not. A family that starts with what it already has is choosing to spend its limited attention on habits and boundaries—the things that actually create shared clarity—rather than on migrating data and learning features. It is choosing a system that respects the household's existing rhythms, which is another way of saying it respects the household.

The motif returns, because it remains the truest guide: inertia. A vault that demands a new identity will be abandoned by the first busy week. A vault that rides existing routines has a chance of becoming part of the home's invisible infrastructure, like keys kept in one place, like a reliable hook by the door. The aim is not to become a different kind of family. The aim is to make the family's current life easier to navigate, with the smallest possible increase in maintenance.

The forward test is therefore not whether the family can build a beautiful system in one evening. It is whether the family can make one promise and keep it: the next time a key detail arrives—deadline, address, requirement—will it be routed into the shared vault using tools already at hand, or will it be left to gravity, drifting back into "somewhere" until it becomes urgent?

Chapter 4
Capturing Everyday Family Inputs

On 15 January 2009, US Airways Flight 1549 struck birds shortly after take-off and lost engine power over New York City. Captain Chesley "Sully" Sullenberger and First Officer Jeffrey Skiles did not survive because they suddenly became better at remembering. They survived because they had rehearsed what to do when the world goes wrong, and because the cockpit's information was designed to be read and acted on in motion. The checklist culture that aviation built over decades exists for one blunt reason: under stress, memory becomes unreliable and improvisation becomes expensive. Families do not face the Hudson, but they do face the domestic equivalent of engine loss: the late message, the lost letter, the forgotten kit, the deadline discovered too late. The drama is smaller. The consequences are still real.

In most homes, the problem is not a lack of intelligence or care. It is a gap between intake and storage. Information arrives continuously—paper in bags, messages in chats, updates in portals, emails with attachments—and the household often does what seems reasonable in the moment: it holds the detail in mind, intending to deal with it later. Later does not arrive. Or it arrives exhausted. The letter slips under a pile. The screenshot sinks into the camera roll. The crucial detail is now "somewhere". A second brain that is not fed becomes a decorative idea. Capture is the act that turns the vault from concept into infrastructure.

Capture is also where families encounter the difference between a system that looks good and a system that lives. Up to this point, the book has insisted on something that can feel almost insulting in its simplicity: clarity is not produced by better intentions; it is produced by reliable externalisation. Designing a vault and choosing tools create the *possibility* of shared memory. Capturing everyday inputs creates the *reality* of it. This chapter sits at that hinge. It is where the household stops asking, "What should our system be?" and starts answering, "Where does this go, right now?"

The difficulty is that "right now" is rarely a calm moment. Family life is not organised into neat blocks of administrative time. It is organised into transitions: the dash out of the door, the drive, the handover at the gate, the shopping queue, the scramble before bedtime. Inputs arrive precisely during those transitions. A system that requires a ritual will fail. Capture must be small enough to fit into the cracks of a day. It must be so light that it feels almost like a reflex—see the thing, put it in the vault—because any capture process that demands a committee meeting with one's own brain will be postponed.

A quiet motif runs through this chapter: the hand-to-hand pass. In sport, a clean pass matters less for its beauty than for what it prevents: a fumble, a turnover, a scramble. The family's week is full of handoffs—paper handed from school to child to parent, messages handed from teacher to app to phone, decisions handed from chat to memory. Most domestic chaos is a fumbled pass: information dropped between intake and storage. Capturing is learning to make the pass cleanly and consistently, so the household's momentum is not interrupted by retrieval panic.

The first movement of the chapter sharpens the core habit: capture as you go. The phrase is deliberately physical, because capture is physical even when it is digital. It is a finger tap to create a quick note. It is a forward of an email. It is a photograph of a piece of paper before it wrinkles into invisibility. It is the difference between "I'll remember" and "It has an address". This is not about becoming obsessive; it is about preventing the predictable loss that occurs when information is carried in working memory during a busy day. The chapter follows a single ordinary artefact—a swimming letter, say—from a damp bag to a stable home, not as a quaint anecdote but as a demonstration of how domestic information moves when it is handled well.

Yet capture cannot be a parental monopoly if the system is to become truly shared. Families often treat children as sources of disruption and adults as sources of organisation. That is a cultural mistake and, over time, a practical one. Children carry information physically. They receive messages socially. Teenagers manage commitments that parents should not have to micromanage. If children are excluded from capture, the vault remains an adult-only archive and the household continues to suffer from the same bottleneck: one person becomes the intake processor. The chapter therefore turns to kid-friendly capture options—ways of making children contributors without turning the second brain into another arena for parental control. The question is not "How do we make children comply?" It is "How do we make participation feel natural, useful, and slightly empowering?"

This matters because children learn what systems *are* from how they encounter them at home. If the vault is presented as surveillance, they will resist. If it is presented as a place where their own ideas and plans have a home, they will often surprise adults with competence. A child recording their own packing list is not a cute story. It is a rehearsal for adulthood: planning, checking, owning the consequences. The chapter explores capture methods that match different ages and temperaments—voice notes for children who think in speech, simple tick-boxes for children who like certainty, photos for children who prefer visual capture—and it treats these methods as a way of distributing agency rather than distributing chores.

Paper, however, remains the great domestic saboteur. Even the most digital families are still assaulted by paper: letters, certificates, forms, receipts, leaflets that arrive as if the twentieth century never ended. Paper's power is that it is tangible and therefore emotionally "real", yet it is also fragile and easy to misplace. A single crumpled letter can dominate a morning. The chapter confronts paper with a practical routine that is neither precious nor punitive: when to scan, when to store physically, when to discard once captured. The aim is not paperlessness. The aim is predictability, so paper stops becoming a slow leak of anxiety. When a family knows what happens to paper on arrival, the kitchen table stops being an unofficial archive.

The final source of overload is the most modern and the most insidious: messages and apps. Families now live inside scrolls. Dates are buried in chat threads. Decisions are hidden between jokes, complaints, and reactions. School portals contain essential documents in awkward interfaces. The household's attention is repeatedly taxed by searching back for the "one message". This chapter insists on a ruthless practice: extract and distil. Turn the noisy thread into three clear notes. Pull the key date out of the portal and put it where it can be searched. Save the document in the vault rather than leaving it stranded behind a login. This is not about rejecting communication channels; it is about refusing to treat them as archives. The vault is the place where meaning is stabilised.

Throughout, the chapter keeps returning to a single standard, because families deserve standards that can be tested rather than admired. Capture should reduce the number of times the household has to re-find the same information. It should reduce the number of repeated questions. It should reduce the number of last-minute recoveries. These are visible outcomes. They can be felt in the body: fewer tight mornings, fewer late-night scrambles, fewer sharp exchanges that have nothing to do with love and everything to do with missing data. The book's thesis has never been that organisation is virtue. The thesis is that shared clarity is kindness, and capture is the daily act that makes that kindness real.

There is also an honest constraint that must be acknowledged, because families who pretend otherwise end up disillusioned. Capture will not be perfect. It cannot be. People will forget. Children will lose papers. Phones will die. Busy weeks will happen. The goal is not a flawless record. The goal is a system that is forgiving enough to recover quickly when a pass is dropped. This is why capture practices must be light and repeatable rather than heroic. It is also why involving children matters: a system that rests on one adult's diligence will fail precisely when that adult most needs support.

By the end of this chapter, the second brain stops being a place the family visits occasionally and becomes a place the family feeds instinctively. That shift is deceptively small. It is also the difference between a vault that stays empty and a vault that becomes trustworthy. The forward tension is therefore practical and slightly bracing: when the next piece of information lands—paper in a bag, message in a chat, update in a portal—will the household make a clean hand-to-hand pass into the vault, or will it gamble, again, on memory and "later"?

Capture As You Go

On 30 October 1935, at Wright Field in Dayton, Ohio, the Boeing Model 299—prototype of what would become the B-17—crashed on take-off after its pilots forgot to release control locks. The aircraft was not "too complicated" in any mystical sense; it was complicated in a way that made memory a brittle control surface. The response that followed was not a sermon about trying harder. It was a checklist: an external memory designed to be used while moving, while distracted, while human. That shift is worth stealing for family life, because the modern home has quietly become a miniature airfield—letters, messages, portal updates, and deadlines arriving at speed, demanding correct action at the worst possible moment.

Capture is the family's checklist culture. It is the habit of taking an input as it arrives and giving it an address in the vault before it can be dropped into the void of "later". *Make the pass clean, now.* The phrase matters because the pass is where families fumble. Information does not usually vanish through drama. It vanishes through transitions: from school bag to kitchen table, from message thread to half-remembered intention, from email to a screenshot that sinks into a camera roll. Capture is the hand-to-hand pass that prevents loss.

The temptation to "just remember" is understandable. It feels efficient. It feels adult. It also fails in patterned ways that can be described, predicted, and therefore designed around. Cognitive psychologists have long distinguished between what people can hold in mind briefly and what they can reliably retrieve later, especially under distraction; George A. Miller's 1956 discussion of limited short-term capacity remains a landmark in that conversation. The household version is blunt: when you hold a detail in mind while doing three other things, you have not stored it—you have merely postponed forgetting. The implication is not only missed deadlines. It is the quiet erosion of trust, because the same avoidable scramble repeats until it begins to feel like character rather than mechanics.

A family vault without capture is a beautifully furnished empty room. It might be structured well. It might be searchable. It might even be shared perfectly. Yet if the household's inputs continue to land elsewhere, the vault becomes a place people admire rather than a place they rely on. Capture turns the vault into a living system by aligning it with the one fact no family can negotiate: information arrives regardless of whether you have time to file it. The aim, then, is not to create more administrative work; it is to perform a smaller action earlier in order to prevent a larger action later. That trade is the only one that consistently pays.

The most useful way to understand capture is through a simple sequence: input, distil, store. "Input" is the raw arrival: a message, an email, a letter, a portal update. "Distil" is the extraction of what future-you will need: the date, the requirement, the link, the document, the decision. "Store" is giving that distilled outcome a stable address in the vault. When families skip distillation, they tend to store noise—screenshots of long threads, photos of letters without titles—and then wonder why retrieval feels like wading through a swamp. When they skip storage, they rely on memory and pay the price later. Capture as you go is the discipline of doing the smallest viable distillation at the moment of arrival, and storing it immediately.

This discipline lives or dies on friction. If capture requires a lengthy ceremony—choosing among many folders, deciding on perfect tags, writing a polished note—families will postpone it until the moment has passed. That is why effective capture is blunt. It favours speed over elegance. A quick note with an obvious title beats a beautifully formatted note written too late. A forwarded email beats a private inbox that only one adult can search. A photograph of a letter, saved into the vault with a clear name, beats a pristine piece of paper that will be lost under a pile. The metric is behavioural: can the capture be completed in under ten seconds, one-handed, while life continues? If not, it will be skipped precisely when it is needed most.

Consider the swimming letter, because it is the perfect domestic input: small, time-sensitive, easy to lose, and oddly consequential once it has been lost. The letter begins its life in a child's bag, slightly damp at the corners, folded twice. The child does not see it as information. They see it as paper. It migrates to the kitchen table. It competes with homework, receipts, a charger, a half-finished drawing. Later, someone notices it and reads: new term dates, payment instructions, a change of pick-up time, an equipment note. The household feels the familiar tug: "I'll deal with this tonight." Then the evening happens, and "tonight" becomes "tomorrow", and the letter becomes one more object absorbed into the house's general drift.

Capture breaks that drift by shortening the distance between noticing and storing. The moment the letter is read, the household performs a small pass: a photograph, a quick note, a decision about where it lives. The vault receives a titled entry—"Swimming term - payment link - pick-up time change"—tagged with the child's name and "Activity". The photo of the letter is attached or stored alongside. The key dates are extracted and placed where the family checks dates. The paper can then be stored or discarded according to the household's routine, because its informational value has already been secured. The implication is subtle but powerful: the next time someone asks, "What time is swimming pick-up now?", the answer is no longer trapped in a piece of paper that might be anywhere. It has an address.

Notice what this example is not. It is not an attempt to eliminate paper, messages, or emails. It is an attempt to stop treating those channels as archives. Families do not need fewer inputs; they need fewer *orphaned* inputs—details that exist but cannot be retrieved when needed. Capture as you go is how you stop inputs becoming orphans.

Email capture deserves special attention because so much family administration still arrives there: attachments, confirmations, instructions, policies. Email feels safe because it is "kept", yet it is not automatically shared, not automatically structured, and not automatically retrievable by anyone other than the account holder. A family can improve its shared clarity simply by treating email as intake rather than storage. The visible behaviour is straightforward: when an email contains a durable reference—an attachment you may need again, a policy, a set of instructions—it is forwarded or saved to the vault's appropriate area, with a title that matches future searches. When an email contains an action with a deadline, the action is extracted into the household's commitment system, while the reference remains in the vault. The implication is reduced dependence on a single person's inbox and reduced time spent hunting for "that email" months later.

There is a named cultural moment that explains why email capture became a topic at all. In 2007, at Google in Mountain View, California, the productivity writer Merlin Mann popularised the phrase "Inbox Zero" through a talk that spread widely online. Whatever one thinks of the slogan, the underlying diagnosis was accurate: an inbox is not a reliable place to store meaning, because its primary function is to receive and queue, not to curate and retrieve. For families, the implication is sharper. An inbox is not merely a personal queue; it is often the household's accidental archive, and accidental archives produce accidental failures. Capture turns "received" into "stored", which is the difference between seeing information and owning it.

Photographs and screenshots are the household's most common capture move, and they are both a gift and a trap. They are a gift because they allow near-instant externalisation: the school letter, the poster, the whiteboard, the portal screen. They are a trap because a camera roll is a terrible vault. It has weak naming, weak sharing, and weak retrieval. Families often feel they have "saved" something when they have merely buried it in a private stream of images. Capture as you go means treating the photo as a temporary container: take the image, then move it into the vault with a clear title and, ideally, a small line of distilled context. Without that second step, the household has not created shared clarity; it has created private hoarding.

The same principle applies to messages and chats. A chat thread is an excellent place to coordinate in the moment and a dreadful place to retrieve later. Chat's core feature—the stream—is precisely what makes it unreliable as a vault. Capture as you go therefore requires a simple extraction reflex. When a key decision is made in a chat—meeting point, time change, what to bring—the household distils that decision into the vault immediately. This can feel almost comically small: one line written down. Yet that line prevents the later ritual of scrolling back through forty messages, squinting at timestamps, and arguing about whether the decision was "final". The implication is fewer disputes about reality and fewer interruptions routed to the person who "probably remembers".

A credible limitation must be admitted, because otherwise capture becomes another perfection fantasy. Real life contains moments when capture is not possible. Phones die. Hands are full. Children melt down. People are driving. A system that assumes uninterrupted capture will fail and then induce guilt, which is a fast route to abandonment. The reconciliation is to design capture as a spectrum rather than a binary. Sometimes capture is immediate and clean: a note created on the spot. Sometimes capture is deferred but bounded: a photo taken as a placeholder, with the promise that it will be moved into the vault at the next available pause. Sometimes capture is delegated: one adult forwards an email with a clear subject line so the other can store it. The principle remains the same: shorten the time between input and address, but accept that the pass will not always be perfect. The system should recover when the pass is dropped, not collapse into shame.

This is also why "good enough" capture is superior to "complete" capture. Complete capture tries to store everything. Good enough capture stores what changes outcomes: dates, requirements, links, documents, decisions. The difference can be measured. Complete capture increases noise and dilutes retrieval. Good enough capture keeps the vault lean and trustworthy. Trust matters more than volume. If a family learns that "the vault usually has the answer", they will check it first, and the checking habit is where the system begins to compound.

The quiet test of capture is not whether the vault contains everything. It is whether the vault contains what the family repeatedly needs when tired. Can the household find the swimming pick-up time in under thirty seconds? Can a second adult retrieve the payment link without asking? Can a child locate the kit requirements without interrupting a stressed parent? These are not abstract virtues. They are observable behaviours, and they reveal whether capture is working as an everyday reflex or remaining a good intention.

The motif of the hand-to-hand pass returns because it keeps the habit honest. Capture is not a grand reorganisation. It is a clean pass performed at the moment of transfer, before the detail can drop. The forward tension is therefore direct and slightly uncomfortable: when the next input arrives—paper in a bag, message in a chat, attachment in an email—will the household make the pass into the vault immediately, accepting a little effort now, or will it gamble again on memory and pay later in search, stress, and re-deciding?

Kid-Friendly Capture Options

In September 1907, in Rome, Maria Montessori opened the first Casa dei Bambini, a "Children's House" designed around a disarming idea: children do not merely need instruction; they need an environment that makes competence possible. The room itself was part of the teaching. Furniture was sized for small bodies. Materials were arranged for independent use. The point was not to force children into adult routines, but to shape conditions in which children could practise real autonomy. A family second brain faces an analogous design challenge. If the vault is built only for adults—adult language, adult patience, adult attention—children will experience it as a place where information goes to be controlled. If the vault makes contribution simple, satisfying, and safe, children can experience it as a place where their own lives have an address.

Most families underestimate what children already do in their heads. Children track games, friendships, assignments, inside jokes, future plans, invented worlds, small anxieties, and a rolling inventory of what matters to them. They are not empty. They are saturated. The issue is not whether children can "organise". The issue is whether the household offers them a structure that feels like *theirs* rather than like homework. That difference is not cosmetic. It determines whether capture becomes shared ownership or becomes another compliance ritual that parents must enforce.

Start by naming the household mistake that turns promising systems sour. Show it in a familiar scene. A parent builds a vault and then tells the child, in a tone that means well but lands badly, "Put your things in there." The child hears: "Do admin." They comply once. Then they forget. The parent repeats. The child resists. The vault becomes a stage for power rather than a tool for calm. Name the failure: administrative outsourcing. Explain why it provokes resistance: children experience imposed organisation as surveillance or as punishment, especially if it is linked to past conflicts about mess, lateness, or forgetting. The implication is that the system remains adult-owned, and the family loses the chance to distribute capture—the very advantage that makes a shared second brain worthwhile.

Kid-friendly capture is therefore less about teaching children to behave and more about giving them interfaces and rituals that match how they already think. Children tend to capture in sensory chunks. They remember in stories. They make lists when lists feel like play. They use voice when writing feels slow. They use images when text feels abstract. Tool choice and capture methods should therefore respect multiple modes of expression. This is not indulgence. It is ergonomic design.

Voice capture is often the most natural entry point, especially for younger children and for children who think quickly and write slowly. Show: a child gets an idea for a science project while walking home, or remembers a requirement for tomorrow's lesson while brushing their teeth. If capture requires typing, the idea will vanish. If capture allows a ten-second voice note, the idea can land somewhere safe. Name: frictionless externalisation. Explain: voice capture reduces the translation cost between thought and record; it allows children to offload details without wrestling with spelling, formatting, or adult expectations of neatness. The implication is that the vault starts to reflect the child's reality rather than only the adults' administrative layer.

Voice capture also has a subtle social benefit. It preserves tone. A child's voice note about why they are excited for a trip, or what they are worried about at school, carries information that text often sanitises. For a family vault that also holds memories and milestones, this matters. A short audio clip is not merely a functional capture method; it is a future artefact. Years later, "What did you pack for your first school residential?" is less interesting than hearing the child list it themselves with the seriousness of someone preparing for an expedition. The vault, at its best, becomes not only a system of obligations but a record of becoming.

For older children and teenagers, forms and tick-box capture can work well when used carefully. A simple structure can be soothing, particularly when life is busy and attention is scattered. The danger is obvious: forms can feel like management. The reconciliation is to align the form with the child's own goals. If a teenager wants to be more independent, a lightweight checklist they control can support that independence without requiring parental nagging. Show: a teenager maintains their own "week checklist" for sports kit, homework items, and a recurring reminder about charging a device. Name: self-managed reliability. Explain: the checklist moves responsibility from parental prompts to a system the teenager can consult privately; it makes competence visible to the teenager themselves. The implication is not only smoother logistics. It is dignity.

This is where the phrase "fun to tap" becomes more than a joke. Interfaces that feel satisfying are used more often, and children respond sharply to whether a system feels like play or like bureaucracy. The behavioural difference can be measured in seconds. A child will willingly tick boxes if the action is immediate and the outcome is visible. They will resist if the process is slow, confusing, or layered with adult judgement. The same principle applies to adults, but children express it without polite concealment.

Photographic capture is another powerful option because it matches how children already use devices: camera-first, text-second. A child can photograph a piece of paper, a poster, a homework assignment written on a board, or a costume requirement for a school event. The photograph becomes a placeholder. The vault then needs the adult-designed part: a place for that photo to live with a title that makes it retrievable. The child's role can be as small as placing the photo into their "School" area or tagging it with their name. The adult's role can be as small as adding context later. Shared systems work best when roles are light and distributed rather than when one person becomes the curator of everything.

A story makes this feel real. Imagine a child preparing for an overnight trip—perhaps a school residential or a weekend away with relatives. The family has decided that the child will own their own packing list, not as a test but as a rehearsal of competence. The child opens the vault and records a list in the way that suits them. Maybe it is a voice note: "Pyjamas, toothbrush, swimming costume, towel, the book, the charger." Maybe it is a list with tick boxes because ticking feels good. The child adds a photo of the trip letter, because it contains the required items, and the child does not want to rely on memory. Then something important happens. On the morning of departure, instead of a parent barking reminders—"Have you got your towel?" "Where's your charger?"—the child checks their own record. They tick. They pack. They leave. The household's tone changes. The parent's role shifts from enforcement to support. The child's role shifts from being managed to managing. That shift is the real prize.

Name what is happening in that story: distributed capture. Explain why it matters: when children contribute to the vault, the system stops being an adult administrative project and becomes a household commons. The implication is scalability. A family with multiple children cannot afford for one adult to be the sole intake processor forever. Shared ownership is not an optional philosophical flourish; it is how the system survives growth.

There is also a privacy dimension that must be treated with care, particularly for teenagers. Teen participation depends on safety. If a teenager suspects their contributions will be read, scrutinised, or used in arguments, they will either withhold or move to private channels. The vault must therefore offer spaces that are clearly the teenager's, with agreed boundaries that are honoured. This is not permissiveness. It is respect. The visible behaviour is participation: teens add to their own planning space, maintain their own checklists, store their own reference notes, and share what they choose to share into the family commons when it affects coordination. The implication is trust that compounds. Each respected boundary makes the next contribution easier.

A credible counter-example should be acknowledged, because families vary. Some children dislike digital capture. Some find it distracting. Some families prefer paper systems for children—physical checklists, wall planners, fridge calendars—because they reduce screen time and because they are visible without devices. This can work exceptionally well. The reconciliation is simple: the vault is a household system, not a screen-based ideology. The child's capture method should match what is sustainable and what respects family values. The underlying principle remains: capture should move obligations and reference out of fragile memory and into a shared, reliable home. Whether the capture is a paper checklist photographed into the vault, or a digital tick-box list, the aim is the same: stable retrieval and shared ownership.

Modern relevance sharpens the argument further. Children now receive information through channels adults do not fully see: school platforms, class group chats, online learning systems, club announcements. The household cannot rely on adults as gatekeepers of all inputs. It is therefore more realistic—and kinder—to equip children with capture habits that reduce the cost of forgotten details. A child who learns to capture their own commitments is not merely helping the household. They are learning an adult skill that will serve them in education, work, and relationships: the ability to externalise commitments and consult them rather than improvising under pressure.

The practical trick is to link capture to what children already care about, not to what adults wish they cared about. Wish lists are an obvious bridge. A child who enjoys making a list of things they want is practising capture. Game ideas are another.

A child who records strategies, character designs, or creative plans is practising structure. Even a "things I want to remember" note—jokes, phrases, drawings, photos—turns the vault into a place where the child's identity has a home. Once the vault holds what delights them, it is easier for it also to hold what obliges them. The vault becomes a friendly place, not an administrative dungeon.

This is why kid-friendly capture should begin with low-stakes material. Start with the child's world. Let them see that the system is for them, too. Then, gently, allow the system to help with school and logistics. The household does not need to announce a new regime. It needs to create a habit loop: capture something you care about, retrieve it later, feel the benefit, repeat. Benefits create adoption. Adoption creates shared ownership.

The motif returns: an address. When children can give their own ideas and obligations an address, they experience a quiet form of agency. They stop living in the constant churn of "I think I have to..." and start living with a record they can consult. The forward test is therefore not whether children can be made to participate. It is whether the family can design participation so it feels like autonomy rather than compliance: will the next child-held detail—tomorrow's kit, a new club time, a creative idea, a personal plan—be captured by the child in a way that fits them, or will it continue to live precariously in a backpack and a memory, waiting to become urgent?

Handling Paper and Post

On 6 May 1840, in London, the first Penny Black stamps went on sale and Britain's postal system entered its modern phase: cheaper postage, more letters, more paper moving through ordinary lives. What followed was not merely a communications revolution; it was an administrative one. When letters become easy to send, obligations travel more readily. Instructions travel more readily. Evidence travels more readily. A century and a half later, families still live with the legacy. The paper has changed its costumes—school letters, certificates, prescriptions, warranty leaflets—but it retains the same power: it arrives as a physical fact and demands to be dealt with.

Paper has its own gravity.

That gravity is not poetic; it is practical. Paper lands on the kitchen table, the hallway console, the top of the microwave—wherever the household's circulation naturally slows. It stacks because stacking is frictionless. It becomes the home's unofficial memory, which works until it does not. One slip, one tidy-up, one curious toddler, and the "system" dissolves into a frantic hunt. The family vault can absorb paper's informational value, but only if the household develops a predictable way to catch paper before gravity turns it into a pile.

Show the ordinary failure. A child brings home a letter in a bag. The bag smells faintly of rain and pencil shavings. The paper is slightly crumpled at the corners. A parent reads it quickly and thinks, sensibly, that they will respond later. They put it down. It slides under another sheet. Days pass. The deadline arrives with no warning except a sudden, sharp sense that something has been missed. Name what happened: paper drift. Explain why it is so reliable: paper requires a physical decision—keep, act, store, discard—and physical decisions are postponed when life is busy. The implication is disproportionate stress. A small piece of paper can derail a morning, not because it is powerful in itself, but because it holds a detail the household failed to give an address.

Handling paper well is therefore not about becoming tidy. It is about establishing a routine that turns paper into either a digital reference, a deliberately stored physical artefact, or a deliberately discarded item. Deliberate is the key word. The enemy is not paper. The enemy is ambiguity. When paper's destination is ambiguous, it becomes clutter by default. When paper's destination is predictable, it stops being a source of low-grade dread and becomes just another input to be processed.

A useful way to think about paper is to separate three questions that families often mash together. What does the paper *say*? What does the paper *trigger*? What does the paper *need to remain*? A school letter, for example, says a set of instructions and dates. It triggers an action: payment, consent, kit preparation, calendar changes. And it may or may not need to remain in physical form afterwards. Many papers do not. Some do. The routine should therefore be designed to extract what matters—content and trigger—while making a clear decision about physical retention.

Start with capture, because capture neutralises gravity. Capture does not mean building an archive of every scrap. It means preserving the information in a form the vault can hold and search. For paper, the lowest-friction capture method is often a photograph or scan taken at the moment the paper is first handled. The photograph is not the end state; it is a handoff. The household's aim is to move the paper's meaning into the vault where it can be retrieved without rummaging. When capture happens quickly, paper stops being a single point of failure.

Now add distillation, because images alone can create a new kind of mess. A camera roll full of unlabelled letter photos is simply a digital pile with better lighting. Distillation is what prevents that. It is the act of extracting the line future-you will need: the date, the requirement, the link, the name of the teacher, the time of pick-up. Distillation can be short. It should be short. The point is not to reproduce the letter. The point is to translate the letter into the family's retrieval language. If, three weeks later, someone searches "Year 4 trip payment", the vault should answer with one clear note rather than twenty near-identical photos.

Consider a worked example: a school letter about a day trip. It arrives on paper because schools still do this, even when they also post the same content in an app that is difficult to search. The letter states the date, the cost, the deadline for consent, and a kit list. The paper is read at the kitchen table. Instead of leaving it there "to deal with later", one adult takes a quick photo or scan. Then they create a short vault entry in the school area, titled in the words the family will later use: "Year 4 trip – 18 June – consent by 4 June – £12 – trainers". The photo is attached or stored alongside, and the note is tagged with the child's name and "School" and "Trip". The date is entered into the shared calendar, and the consent deadline is recorded as a commitment if the family uses a task layer. The paper is now informationally redundant. It can be stored briefly in a known place until the action is complete, then discarded. The important detail is not the app used. The important detail is that the paper's gravity has been defied: the information has been given an address.

Name what this routine achieves: canonical capture. Explain how it reduces failure: once the vault holds the authoritative record, the household no longer depends on the continued physical existence of a fragile sheet of paper. The implication is calmer follow-through. The family can find the kit list the night before without rummaging. They can confirm the deadline without searching through piles. They can answer a grandparent's question without lifting a finger to dig through a drawer.

This is the core principle: paper is allowed to be temporary once its meaning has been captured. Families often treat paper as if it is the only "real" version of information. That instinct has a history. Paper feels official because institutions have long used it as proof. Yet much household paper is not proof; it is instruction. When instruction is digitised into a vault, it becomes easier to retrieve and easier to share. The household can then reserve physical storage for the smaller category of paper that truly needs to remain physical: documents that are hard to replace, documents that are required in original form by an institution, or documents that carry sentimental value in their materiality.

At this point, a credible limitation must be faced honestly. Not all paper can be treated as informationally redundant. Some items are best kept physically, and families should not pretend otherwise. A child's certificate, for example, may have little administrative value but considerable emotional value; its meaning is partly in the object itself. Certain formal documents can also have requirements attached that families should respect, which means keeping originals in a safe place even if a digital copy exists for convenience. The reconciliation is simple: the vault is not a bonfire. It is a memory and reference system. Keeping an original does not contradict the vault; it strengthens it, because the vault can record where the original lives and provide a digital copy for quick retrieval. The household gains both security and speed.

This brings us to the physical routine, which matters because the vault lives in the digital realm while paper lives in the physical one. Families do not need a complex physical filing system. They need a stable landing zone: one place where paper goes immediately on entering the home, so paper is not scattered across surfaces. Scatter produces search. Search produces stress. A stable landing zone produces processing. Processing produces clarity. The landing zone should be boring and visible. Not hidden. Hidden zones become forgotten zones.

From there, paper can be processed in small bursts rather than heroic sessions. The error families make is to imagine a single big "organising day" after which paper will behave. Paper does not behave. Paper continues arriving. A sustainable routine therefore treats paper as a stream, not as a one-off backlog. The household processes paper when attention is briefly available—perhaps at the end of the day, perhaps during a weekly review—using the same few decisions each time: capture and distil; store physically if it must remain; discard when safe; record actions and dates in the appropriate systems. The benefit is not perfection. It is predictability.

Research on paper in everyday work helps explain why this predictability matters. Abigail Sellen and Richard Harper's *The Myth of the Paperless Office* (2002), based on close observation of how people manage information, argues that paper persists because it is flexible, glanceable, and easy to annotate. Families experience the same thing. Paper is fast. It can be spread on a table. It can be pinned to a fridge. It can be handed to another adult without worrying about permissions. These are genuine advantages. The household routine should not fight paper's strengths. It should harvest them and then stabilise the content digitally so the information is not lost when the paper is lost.

One practical implication follows: scanning is not always necessary. Photographs are often sufficient. The goal is retrieval, not archival perfection. Families sometimes become stuck because they think paper capture requires special equipment or pristine scanning. It does not. A legible image paired with a clear title and a short distilled summary is enough to prevent most paper-driven failures. The vault needs accuracy at the point of retrieval, not museum-grade digitisation. When families accept this, capture becomes easier and more frequent, which is precisely what keeps paper from accumulating.

Receipts are a useful test case because they combine paper's worst traits: they are small, easy to lose, and often relevant only later when memory has faded. Many receipts are disposable. Some are not. The vault's role is not to create a comprehensive accounting system; it is to ensure that when a receipt is needed—warranty claims, returns, household reference—it can be found. The pattern remains: capture quickly, name clearly, store in one stable place. The physical receipt can then be kept briefly in a known envelope or tray until it is clear it is not needed, or kept longer when it relates to something valuable. The household does not need to hold every scrap. It needs to avoid the particular pain of needing a scrap and not having it.

Certificates and children's paper achievements introduce a different complexity: sentiment. Parents often feel guilty discarding anything that signals a child's progress. Children often feel differently; sometimes they care deeply, sometimes they do not. A vault can reduce the emotional pressure by allowing a light curation practice: photograph the certificate, record the date and what it was for, and keep the physical version only when it truly matters. The implication is that memory is preserved without the home becoming a warehouse of paper. The vault also allows context. A certificate without a story is a piece of card. A certificate with a line—"first time they swam a length without stopping"—becomes a small piece of family history.

The same logic applies to post more broadly. Post arrives with a social signal of importance: it looks official. It is printed. It has an envelope. Yet much post is advertising, noise, or information that can be dealt with quickly. A routine that treats all post as equally worthy creates piles. A routine that sorts by consequence reduces piles. Consequence can be seen, not guessed: does the item require action? does it contain a detail the family will need later? does it need to be kept physically? When the answers are no, the best action is often immediate discarding. Not because discarding is virtuous, but because keeping low-consequence paper is how the home's surfaces become an archive of noise. Noise makes the important thing harder to see.

A second named example from outside family life sharpens the point about predictable handling. In many offices, the "in-tray" persists even in digital settings for a reason: it gives incoming items a clear temporary home so that work can be processed rather than scattered. The household needs its own version of the in-tray. Not as an emblem of corporate life, but as a simple defence against gravity. When paper has an in-tray, paper's arrival stops being an invasion of every surface. It becomes a controllable flow.

The motif returns because it is the real adversary: gravity. Paper will always fall into piles if the household allows it to. The vault cannot prevent paper from arriving. It can prevent paper from becoming a permanent, anxiety-inducing presence by giving paper a predictable route: landing zone, capture, distil, decide physical fate. When that route is established, the household gains a strange new freedom: the freedom to tidy without fear. When a parent clears the kitchen table, they are no longer terrified of throwing away something vital, because the vital things have already been captured and given addresses.

The forward test is deliberately simple, because simplicity is what survives. The next time a letter, certificate, or receipt crosses the threshold, will it be allowed to obey gravity—landing on a surface and joining a pile—or will it be routed through a predictable pass into the vault, so its meaning can be retrieved without rummaging? The answer will determine whether paper remains the household's quiet saboteur or becomes just another input, handled with calm competence.

Dealing With Messages and Apps

In March 2011, in Sendai, Japan, the Tōhoku earthquake and tsunami shattered infrastructure and flooded communication channels with noise, rumour, and partial signals. One of the lessons emergency managers have repeated since is not romantic: in crises, information must be triaged. Signals must be separated from chatter. Decisions must be stabilised in forms people can retrieve under pressure. Families do not face tsunamis as a rule, but they do face informational surges that behave similarly on a smaller scale: the school app update at 9.47 pm, the parents' group chat that explodes before a trip, the portal that hides a PDF behind three taps and a password you can never quite remember. The household is forced into triage without calling it that.

Scrolls are not archives.

That sentence matters because modern family information increasingly lives inside scrolls. Messaging apps, school platforms, and portals are designed for delivery and engagement, not for long-term retrieval. They are fast at getting something to you. They are bad at helping you find it again, especially when you are tired, distracted, and trying not to snap at anyone. Families therefore develop a peculiar habit: they keep re-finding the same information, repeatedly paying the cost of search. The cost is not only time. It is the emotional charge that comes with hunting: the sense of being behind, the irritability of "I saw that somewhere", the sharpness of "It was in the thread". The vault exists to end that cycle, but only if the family learns to extract and stabilise what matters from the noisy channels where it first appears.

The structural problem is easy to describe. Messaging apps are rivers. They carry everything: logistics, jokes, complaints, reactions, speculation, social bonding. School apps and portals are labyrinths. They hide essential documents inside interfaces built for compliance rather than ease. Both are forms of information delivery that are optimised for institutions, not households. When a family treats them as storage, it accepts a fragile arrangement: a crucial detail survives only if someone remembers it exists, remembers where it was posted, and has the time and patience to scroll back until they find it. That is not "being disorganised". That is using a river as a filing cabinet.

Name the better move: distil and pin. Distillation is the extraction of the minimum information that changes outcomes: date, time, place, requirement, link, document, decision. Pinning is giving that distilled outcome an address in the vault, where it can be searched and shared. The implication is decisive. Once the family has pinned the outcome, the scroll can return to being what it is good at:

conversation and short-term coordination. The vault becomes what it is good at: reference and shared clarity.

A household example makes the mechanism unmissable. A parents' group thread begins on a Thursday evening. Someone asks about Saturday's football match. Another parent replies with a time. Someone else mentions a location change. Someone asks what kit is needed because the weather looks uncertain. Someone adds a screenshot from the club app. The thread grows: twenty messages, then forty. Amid the noise, the key facts shift and settle: the match is at 10.30, not 10.00; the location is a different pitch; the kit includes a water bottle and a dark top. By Friday morning, half the parents are still unsure because the information is buried beneath banter and updates.

A family practising vault behaviour treats this thread as intake, not as storage. One adult reads the thread once, not repeatedly, and extracts three stable notes into the vault. The first note is "Football – Saturday 10.30 – Pitch B – drop-off details", tagged with the child's name and the club. The second is "Kit list – football – cold weather", with a short, reusable checklist. The third is "Club link / screenshot", stored as reference with a title that will be searchable later. The calendar event is updated. The paper doesn't matter. The specific app doesn't matter. What matters is that the thread's outcome has been converted into a stable, retrievable form. Name what happened: outcome stabilisation. Explain: the family took a river of messages and turned it into three addressable artefacts; it replaced repeated scrolling with a one-time extraction. The implication is relief: on Saturday morning, the household does not argue about what was "said"; it checks the vault and leaves.

This is not merely a productivity trick. It is a shift in what the household treats as authoritative. When the scroll is authoritative, reality is mutable, because messages can be missed and interpretations can differ. When the vault holds the authoritative distilled outcome, the family has a single source of truth, and that reduces conflict. Conflict reduction is not abstract. It shows up as fewer sharp exchanges at the threshold of the day, fewer frantic last-minute messages to other parents, fewer interruptions to whichever adult tends to remember things.

The same logic applies to school apps and portals, which introduce an extra layer of friction: access. A portal hides information behind logins, passwords, and awkward navigation. That friction makes families postpone retrieval until the last moment. The vault's job is to pull out what will be needed later, while the portal is open and the information is visible, and to store it where the family can reach it without repeating the login ritual. Show: a parent finally logs into a school portal to find a policy about uniform or a PDF about an upcoming trip. Instead of promising themselves they will remember where it is, they capture the PDF (or a screenshot), create a short vault note with the key details, and store the link and the document in the family's stable file home. Name: access neutralisation. Explain: the vault reduces dependence on brittle access pathways by preserving the necessary information in a place the family controls. The implication is fewer late-night logins and fewer instances of "I can't get into the portal right now".

Here, a named example from the wider world helps clarify why portals feel so hostile. In 2013, the United States saw a high-profile failure in the rollout of HealthCare.gov, in part because complex systems exposed to heavy use can behave unpredictably. Families experience their own version: portals that time out, apps that update, interfaces that change mid-term. The point is not to criticise any particular institution. The point is to recognise that families should not base their shared memory on systems they do not control. A second brain is, in part, a resilience strategy: it reduces the household's dependence on a brittle interface by capturing what matters while access is available.

The psychological dimension of message overload is also worth naming because it explains why scrolling feels both necessary and draining. Research on attention and interruption has repeatedly shown that task switching carries a cost; Gloria Mark's work on interruptions in knowledge work, for example, has documented how disruptions fragment attention and increase time to complete tasks. Family life is not an office, but it shares the same cognitive mechanics: each scroll back through a thread is a small interruption that taxes attention and mood. The vault's value, then, is not only retrieval speed. It is attentional protection. When the family extracts outcomes once, it reduces repeated interruptions later.

There is a temptation to treat this as a call to strictness—no messages, no group chats, no informal coordination. That would be a misunderstanding. Group chats are social infrastructure. They create belonging. They share small kindnesses. They enable rapid coordination. The credible limitation is that families cannot and should not eliminate noisy channels. The reconciliation is to respect each channel's nature. Use messaging for what it is good at: social glue and immediate coordination. Use the vault for what it is good at: stable reference and evolving plans. The boundary prevents the second brain becoming yet another noisy channel, because it refuses to carry chatter. It carries outcomes.

This boundary also protects children. Children and teenagers increasingly coordinate through their own messaging channels. They may not show parents every thread, and they should not have to. What the family needs is not access to every message. It needs stable shared reality for the parts that affect household coordination: times, locations, requirements, permissions. A teenager can contribute the distilled outcome without exposing the full conversation. That preserves autonomy while maintaining shared clarity. The visible behaviour is more mature than it sounds: a teenager says, "The cinema is at 6.30; I need £10 and I'll be picked up at 9.15," and records it in the shared place. The family stops asking to see the chat. The system reduces intrusion by reducing uncertainty.

The practical craft of extraction rests on a small set of recognisable triggers. A message becomes vault-worthy when it contains a date, a time, a location, a requirement, a payment link, a document, or a decision that would otherwise be re-litigated. That is not an exhaustive taxonomy. It is an attention cue. Once the household recognises these triggers, capture becomes faster because the decision "should this go in the vault?" stops being a debate. It becomes a reflex.

The danger, again, is over-capture. Families can respond to scroll pain by dumping entire threads into the vault as screenshots, thinking they have "saved" the information. They have saved the noise. The vault then becomes crowded with unreadable fragments, and trust collapses. Name: screenshot sediment. Explain: raw captures without distillation create a new scroll inside the vault; search results fill with indistinguishable images, and retrieval becomes slow. The implication is that the family stops checking the vault and reverts to asking or scrolling. The solution is not to stop capturing. It is to capture *less* and distil *more*—a short note plus a single relevant screenshot, rather than twenty screenshots without context.

This is where the earlier motif of the hand-to-hand pass returns, now sharpened. Messages and apps are fast-moving hands in a crowded room. Details are passed quickly, sometimes clumsily. The vault is the place where the pass becomes secure. The family's job is not to catch every ball. It is to catch the ones that will matter later. That selectivity is what keeps the vault calm. Calm is not aesthetic; it is functional. A calm vault is one people trust under stress.

End with the forward test, because this is where families either change their daily experience or continue paying the same tax. The next time a thread erupts, a portal hides a document, or an app posts a late update, will the household accept the scroll as the archive and risk re-finding later, or will it distil the outcome into a small number of clear, searchable notes that stabilise reality? The choice is not between being "organised" and being "relaxed". The choice is between repeated searching and one-time extraction—between living inside rivers and building a reliable shore.

Chapter 5
Tags, Templates, and Checklists

In 1760, in London, John Harrison presented his H4 marine chronometer to the Board of Longitude after years of refinement, proving—decisively—that precise timekeeping at sea could be made portable and trustworthy. The romance in that story is not brass and gears. It is a design lesson about reliability under motion. Sailors did not need grand theories while the deck pitched beneath them; they needed a device that performed one small job faithfully, every time, so navigation could stop being guesswork. Families face their own less glamorous ocean: the week. The home's problems rarely come from ignorance of what to do. They come from the failure to do the right small thing at the right moment, especially when attention is torn.

There is a paradox at the heart of family organisation. The household can build a shared vault, capture diligently, and still feel disordered if the information is hard to retrieve and the routines are hard to repeat. At that point, families often respond with the wrong cure: more folders, more categories, more elaborate structure. The result is usually a deeper maze. What the household needs instead is a small set of tools that behave like Harrison's chronometer: simple, consistent instruments that convert chaos into something navigable. Tags, templates, and checklists are those instruments. They do not add weight to the system. They reduce drag.

A quiet motif runs through this chapter: the hook. A hook is a small, sturdy attachment point—something you can trust without thinking. Keys on a hook do not require memory. A coat on a hook does not require negotiation. In a second brain, tags are hooks for retrieval, templates are hooks for repetition, and checklists are hooks for execution. Each is modest. Each changes behaviour. Together, they turn a vault from a place where information is stored into a place where life becomes easier to run.

Tags arrive first because families live in overlapping realities. One document rarely belongs to a single category. A camp form belongs to a child, to an activity, to a date range, and perhaps to a health note about allergies. Put it in one folder and you have hidden it from the other contexts that will later matter. Duplicate it into multiple folders and you create a different problem: multiple versions that drift apart. Tags are the elegant escape from that trap. They allow one item to wear several identities at once without duplication. The benefit is not theoretical. It is the difference between searching once and searching three times in three different places.

Yet tags are only powerful when they are shared. A private tag language inside one person's head recreates the old bottleneck: one person knows how things are filed, everyone else guesses. Designing a family tag system therefore becomes an act of translation. The tags must be memorable, speakable, and limited. They must reflect how the family refers to itself—names people actually use, places that matter, themes that recur, time markers that make sense in household life. The chapter treats this not as a taxonomy exercise but as a gentle negotiation of a shared vocabulary, because the vault's purpose is coordination, and coordination requires common terms. A tag system that is brilliant but idiosyncratic is not brilliant. It is private.

Tags solve retrieval. Templates solve repetition. Families suffer not only because they forget facts, but because they repeatedly reinvent the same plans: the holiday packing scramble, the birthday preparations, the start-of-term reset, the recurring health appointment dance. Each time, the household pays the full cost again, as if experience counts for nothing. Templates are how experience begins to compound. A template is not a form to be filled in obediently; it is a starting map that prevents the family from beginning in fog. It captures the shape of a recurring event—the headings, the common tasks, the standard documents—so the household can focus on the particulars rather than recreating the basics. Done well, templates feel like a kindness from past-you. They are the domestic equivalent of a well-designed cockpit: not decorative, simply supportive.

Then come checklists, the most misunderstood of the trio. Many intelligent people flinch at checklists because they associate them with rigidity or with incompetence. Yet the modern checklist, as a cultural technology, has earned respect in fields where mistakes are costly. Atul Gawande's *The Checklist Manifesto* (2009) popularised this idea in healthcare, arguing that even experts benefit from simple, well-designed prompts because complexity makes omission likely. Families live inside complexity too, especially during transitions: leaving the house, preparing for exams, managing routines that must not be missed. A checklist does not insult the household. It protects it. It moves responsibility from a stressed brain to a visible prompt that any family member can follow. It also has a moral dimension that is easy to overlook: checklists reduce the need for nagging by making expectations explicit and shared.

This chapter, then, is about making the vault usable at speed and reliable over time. It is about turning the information the family has already captured into something that can be found in seconds, reused without fuss, and acted upon without argument. It stays grounded in small scenes rather than grand claims: the parent searching for a form and finding it immediately because it is tagged with the right names; the family preparing for a trip with a template that prevents the usual forgotten chargers and last-minute document hunts; the child following a short "get ready" checklist that replaces a vague command with concrete steps. These are not organisational triumphs. They are frictions removed.

Modern relevance sharpens the necessity. Families now operate in mixed media: paper, email, portals, chats, calendars. Information is not merely abundant; it is fragmented. Retrieval therefore matters more than storage. Repetition matters more than planning. Execution matters more than good intentions. Tags, templates, and checklists are the three mechanisms that allow a second brain to scale under those conditions without becoming heavy. They offer something that families quietly crave: not control, but predictability.

The closing tension of the chapter is not whether these tools work. They do, when used with restraint. The tension is whether families will be tempted into over-building. Tags can multiply until they become a private dialect. Templates can become elaborate documents no one consults. Checklists can expand until they feel punitive. The chapter therefore keeps returning to the hook: small, sturdy, used. A hook is valuable only when it is placed where hands reach naturally. The question that hovers over every page ahead is simple enough to measure: will the family build hooks that genuinely catch what matters—retrieval, repetition, reliability—or will the system drift back into the old pattern where memory does the work, and memory, under load, quietly drops things?

Why Tags Beat Folders

In 1931, in New Delhi, the Indian civil servant S. R. Ranganathan published *The Five Laws of Library Science* and began pushing librarians to think less like custodians of shelves and more like designers of access. A book, he argued in essence, should not merely exist in a building; it should be findable by the reader who needs it. The implication was radical in a quiet way: classification is not about tidiness. It is about retrieval under real human conditions—partial memory, uncertain vocabulary, limited time. Families, building their own vaults, are not running libraries, but they are facing the same problem with less staff and more distractions. A household record is valuable only when the right person can find it at the right moment without a debate about where it "ought" to be.

Folders appeal because they promise order. One item, one place, clean hierarchy. They also carry a hidden demand: you must remember the place. The moment a family relies on deep folders, it asks every member to recall a path, often chosen months earlier by someone else, under different circumstances, with different assumptions. That is an expensive requirement in a home where information arrives mid-commute and retrieval happens while a child waits by the door. Tags beat folders because they align with how families actually retrieve: not by path, but by cues.

Here is the paradox that defeats folder systems in family life: the same item is relevant in more than one way, and those ways change depending on the question asked. A camp form is not merely "School". It is "Ava". It is "Summer". It is "Consent". It is "Medical info". It is "Payment deadline". It is "Packing list". If the form is filed under one folder—say, School > Trips > Camp—then it disappears from the view of whoever later searches by health needs or by the child's name. If it is duplicated into Health > Ava and also into School > Trips and also into Money > Payments, then versions diverge, and the family begins to live with a new, uglier uncertainty: which copy is current? A tidy hierarchy has produced a messy truth.

Show this failure in a scene. A parent is asked, the night before camp, whether the child needs an inhaler, and whether the school already has that information. The parent remembers that the form exists. They do not remember where it lives. They open the vault's folder tree and begin guessing. School? Health? Activities? Trips? They open one folder, then another. They search within a folder. They back out. Meanwhile, the child grows restless, and the parent's tone tightens. Name what is happening: path dependence. Explain why it bites: folders require the user to remember the filing decision, not merely the item; in family life, the filing decision is rarely memorable. The implication is that the vault feels slower than asking, and asking returns as the household default.

Tags interrupt this failure by allowing one item to be retrieved through multiple cues without duplication. The camp form can be stored once—in one sensible home within the vault—and tagged with the child's name, the activity, and the relevant themes, including health. Now the parent can retrieve it by searching "Ava + camp", or "camp + inhaler", or "school trip + consent", and the same artefact appears each time. The system behaves as if it understands that items have more than one identity. Name the mechanism: multi-context retrieval. Explain: tags are metadata—small labels attached to an item—that allow the vault to present different "views" of the same thing. The implication is speed and confidence: the family can find the form under pressure without remembering a path.

This is not merely an aesthetic preference. It is a structural truth about domestic life. Family information is cross-cutting. A single event touches school, health, logistics, money basics, and time. A single document can answer several questions. A single decision can sit in multiple contexts. Folder systems were designed for environments where categories are stable and roles are clear: departments, projects, years, client files. Families are not departments. Their categories are porous because life is porous. Tags beat folders because tags accept porosity rather than fighting it.

The most powerful demonstration of this comes from how people search. Rarely does a family member remember the exact name of a document or the exact place it was filed. They remember fragments: "that thing about swimming", "the letter with the payment link", "the allergy form", "the pitch change", "the trip in June". Tags convert fragments into retrieval. They allow a search to behave like a conversation with partial memory. If the household uses a child tag for each child, an activity tag for recurring commitments, and a few theme tags for things like "Health" or "Payments", then a vague search becomes precise enough to work. A folder tree cannot offer that without either duplication or deep complexity.

The library world offers a named example of why multi-context classification became essential. Faceted classification—the idea that an item can be categorised across multiple independent dimensions—was central to Ranganathan's own thinking. In plain language, "facets" are independent angles: author, subject, time, place, format. A book about Indian architecture can be found via architecture, via India, via a particular period, via a particular style. That is not because librarians enjoyed complexity. It is because readers search by different cues. Families do too. They search by person, by event, by place, by requirement, by time. A folder path is a single angle pretending to be the only angle that matters. Tags are multiple angles held lightly.

A second named example comes from the design of the modern web itself. In 1998, at Stanford University, Larry Page and Sergey Brin described Google's PageRank, a method for ranking web pages by link structure rather than by a single categorical directory. Early web directories tried to behave like folder trees; they were quickly overwhelmed. The web was too large and too cross-linked for a single hierarchy to serve real retrieval. Families have their own smaller web. School, health, and home life link to one another constantly. A hierarchy works until the links overwhelm it. Tags are how you admit the links exist.

Still, folders are not useless, and pretending they are would be dishonest. Families benefit from broad domains because domains reduce the search space. A "School" area, a "Health" area, a "Home" area—these are sensible containers that give information a home and prevent the vault becoming an unbounded dump. The limitation appears when families treat the folder tree as the primary retrieval method, pushing it deeper and deeper in an attempt to capture nuance. The reconciliation is to use folders shallowly for domains and tags for cross-cutting nuance. Folders answer "roughly where does this live?" Tags answer "in what ways is this relevant?" The two can cooperate without competing.

Consider a worked scenario that shows the co-operation rather than the rivalry. The family captures a school email about a residential trip. They store it in the School domain because that is the institutional source and the stable home. Then they tag it with the child's name, "Residential", "Payments", and "Health" if it includes medication instructions. The email can now be found through School, through the child's tag, through "Payments" when the fee is due, and through "Health" when the medication question arises. One artefact. Multiple handles. No duplication. No guesswork.

The behavioural effect is measurable. A family that relies on deep folders will often experience more "search churn": repeated opening and closing of folders, repeated guessing, repeated requests for help from the person who set it up. A family that uses tags well will experience more direct search: type a name and a keyword, find the item, move on. The difference is not small. It changes the emotional temperature of ordinary moments. Searching within a folder tree invites frustration because it feels like you are *nearly* there while remaining lost. Searching with tags feels like narrowing in, because each tag reduces the field without requiring you to remember where the item lives.

Tags also protect shared clarity, because they are easier to standardise across people than folder paths are. Two adults can agree on the child tags and the activity tags more easily than they can agree on whether "School" should be under "Kids" or "Admin", whether "Trips" belongs under "School" or "Family", or whether "Health" belongs under "Home" or "Personal". Folder debates become endless because they are debates about the "true" structure of life. Tags sidestep that metaphysical argument. A child's name is not a metaphysical question. It is a practical label.

There is, however, a credible counter-example: some families become over-enthusiastic with tags and create a tag soup. Everything receives ten tags. Tags proliferate with near-synonyms. People disagree about spelling. Searches become noisy. The system begins to feel like an inside joke for whoever designed it. Name the failure: taxonomy drift. Explain: when tags multiply without constraint, they lose their value as retrieval handles; they become decorative rather than functional. The implication is the same as with deep folders: people stop trusting retrieval and return to asking.

The reconciliation is restraint and shared language. Tags should be few, memorable, and tied to questions the household actually asks. People, places, activities, and a small number of themes. That is enough to unlock multi-context retrieval without creating an arcane dialect. The point is not to label everything. The point is to label the things you will later hunt for under pressure. Tags are hooks. Hooks work because there are not too many of them and because they are placed where hands naturally reach.

This returns us to the core claim: tags beat folders because families do not live in a tree. They live in a mesh. A child is connected to a school, to activities, to health needs, to relatives, to places, to recurring seasons and term rhythms. A folder tree insists on one primary location for each item. A tag mesh allows the item to be found through multiple realities without being copied and without demanding perfect memory of filing choices.

The forward test is therefore not whether the household can create a beautiful folder structure. Many can. The test is whether the household can retrieve under strain. When the next multi-context item arrives—a camp form that touches school, activity, and health; a trip document that touches money, dates, and packing—will the family force it into a single folder path and hope they remember, or will they store it once and attach the few tags that let it surface whenever any of its identities becomes the one that matters?

Designing Family Tag Systems

In 1755, in London, Samuel Johnson published *A Dictionary of the English Language* after years of labour, attempting to stabilise spelling and meaning in a language that refused to sit still. The dictionary did not "fix" English; it made English easier to share. That distinction is the heart of a family tag system. Tags are not about perfect classification. They are about shared language. A household needs a small set of words that everyone can use to attach meaning to information, so that later retrieval does not depend on one person's private logic. When a tag system works, it feels almost invisible. When it fails, it produces the most irritating kind of domestic confusion: everyone is looking for the same thing, and everyone is using different words.

Families already have a tag system. It lives in speech. It is the set of names, nicknames, places, and shorthand that structure daily life: "Gran's", "PE kit", "the blue folder", "after-school club", "dentist", "the trip". The problem is that this language is rarely formalised in the vault, so the system remains half-shared and half-implicit. One adult writes "Physical Education", another writes "PE", a child writes "sports", and search becomes a lottery. Designing a family tag system is the act of turning the household's spoken shorthand into a stable set of hooks that the vault can use for retrieval.

Five words can suffice.

That sentence is not a trick. It is a reminder that tags should begin small. A family does not need fifty tags to gain the power of multi-context retrieval. It needs a handful that map to the questions the household repeatedly asks under time pressure. The most robust approach is to design tags around four dimensions that match how families retrieve: people, places, themes, and time markers. Each dimension is a different angle on reality. Together, they allow the same item to be found through multiple cues without duplication. The moment you add a fifth or sixth dimension, you should be able to name the recurring question it answers. If you cannot, you are building a taxonomy to feel organised rather than to become findable.

Start with people, because families search by person constantly and because person tags are easy to agree on. Show the retrieval need. A parent wants "everything relevant to Ava": school letters, medical notes, club schedules, trip documents, emergency details. Without a person tag, that retrieval requires either a maze of folders or repeated search terms that miss items phrased differently. Name the concept: anchor tags. Explain why person tags work: they are stable, unambiguous, and meaningful to every household member; they reduce search space quickly. The implication is immediate convenience. A person tag turns the vault into something closer to a dossier: not in the sinister sense, but in the sense of a coherent set of references that can be surfaced quickly when needed.

Person tags sound easy until they collide with household reality: nicknames, changing names, and blended family structures. The way through is not to impose formality; it is to choose the name the household naturally says, then keep it consistent. If the family calls a child "Sam", tagging everything "Samuel" introduces friction and invites divergence. Consistency beats correctness. This is where a shared tag language behaves like Johnson's dictionary: it privileges common use over private preference. A teenager who insists on a particular name should be respected, not only for ethical reasons but for system integrity; a tag system that ignores identity will be resisted and therefore will decay.

Now move to places. Place tags can be literal—home, school, Gran's—or functional—"the surgery", "the club", "the dentist". Place tags answer a different retrieval question: "everything connected to this location or institution". This is more powerful than it first appears because place often acts as a proxy for an entire set of constraints: different pick-up rules, different contact numbers, different documents, different rhythms. Show: a parent needing the address for a new dentist or the details for a school event held offsite. Name: context tags. Explain: place tags allow the vault to represent a family's geography and institutional landscape; they reduce the cost of switching contexts because the relevant information can be filtered by where it belongs. The implication is smoother coordination, especially when multiple carers and relatives are involved.

Themes come next, and this is where families often overbuild. Themes are broad categories that cut across people and places: "Health", "School", "Payments", "Travel", "Home", "Admin", "Emergency". The danger is to treat themes as an opportunity to reproduce a folder tree in tag form, creating dozens of overlapping labels. The better approach is to treat themes as a small set of recurring concerns that genuinely change how you search. A theme tag should exist because it answers a recurring question. If no one ever searches "Payments", it does not need to be a tag. If people repeatedly need to surface anything time-sensitive involving money—fees, invoices, renewals—then "Payments" becomes valuable. Show: a family looking for all upcoming costs related to school and clubs. Name: cross-cutting retrieval. Explain: theme tags cut across domains, allowing the family to surface items that share a property even when they live in different areas. The implication is fewer surprises, because patterns become visible.

Time markers are the final dimension, and they should be used with restraint. Families already have time represented in calendars. Time tags serve a different purpose: they allow retrieval by season, term, or year, especially for reference and memory. "2025", "Summer", "Term 2", "Year 6" can be useful when people search retrospectively: "the form from last summer", "the photos from Year 3", "the policy we used last term". The risk is that time tags become a substitute for good titles and good capture, or that they proliferate into a confusing calendar system inside the vault. The reconciliation is to use time tags only when they genuinely aid retrieval across many items, such as annual cycles or school-year structures. The implication, when done well, is continuity. Families can look back without rummaging.

At this point, the tag system is not yet designed. It is merely sketched. Design requires agreement, because a tag system that only one person understands recreates the bottleneck it was meant to remove. Agreement is not a meeting with minutes. It is a short shared decision: "These are the tags we will use." The household's aim is not to satisfy everyone's sense of order. It is to ensure that two adults and at least one child can apply tags consistently without thinking too hard. That is why smallness matters. When tags are few, they are used. When tags are many, they become someone's hobby.

A worked example makes the dimensions concrete and shows how tags enable flexible queries. Imagine a school email: a message about a Year 6 residential trip, including a PDF, a payment schedule, and a note about medication forms. The family captures the email into the vault and stores the PDF in the family's stable file home. They then apply tags. Person: "Ava". Place: "School". Theme: "Trip", "Payments", "Health". Time marker: "Year 6" or "Summer 2026", depending on what the family uses. Now retrieval becomes flexible. If a parent searches for "Ava + Payments", the trip fee appears alongside other fees. If a parent searches "Health + School", the medication form appears alongside allergy notes. If someone searches "Trip + Summer 2026", the residential information appears alongside holiday plans. The same artefact surfaces under different questions without duplication and without requiring path memory. That is the practical magic: a tag system converts one stored item into multiple useful views.

This example also reveals a subtle point. Tags are not merely for retrieval; they are for thinking. When a family tags an item, it is forced—briefly—to name what the item is about. That naming can prevent errors. If a school letter has a health implication, tagging it "Health" makes that implication visible. If a document involves a payment deadline, tagging it "Payments" surfaces it during financial review. Tags, used sparingly, act as cognitive guardrails. They reduce the chance that a detail is treated as purely logistical when it has broader consequences.

There is, however, a credible counter-example, and it deserves more than a footnote. Some families find tagging too fiddly. They do not apply tags consistently. They capture items but neglect metadata. Over time, the tag system becomes patchy, and search becomes unreliable. The household concludes that tags "don't work". The reconciliation is to recognise what tags are competing with: not perfection, but fatigue. Tagging must therefore be designed around the minimum viable tagging behaviour. The household can decide that person tags are non-negotiable, because they provide the highest retrieval value, while other tags are optional. Or the household can decide that only certain kinds of items get full tagging: school documents, health notes, trip planning, and anything time-sensitive. The point is to match tag discipline to household bandwidth. A small, consistently used tag set beats a perfect tag system that exists mostly in theory.

Language drift is another failure mode, and it appears even in homes with good intentions. People invent near-synonyms. One adult uses "Trip", another uses "Travel". One child uses "Football", another uses "Soccer" after hearing a YouTuber. Small divergences multiply until search requires guessing. Name: vocabulary divergence. Explain: without a shared tag language, metadata fragments; retrieval becomes probabilistic. The implication is backsliding into asking and scrolling. The remedy is not to police language harshly. It is to choose tag names that feel natural to the household and to keep them visible. A "Tag guide" note in the vault, listing the small set of official tags, can act as a quiet reference. Again, the point is not bureaucracy. It is shared clarity.

Modern relevance makes this more urgent because family information now arrives from multiple institutions that use different labels. Schools use different term names. Clubs use different age categories. Health systems use formal terminology. The vault is where the family translates institutional language into household language. Tags are the translation layer. They allow the family to search in its own words rather than in the institution's categories. That is not merely convenient; it is empowering. The household stops being dependent on remembering the school's phrasing or the portal's menu layout.

The motif of the hook returns because tags are, ultimately, hooks for attention. A hook is useful when it is placed where you naturally reach and when it holds reliably. A tag is useful when it is memorable and when it retrieves reliably. Both fail when overcomplicated. Designing a family tag system therefore requires a certain intellectual humility: the recognition that the most elegant schema is not the best schema, and that the best schema is the one that the least interested household member can use consistently.

The forward test is a trade-off, and it will not disappear. A family can choose a small, shared tag language and accept that some nuance will be lost, or it can pursue nuance and accept that consistency will decline. The diagnostic question is simple enough to keep in mind during every tagging decision: will another person in the household use this tag a month from now without thinking, and will it help them find something under pressure? If the answer is yes, the tag belongs. If the answer is no, the tag is noise dressed as order.

Reusable Templates for Families

In April 1970, after an oxygen tank explosion crippled Apollo 13, NASA engineers in Houston worked with what they had: existing parts, limited power, limited time. One of the most famous phrases from the mission—"failure is not an option", attributed in popular retellings—matters less than the real operational truth. Survival depended on procedures that could be reused under pressure, adapted quickly, and executed without reinventing physics in the moment. Families do not navigate spacecraft, but they do repeatedly face situations where invention is the enemy: trips that provoke last-minute scrambles, birthdays that arrive like a surprise every year, term starts that somehow catch everyone unprepared, health appointments where the same details must be gathered again and again. The household keeps paying for the same chaos as if it is new.

Templates are the household's way of refusing that tax.

A template, in the family sense, is not a stiff form that tells people how to live. It is a starting shape—headings, prompts, and a small amount of structure—that captures what the household has learned from doing the same kind of thing before. The point is not to eliminate spontaneity. The point is to stop wasting attention on predictable basics. Families often resist templates because they sound corporate, as if life is being turned into a project plan. Yet families already run repeated projects. They just do so with poor tooling: frantic memory, last-minute lists on scraps of paper, and shared stress. A template turns an experience into an asset.

Make it light.

That sentence is the governing rule. A heavy template becomes a monument. A light template becomes a tool. The family should be able to duplicate a template and begin filling it out in seconds, using it as a prompt rather than a demand. The template should feel like a well-labelled drawer: you open it, and the right categories are waiting. You can ignore what you do not need. You can add what is missing. You do not have to re-remember what you forgot last time.

The logic of templates follows a simple engine that mirrors how the vault already works: show, name, explain, imply. Show: a family preparing for a trip and discovering, at 10.30 pm, that the child's swimming costume is missing, the travel insurance details are nowhere, and someone has forgotten to cancel a weekly activity. Name: repeated failure points. Explain: repeated events generate repeated omissions because attention is finite and because the household tries to hold the plan in mind rather than in a stable place. The implication is that the same stress repeats, and people begin to believe the stress is inevitable, part of the trip's "nature", rather than a predictable result of improvising the same plan each time.

A template changes that by shifting the unit of work. Instead of planning a trip from scratch, the family begins with a trip template that already contains the categories that matter: bookings, documents, packing, money, cancellations, contact details, contingencies. Those categories are not an aesthetic preference. They are based on what actually breaks trips. Bookings break when references are lost. Documents break when passports are forgotten or details cannot be found at the airport. Packing breaks when the family relies on a vague mental model of "everything" rather than on a list that reflects what the trip requires. Money breaks when costs are scattered across apps and receipts. Cancellations break when standing commitments are forgotten and fees are incurred. A template is therefore an instrument for memory, but also an instrument for risk reduction in the ordinary sense: fewer avoidable problems.

The same logic applies to birthdays, which families often treat as both joyful and oddly draining. A birthday is predictable in date and unpredictable in execution, because it contains social obligations, planning, and purchases that can expand quickly. Show: two days before a birthday, someone remembers the cake, someone remembers the gift, and then the family realises they have not invited the right people, booked the venue, checked dietary needs, or arranged transport. The joy becomes logistics. Name: celebration load. Explain: celebrations are emotionally charged and therefore difficult to run calmly when the planning is improvised; the household's attention is split between meaning and management. The implication is that adults experience birthdays as work and children experience the stress around them as part of the celebration. A light birthday template—guest list, cake notes, gift ideas, timing, messages to send, photos to take—does not diminish joy. It creates space for it.

Term times, too, are repeated shocks. Every new term brings timetable changes, new teachers, new clubs, new uniform requirements, new dates. Families often treat each term as a new crisis because the information arrives through multiple channels and is processed late. Show: the Sunday night before term, the household scrambles for kit, tries to remember which day PE happens, and searches for the list of required items. Name: reset friction. Explain: resets are cognitively costly because they require rebuilding routines; without a template, the family repeats the same reconstruction labour each time. The implication is a predictable spike in stress at the least convenient moment. A term-start template—contacts, uniform notes, timetable, key dates, reminders to check clubs and transport—turns the reset into a repeatable process.

Health appointments introduce a different kind of repetition: repeated information transfer under conditions that can already be tense. Families are often asked the same details: medications, allergies, symptom history, prior appointments, relevant documents, contact details. Show: arriving at an appointment and realising that the last letter is in a different app, the medication name is remembered approximately, and the previous notes are scattered. Name: recall pressure. Explain: health-related contexts often increase cognitive load; stress reduces recall accuracy; scattered information becomes harder to retrieve precisely when precision matters. The implication is frustration and inefficiency, and sometimes the need to repeat conversations later. A health appointment template—key facts, questions, documents to bring, notes after the appointment—does not offer medical advice. It offers an information scaffold that reduces repeated scrambling.

None of this works if templates are stored in obscure places. Templates must have a home that is both obvious and stable. Many families make a simple mistake: they create a template once, then cannot find it the next time. That is not a failure of discipline. It is a design failure. Templates should live in a clearly labelled "Templates" area in the vault, close to the system's front door, and they should be named in a way that makes them searchable: "Trip Template", "Birthday Template", "Term Start Template", "Health Appointment Template". Plain names win. Decorative names lose. The metric is simple: can a tired adult locate the template in under ten seconds? If not, the template is not truly a tool.

A worked trip template example brings the idea down to the level of behaviour. Imagine the family duplicating the trip template for a weekend away. They begin not with a blank page but with prompts that force decisions early, when there is still time. Booking references are recorded. Addresses are pasted. Check-in rules are noted. A section prompts the family to list documents: confirmation emails, tickets, any needed IDs. Another prompts packing, not as a single overwhelming list but as a few recognisable buckets: clothing, toiletries, chargers, special items. Another prompts money: budget notes, payment deadlines, cash needs, fees. Another prompts cancellations: which standing commitments need pausing, which pets need care, which deliveries need rerouting. The family does not fill every line. They fill what is relevant. That is the point. The template is a prompt, not a contract.

Now show the payoff. The night before departure is still busy. Children still misplace things. That is family life. Yet the family no longer experiences the particular panic of uncertainty:

"Have we forgotten something important?" The template has made the key categories visible, and the act of checking categories is faster than the act of improvising. The system provides calm not through control but through coverage. Coverage is a better word than organisation because it suggests what templates actually do: they cover the common failure points so the family's attention can go to the human parts.

A named, checkable example from outside domestic life underlines why templates work. In software and operations, "runbooks" are written guides for recurring incidents—what to check, what to do, where to find information. Their value is not that they prevent incidents; it is that they reduce the cost of response and make performance more consistent across people. Families are, in effect, running a small operation. A trip template is a runbook for travel. A term-start template is a runbook for seasonal reset. A birthday template is a runbook for celebration logistics. The language can be softened, but the function is the same: reduce repeated improvisation and allow shared execution.

A credible limitation must be handled honestly. Templates can become stale. They can preserve yesterday's life. A family changes—children grow, routines shift, priorities evolve—and a template can quietly become wrong if it is never reviewed. The reconciliation is to treat templates as living artefacts. Each time a template is used, the family has a chance to learn: "We forgot chargers again," or "This section is irrelevant now," or "We always argue about this step." Those observations can be folded back into the template with small edits. The point is not to perfect templates; it is to let them improve gradually so they reflect the family's current reality rather than an idealised one.

There is also a risk of over-templating. Some households respond to the promise of calm by templating everything: every outing, every weekend, every meal. The system becomes heavy and starts to feel like living inside paperwork. The reconciliation is to template only what repeats and only what hurts when improvised. The signal is emotional. If the absence of a template creates repeated conflict or repeated forgetting, a template is worth it. If a template feels like administration without payoff, discard it. The vault should serve life, not replace it.

Modern relevance makes templates unusually powerful because modern family life has become more modular and more fragmented. Parents coordinate across jobs, carers, clubs, schools, and extended family. Information arrives through multiple channels. Routines are repeatedly disrupted by changes. Templates provide continuity across that fragmentation. They allow the family to restart quickly after disruptions, because the basic shape is already stored. This is why templates are more than convenience; they are resilience.

The motif of the hook returns here in a different form. A template is a hook into the future. It is a way for past-you to catch future-you before they fall into the same familiar scramble. It is also a subtle act of generosity. Someone, at some point, did the work of noticing what repeats and writing it down so that the household can stop paying the same cost. When templates are shared, that generosity becomes collective.

The forward test is not whether templates can make life "smooth". Life will not comply. The test is whether the family will choose to turn experience into an asset. After the next trip, birthday, term start, or appointment, will the household store the lessons in a reusable shape that makes the next iteration calmer, or will it accept repeated chaos as the natural price of family life, paying again with time, mood, and last-minute improvisation?

Simple Checklists for Reliability

On 15 November 1990, at Burbank in California, a patient named Martin Memmott underwent surgery intended to relieve a chronic problem and instead suffered a catastrophic error. The case later became one of the examples discussed in the patient-safety movement that gathered pace in the 1990s and 2000s, as clinicians began to confront a brutal fact: intelligent, conscientious professionals still make predictable omissions when systems are complex and attention is divided. The response was not moral outrage alone. It was design. Hospitals began adopting checklists not because surgeons were careless, but because memory is not a reliable instrument under pressure. The family home, in quieter ways, runs on the same cognitive physics.

For moments that must not be missed, hope is a weak strategy.

That sentence can sound harsh until you notice how gently it treats people. It blames no one. It simply recognises that the conditions in which omissions occur are ordinary: fatigue, hurry, interrupted attention, competing demands, emotional weather. A checklist is a small, visible prompt that turns those conditions from a personal failing into a manageable system. It does not make the day calm. It makes the day less brittle.

Families often resist checklists for the same reason professionals once did: they feel like an insult. A competent adult should not need to be told to take keys. A capable teenager should not need a list for exam morning. A parent should not need a prompt about medication routines. Yet competence in real life is not the ability to remember everything. It is the ability to offload what should not depend on memory so that attention can be spent where it is most needed: on judgement, on care, on presence. Checklists are not for fools. They are for humans.

Show the classic household failure. The instruction is vague: "Get ready." A parent says it while packing lunches, answering messages, and watching the clock. The child hears it and does what children do: they move towards readiness in a cloud of partial tasks. They put on one sock. They forget the other. They brush teeth and forget hair. They remember a book and forget the water bottle. The parent notices the omissions, feels irritation rise, repeats themselves more sharply, and the morning becomes a low-grade conflict about responsibility. Name the problem: ambiguous prompts. Explain: a vague instruction forces the child to invent a plan on the fly, and invention is cognitively demanding under time pressure; omissions are therefore not surprising. The implication is not merely a forgotten item. It is a predictable emotional pattern: nagging and defensiveness, which neither side enjoys.

Now show the alternative. The instruction becomes concrete, visible, and shared: a short list that the child can follow without interpretation. It is not a lecture. It is a sequence of observable actions. The parent does not have to hold it in mind. The child does not have to translate "get ready" into ten separate tasks while half-asleep. The list shifts responsibility from a contest of wills to a simple process. Name: execution scaffolding. Explain: a checklist reduces the cognitive load of planning by externalising the steps; it converts a vague goal into a set of verifiable actions. The implication is both practical and emotional: fewer omissions and fewer arguments, because the household is no longer negotiating what "ready" means every morning.

This is the essential move of a checklist: it makes success easy to recognise. Families often live in a fog of implicit expectations. Adults carry mental models of what should happen. Children carry different models, shaped by what they notice and what they value. Checklists turn implicit models into explicit prompts. That is not control. It is clarity. It is also fairness. A child cannot meet an expectation they cannot see.

Checklists also create a quiet kind of independence. When a child follows a list, they experience the satisfaction of completion and the dignity of self-management. Adults, meanwhile, experience a reduction in micromanagement. The parent stops being a human reminder system and becomes a supporter. The child stops being the object of correction and becomes an agent. That shift is, in many households, the beginning of calmer routines.

The reliability gained is not mystical. It can be measured. Families can count "returns to the house" after leaving because something was forgotten. They can count late arrivals caused by missing items. They can count the number of times the same reminder is repeated. When a checklist is used consistently, those counts tend to drop. The household feels this as time regained and stress reduced. It also feels it as a change in tone. Mornings become less spiky. Evenings become less frantic. That is the practical moral of checklists: they reduce the number of moments in which family members treat one another as obstacles rather than as allies.

A checklist's power, however, depends on its design. Show the common failure. A family creates a long checklist—twenty items for leaving the house—and posts it somewhere. No one reads it. Or they read it once and then it becomes wallpaper. Name the problem: checklist dilution. Explain: long lists are cognitively heavy; they feel punitive; they invite skipping; they become background noise. The implication is that the checklist fails, and the household concludes that "lists don't work". In reality, the list was poorly designed for the way attention works under time pressure.

This is where research and practice meet. Atul Gawande's account of checklists in complex environments (2009) emphasises brevity and clarity: checklists should capture the critical steps most likely to be missed, not every possible step. The family translation is direct. A leaving-the-house checklist should include the few items that cause disproportionate pain when forgotten: keys, phone, wallet, medication, school bag, specific kit. It should not include "put on shoes" unless that is genuinely a recurring failure point. A good checklist is not exhaustive; it is strategic. It targets the household's most expensive omissions.

The same principle applies to medicine routines, though the tone must remain careful. Families handle health information with sensitivity, and a book cannot and should not offer medical advice. Still, as an educational point about systems, it is clear that recurring routines with consequences benefit from reliable prompts. The checklist here is not a substitute for professional guidance. It is an organisational support that ensures agreed steps are visible and trackable within the household's own system. The observable behaviour is that the routine is recorded consistently rather than being left to memory. The implication is reduced uncertainty and reduced household conflict about whether something was done. The checklist becomes a shared record of action, not a moral judgement.

Exam mornings provide another vivid case because they combine high stakes, anxiety, and time pressure. Show: a teenager wakes late, panics, and forgets a calculator or an ID card. The omission is not a character flaw; it is the predictable result of stress compressing attention. A short exam-morning checklist—again, not a manifesto—can reduce that risk. The child experiences it as a safety net rather than as a parental intervention, provided the list is theirs as much as the parent's. Name: anticipatory support. Explain: a checklist created during a calm moment serves the stressed version of the same person later; it externalises what must be remembered when stress makes memory unreliable. The implication is a smoother morning and a better emotional state entering the exam room.

It is also worth naming what checklists are not. They are not a replacement for thought. They are not a rigid script. They are prompts for the basics, so judgement can be spent on what is truly variable. This is why checklists do not belong everywhere. They belong at points of repeated failure and high consequence: transitions, routines, and events where omissions carry a cost. When families over-apply checklists, they create a household that feels bureaucratic. The reconciliation is restraint: checklists for what must not be missed, not for everything that could be done.

A named, checkable counter-example helps keep this honest. Some families prefer visible physical prompts rather than digital checklists, especially when trying to reduce screen time and keep routines glanceable. A laminated checklist by the door can outperform a beautifully designed digital list if the physical version is where eyes naturally land. The vault still has a role: it can store the canonical list, allow edits, and provide a reference when the physical copy needs updating. The reconciliation is pragmatic: the checklist should live where it is used, whether that is on a phone, on a fridge, or on a wall. A checklist hidden behind taps is a checklist that will not be used.

Visibility, then, is not a minor detail. It is the whole game. A checklist must be in the line of action. A leaving-the-house checklist belongs near the exit. A bedtime routine belongs where bedtime happens. An exam checklist belongs with the bag or the desk. Digital checklists can achieve this with placement—pinning, favouriting, making the checklist part of a dashboard—but the principle remains physical: the prompt should appear at the moment of decision. Otherwise it becomes one more thing the family must remember to remember, which defeats the purpose.

The motif of the hook returns because checklists are hooks for behaviour. They catch the moment just before it slips. They reduce the need for last-minute mental rummaging. They also change the household's emotional choreography. Instead of a parent hovering and correcting, the checklist becomes the third party that holds the standard. The family can blame the list rather than one another. That is not a trick; it is a way of removing personal accusation from routine friction.

End with the forward test, because checklists ultimately ask the household to make a trade. They trade a small amount of upfront clarity—writing down the critical steps during a calm moment—for a reduction in repeated stress during chaotic moments. The diagnostic question is simple and sharp: at the next high-friction transition—leaving the house, managing a recurring routine, preparing for an exam—will the family rely on vague commands and brittle memory, or will it place a short, visible checklist in the line of action and let the system carry what people should not have to carry in their heads?

Chapter 6
Managing School and Health Records

On 29 October 1998, in Bristol, the UK government published the first annual report of the new National Health Service clinical governance framework, formalising a simple institutional truth: when care is complex, information must be reliable, traceable, and shareable. The policy language was public-sector plain, but the underlying logic was intimate. Someone's wellbeing depends on whether the right detail can be retrieved at the right moment. In homes, the stakes are smaller and often private, yet the same logic applies every weekday morning when a parent tries to recall PE days, locate a trip letter, find a login for a school portal, or summarise a child's relevant medical history for an appointment. The home, too, runs on records. It simply pretends not to.

Families tend to treat administration as an optional layer hovering above "real life". School and health quietly contradict that fantasy. They are not merely domains of paperwork; they are the interfaces through which children move into institutions and through which families navigate care. Those interfaces have expanded. Schools use multiple platforms. Clubs use their own apps. Clinics and surgeries send messages through different channels. Information arrives as a scatter of dates, policies, attachments, instructions, and forms, and the household's success depends less on remembering and more on retrieving. A family second brain without a disciplined approach to school and health records remains incomplete, because these are precisely the areas where consequences bite when information is missing.

A quiet motif runs through this chapter: the pocket file. It is the slim folder one keeps for documents that matter—light enough to carry, structured enough to trust, ready when asked. The family vault should behave like that pocket file, but more powerful: searchable, shareable, and resilient to the whims of paper and portal. The aim is not to turn the home into an office. The aim is to stop treating the most consequential household information as if it could safely drift.

The chapter opens with school, because school is where modern family life often becomes administratively dense. Term dates, timetables, policies, portals, contacts, trip documents, uniform rules, and an ever-moving calendar of events arrive through multiple channels and in multiple formats. The familiar stress is not caused by the existence of these details; it is caused by their fragmentation. A parent knows the information exists somewhere, yet retrieval is slow, and slowness becomes panic when the question is asked at 7.55 am. The chapter shows how to design a school area that behaves like a compact system rather than a pile: a structure where notes, documents, and tags are linked so that one quick search surfaces what matters. The scenario is deliberately ordinary—checking PE days and upcoming trips—because ordinary is where families pay their daily tax.

From there, the chapter widens into activities and homework, the second ring of school life that often becomes a source of hidden resentment. Clubs, lessons, and homework can turn one adult into a household project manager, quietly tracking deadlines and kit requirements while everyone else assumes it will somehow be handled. That arrangement is fragile and unfair. Yet the solution is not to intensify parental oversight. It is to create light-touch systems that allow commitments to be visible without making the home feel like a compliance machine. The chapter explores ways to log activities and due dates that respect a child's growing autonomy—often by placing responsibility in the child's own space—while keeping adults sufficiently informed to support, not control. A simple homework checklist linked to reference notes becomes less a tool of enforcement and more a scaffold for independence.

Health records then shift the tone, because health information carries a different weight. Even in the calmest families, health details are the kind of information people wish they could forget, and yet must be able to produce accurately when asked. Allergies, medications, relevant history, appointment notes, and care instructions do not belong to memory alone, not because family members are careless, but because stress degrades recall and because the consequences of omission can be serious. The chapter treats health organisation with the seriousness it deserves while keeping the method humane: secure, reachable storage; naming conventions that allow quick retrieval; tagging by person so a family can surface a coherent picture without rummaging. A small scenario shows how quickly a clear summary can be produced for a new clinician or an unfamiliar setting, reducing the cognitive load at precisely the moment when the family's attention should be on listening and deciding rather than on reconstructing facts.

There is also an honesty required here about privacy and dignity. Health information is sensitive. Children grow into teenagers who deserve boundaries. Families vary in how they share and who needs access. The chapter therefore treats "secure yet reachable" as more than a slogan. It is a design tension: too open, and trust is damaged; too locked away, and retrieval fails when it matters. The second brain's promise is not merely storage; it is *appropriate access*. Done well, health records become an act of care for the whole family, including the future adult the child will become.

The final movement of the chapter takes a turn that is emotionally uncomfortable but practically essential: emergencies. This is not about fear-mongering. It is about acknowledging that households rely on tacit knowledge until the day they cannot. When a parent is ill, away, or simply unavailable, someone else may have to step in—another parent, a relative, a trusted friend—and the difference between chaos and continuity often comes down to whether essential information is packaged in a form that can be used. Emergency contacts, care instructions, key documents, and a handful of practical notes can be assembled into a concise "in case of" bundle inside the vault. The best thing about such a bundle is that it almost never needs to be used. The second-best thing is that if it is needed, it works.

Modern relevance sharpens the stakes. Institutions increasingly assume digital competence: logins, portals, PDFs, online forms. They also assume uninterrupted attention, which families rarely have. The second brain provides a counterbalance: it allows the household to translate institutional demands into a stable internal system. It reduces dependence on the memory of the one person who remembers passwords. It reduces dependence on the latest message in a thread. It reduces dependence on paper that can be lost. In doing so, it changes the household's relationship with school and health from reactive to prepared. Prepared does not mean anxious. It means able to retrieve.

The emotional payoff of this chapter is subtle. It is the relief of knowing that important information is not balanced precariously on one mind. It is the shift from "I hope we can find it" to "We know where it is." That shift is not merely convenient; it changes family dynamics. It reduces blame. It increases follow-through. It allows children to participate in their own organisation as they grow, without turning them into miniature administrators.

The closing tension, then, is a question about what a family wants its default mode to be. When the next school message arrives, when the next portal hides a PDF, when the next appointment requires a summary, will the household rely on improvisation and private memory, or will it treat school and health records as part of the shared infrastructure of family life—light enough to maintain, strong enough to trust, ready in the pocket when it is suddenly needed?

Organising School Information

In September 1988, in London, the UK government published the Education Reform Act, reshaping the structure of state education in England and Wales and formalising a new language of curricula, assessment, and institutional accountability. The Act did not merely change classrooms. It amplified paperwork. When institutions become more measured, they become more documented. Families have lived with the downstream effects ever since: policies proliferate, term dates are formalised, communications become more frequent, and the child's education arrives at home not only as learning but as a stream of instructions, forms, portals, and deadlines. School is not one thing. It is a web of information that must be retrieved quickly, often under pressure.

Mornings reveal the truth.

A parent stands by the door at 7.52 am, holding a shoe, listening to a child insist that today is PE day. The parent is not sure. The timetable changed last term, and there was a message about a rotation. The parent's phone is already open, thumb hovering, trying to remember where the information might be: the school app, the email, a PDF, a screenshot, a note scribbled on a calendar. In the background, the kettle clicks off. The child is impatient. The parent feels the familiar tension: this should be easy, yet it is not. The problem is not ignorance. The problem is retrieval.

Show the pattern plainly. School information arrives through multiple channels: email, messaging threads, school apps, portals, paper letters, printed calendars, posters photographed at pick-up, verbal instructions passed through children. Each channel is optimised for delivery, not for later finding. Families therefore live in a perpetual state of partial knowledge: the information exists somewhere, but not in a form that the household can reliably locate in the moment it is needed. Name the problem: fragmented authority. Explain: when school information has no single trusted home, the household cannot treat any record as definitive; people keep re-checking and re-asking, which costs time and mood. The implication is an invisible tax on family life: repeated micro-emergencies that feel personal but are structural.

A school area inside the family vault is an attempt to create one stable "pocket file" for the institution that touches the household most often. The pocket file metaphor matters because it keeps the design honest. A pocket file holds only what you repeatedly need and need to reach quickly. It does not try to store the universe. It does not attempt to preserve every message. It offers fast retrieval of the essentials: term dates, timetables, policies that govern decisions, portal access, contact details, and the documents that routinely trigger action—trip forms, consent letters, payment links, kit lists. The aim is not to organise school life into a beautiful archive.

The aim is to reduce last-minute scrambles by making the right information easy to surface.

The structure begins with a small act of naming. Families should store school information in a way that mirrors how they actually speak about it. If there are multiple schools, each school gets its own clearly named home. If the child is in a particular year group, that year becomes a useful tag or sub-area, not because it is bureaucratic but because it matches how information is issued: "Year 6 trip", "Year 3 timetable", "Reception newsletter". The household is building an access path, not writing a thesis. The visible behaviour to aim for is simple: when a school item arrives, the family can place it in the school area without hesitating, and later retrieve it by searching with the words they naturally use.

Within that school home, the most useful ingredients are stable anchors rather than elaborate categories. An anchor is a note or document that other items can point to. Anchors reduce search because they become reliable gateways. The first anchor is contacts: phone numbers, email addresses, key staff roles, and any relevant links. Families often discover how vital this is at the moment they need it—when a child is unwell, when transport changes, when someone needs to call quickly—and by then they are hunting. Having a single contact note reduces that hunting. The second anchor is access: portal logins, links, and a record of where key information tends to live. Even when families do not store passwords in the vault for privacy reasons, the vault can still store the link and a note about which account is used, reducing the cognitive friction of "how do we get into this again?" The third anchor is the current timetable and term dates: the rhythms that govern everything else.

Now connect anchors to the earlier chapters' lessons: tags and retrieval. A school item is rarely "just school". It belongs to a child and to a theme: trip, payment, health, homework, uniform, policy. Tags allow one artefact to be retrieved under multiple questions without duplication. A timetable document tagged with the child's name and "School" becomes instantly findable. A policy document tagged "Uniform" or "Behaviour" becomes retrievable when a decision or dispute arises. A trip letter tagged "Trip", "Payments", and the child's name becomes visible both during planning and during financial review. Tags turn the school area into a living system rather than a filing cabinet.

A scenario shows how the pieces work together. The parent by the door opens the vault and searches using two cues: the child's name and "PE". The search surfaces a small note titled "PE days and kit – Spring term", linked to the current timetable and tagged with the child's name and "School". The note contains the one line the parent actually needs in that moment: the day and any rotation detail. The parent checks it, hands over the kit, and the morning continues without argument. The system has not made the family calmer by magic. It has made the correct answer easy to retrieve quickly.

This scenario is mundane by design, because school organisation should deliver mundane wins. Families often chase "big" improvements and miss the fact that most stress comes from repeated small frictions. PE days are a small friction until they are not—until the child is embarrassed, until a note is sent home, until the morning is derailed. A clear school area prevents dozens of such moments across a term. It also changes family dynamics. When the vault can answer the question, the parent does not have to. The household moves away from dependence on a single adult memory-holder.

The same retrieval logic applies to trips, which are the school's most reliable source of logistical chaos. A school trip letter contains dates, deadlines, kit lists, and often payment instructions. The letter arrives via paper or app, and the family's risk is predictable: the deadline is missed or the kit requirement is discovered too late. A well-organised school area treats trip information as a distinct pattern. Capture the letter, distil the key details, store the document, tag it with child, school, and "Trip", and link it to the child's trip template if the family uses templates. Now the trip ceases to be a scattered set of messages. It becomes a small project with an address. The implication is reduced last-minute searching and a higher likelihood of calm preparation.

Not all school information deserves the same level of preservation. This is where a credible limitation must be admitted. Schools send a lot of communication that is informational in the moment and irrelevant later—general reminders, duplicate announcements, routine newsletters. If families attempt to store everything, the vault becomes noisy and retrieval becomes harder. The reconciliation is to treat school information in two layers: durable reference and transient chatter. Durable reference includes timetables, term dates, policies, portal links, contacts, and documents tied to action. Transient chatter can remain in the school's native channels, because its value decays quickly. This boundary keeps the vault lean and protects trust: when someone searches the school area, they find what matters, not yesterday's noise.

This distinction also keeps families from becoming unwilling archivists of institutional life. A family second brain is a domestic tool, not an external compliance system. Its job is to support the household's decisions and reduce avoidable stress. That job requires selectivity. Selectivity is not laziness. It is design. The household should store what it repeatedly needs for action and retrieval, not what merely passes through.

A second named, checkable example sharpens the point about access and design. In 2003, the UK government launched the National Pupil Database, a large-scale system for collecting pupil-level data. Whatever one thinks of such systems, they reveal an institutional orientation: schools increasingly depend on data systems to operate. Families feel this as portals, apps, and formalised processes. The implication for the home is simple: the household cannot rely on being able to reconstruct information later through institutional interfaces that change, that require logins, that may be inaccessible at the worst moment. The family vault becomes the household's stable interface to an unstable institutional environment.

This is also why linking matters. A school area should not be a pile of isolated items. Links between notes, documents, and tags create a navigable web. A timetable note links to term dates. Term dates link to holiday planning. A uniform policy note links to a shopping list or a "start of term" template. A "portal access" note links to the most used pages. Linking reduces cognitive load because it matches how questions arise: one question triggers another. "Is it PE day?" becomes "What kit?" becomes "Is there a trip coming up?" A linked school area allows the family to follow these questions without leaving the vault and falling back into scrolls.

The motif of the pocket file returns here because it captures the emotional promise. A pocket file is reassuring because it tells you, silently, that you do not need to remember everything. You need only know where to look. When a family builds a school area that is anchored, linked, and tagged, school stops feeling like a constant intrusion of administrative surprise and starts feeling like something that can be handled with calm competence. The child benefits too. A child who can look up PE days or trip details begins to practise autonomy. The household benefits because fewer questions become urgent. Urgency is often just missing information.

The forward test is straightforward and therefore revealing. When the next school item arrives—a timetable change, a trip letter, a policy update, a portal message—will the family treat it as transient noise that must be held in memory until it becomes urgent, or will it be captured into a clear school area with enough structure—anchors, links, tags—that the next frantic morning question can be answered in seconds rather than in stress?

Tracking Activities and Homework

In 1938, in Ames, Iowa, the psychologist Kurt Lewin began developing what would later be called field theory, arguing that behaviour is shaped less by character in isolation than by the total situation—goals, obstacles, social forces, and the structures that make action easier or harder. That claim has been tested and re-tested across decades of behavioural science and organisational practice, and it lands with particular force in family life. Children do not fail to keep track of homework and activities because they are lazy. Parents do not become accidental project managers because they enjoy it. The environment pushes both into predictable patterns, and those patterns can be redesigned.

Small structures change outcomes.

Activities and homework are where family organisation often becomes emotionally charged because they sit at the border between support and control. A child wants autonomy. A parent wants reliability. The household wants evenings that are not consumed by last-minute discoveries. Yet the information involved—club times, kit requirements, homework briefs, due dates, practice schedules—arrives in fragments and changes frequently. It is easy for parents to absorb it "temporarily" in their own minds, because doing so feels protective. Then "temporarily" becomes permanent, and one adult becomes the household's human scheduler: remembering which day is piano, which week is swimming, which evening has a deadline, which kit has to be washed. This is not a moral failure. It is a structural trap.

Show the trap in a familiar domestic scene. It is Wednesday, late afternoon. A child announces that there is a project due tomorrow—something involving printed photos, a costume element, or a worksheet that has to be signed. The parent's body tightens, not because the task is impossible, but because the task arrives as an ambush. The parent asks, "Why didn't you tell me?" The child shrugs, not maliciously, simply because the information existed in a place the parent did not see, or because it was mentioned once and then vanished into the swirl of the day. The parent's tone sharpens. The evening's rhythm collapses. Name what happened: deadline ambush. Explain: when commitments live only in a child's working memory or only in scattered channels, deadlines surface late; the household then pays with urgency, stress, and conflict. The implication is more than a missed task. It is a recurring emotional pattern that teaches both parent and child the wrong lesson: that planning is punishment and that adults are there to catch the fall.

A family second brain offers a different lesson: planning is a shared system, not a personal virtue. The goal in tracking activities and homework is not to produce hyper-managed children. The goal is to create a light-touch record of commitments that makes follow-through likely while preserving the child's dignity. Light-touch matters because heavy systems provoke rebellion or collapse under fatigue. The household is not trying to create a mini office. It is trying to make the basic truth visible: what must happen, when, and what is needed.

Begin with activities, because they are recurring and therefore ideal for system design. Activities have three kinds of information that matter: schedule (when and where), requirements (kit, fees, permissions), and exceptions (changes, cancellations, special events). Families often capture schedule in a calendar and then neglect the rest. The problem shows up when requirements and exceptions surface late—forgotten kit, missed payments, unexpected location changes. The vault can hold these details as stable reference attached to the activity. When a club has a standing kit list, that list should not live in a chat thread. It should live as a short note in the child's space, tagged with the activity and linked to the calendar entry or at least to the activity's reference note. The point is not to produce more documentation. The point is to create a single reliable place for "what does this activity require?" so the family stops relearning it repeatedly.

Now add the child's own space, because independence is the real prize. If the adult is the only person who logs activities, the system remains adult-owned. The child stays passive. The household keeps the same bottleneck. A light-touch approach places the activity notes and homework prompts where the child can see and update them, with parents retaining enough visibility to support. The design tension is delicate: too much parental monitoring and the child withdraws; too little structure and the child floats. The solution is not surveillance. It is shared infrastructure: a common place where commitments are recorded and can be checked without drama.

Homework introduces a different challenge because it is often variable and sometimes poorly specified. One child receives a clear assignment with a date. Another receives an ambiguous instruction delivered verbally at the end of the day. Digital homework platforms can help, yet they also create a new retrieval problem: homework exists behind logins and inside interfaces that are not built for family use. The household needs a simple system that can capture homework requirements quickly and connect them to the reference material required to complete them. That connection—between "what to do" and "how to do it"—is where second brains shine.

A worked example makes this concrete. A child has a weekly set of tasks: reading, spelling practice, a maths assignment, and a small research task. Instead of relying on memory and nightly questions, the child has a simple homework checklist in their space, with tick boxes. Each item links to a reference note: the spelling list, the reading log instructions, the maths platform link, the teacher's research guidelines. The checklist is short enough to be usable and visible enough to be checked without prompting. The child updates it. The parent can glance, not to police, but to know when support might be needed. When the child sits down to work, the system reduces friction. They do not have to search for the spelling list; it is one tap away. They do not have to ask which book to read; the reference note says. Name what is happening: task-to-reference linking. Explain: homework is easier when the action prompt is directly connected to the relevant materials; the child spends less time searching and more time doing. The implication is fewer arguments and more autonomy, because the child can proceed without constant adult mediation.

This linkage also alters the moral economy of homework. When homework is vague and adults repeatedly remind, homework becomes a site of power. Children experience reminders as nagging. Adults experience silence as irresponsibility. A checklist makes expectations explicit and therefore less personal. The parent is no longer saying, "You should..." The system is saying, "This is what's due." That shift is not cold. It is kind. It reduces the emotional heat around routine obligations and makes the parent-child relationship less entangled with admin.

Of course, not every child will adopt a checklist willingly, and pretending otherwise would be naive. A credible counter-example is the child who finds lists oppressive, who rebels against visible tracking, or who uses avoidance as a coping strategy when tasks feel overwhelming. The reconciliation is to treat the system as a support, not a test. The household can begin with the minimum viable capture: recording only due dates and critical requirements, leaving the rest flexible. The system can also be co-designed with the child, allowing them to choose how they capture—voice notes, simple check marks, or brief text—so they feel ownership rather than imposition. The aim is not perfect compliance. The aim is reduced ambushes and increased agency.

There is also a risk on the adult side: overreach. Parents can turn tracking into micromanagement, particularly when anxious about school performance or social commitments. That anxiety is understandable, but a second brain designed as a monitoring device will quickly become a contested space. The reconciliation is to anchor the system in the household's true objective: reliable logistics and supportive independence. The parent's role is to design the environment, not to run the child's life. The metric is behavioural. If the system results in fewer parent reminders, it is working. If it results in more monitoring and more conflict, it is failing, regardless of how neat it looks.

Modern family life makes this balance harder because children's commitments now extend beyond what parents can easily see. Clubs communicate through apps. Homework can be assigned through platforms. Teachers send updates through portals. Children may receive information directly and forget to relay it. The family second brain is not a substitute for communication, but it provides a stable landing place for the commitments that matter to the household. It also reduces dependence on "Did you tell me?" conversations, which tend to be accusatory even when no one intends them to be.

A second named example helps situate the issue in a broader evidence base. In 1999, psychologists Peter Gollwitzer and Veronika Brandstätter published work on implementation intentions—if-then planning—showing that specifying when and how an action will be taken can increase follow-through. The family translation is simple: children are more likely to complete tasks when the task is not merely "do homework" but tied to a concrete cue and supported by accessible materials. A checklist linked to reference notes is, in effect, an environmental implementation intention. It turns "I should" into "I know what and where." The implication is not guaranteed success. It is improved odds, which is what families need.

The motif that quietly unifies this subchapter is the handrail. A handrail does not drag anyone upstairs. It does not remove the stairs. It makes the climb safer and more predictable, especially when carrying things. Activities and homework are stairs. They repeat. They are sometimes steep. A light-touch tracking system is a handrail: a support that makes follow-through easier without taking over the climb.

The forward test is therefore not whether the household can record every activity and every homework task perfectly. Perfection is irrelevant. The test is whether the family will choose systems that distribute responsibility rather than concentrating it in one adult's mind. When the next club change arrives, when the next homework brief appears, will it be captured into the child's space with a simple record and links to what's needed, or will it continue to float in messages and memory until it resurfaces as a deadline ambush, costing time, mood, and trust?

Storing Health and Medical Details

In January 2018, in London, the NHS introduced a new national "Allergy Safety" initiative within parts of its patient-safety work, reflecting a recognition that allergy information is not a nice-to-have annotation but a detail that can change outcomes. The lesson is unromantic and widely applicable: in healthcare, the smallest facts are sometimes the most consequential, and the worst time to reconstruct those facts is when someone is unwell, frightened, or in a hurry. Families encounter a domestic version of that constraint whenever they have to answer questions quickly: What medications are being taken? What allergies exist? What happened last time? Who is the clinician? What was decided? In those moments, memory feels like it should be enough. It often is not.

Stress steals recall.

That is not a slogan; it is a description of how attention works. Under stress, people narrow focus. They recall the dramatic bits and lose the precise ones. They confuse dates. They forget names. They remember "the blue inhaler" but not the dosage or the schedule. They recall that a reaction happened but not what triggered it. This is not incompetence. It is the mind doing what minds do in urgent situations: prioritising survival over administration. A family second brain exists, in part, to protect households from this cognitive physics by externalising the facts that should not depend on stressed recall.

Before anything else, it helps to name the design tension clearly: health information must be both secure and reachable. Secure, because it is sensitive. Reachable, because it is useless if buried behind friction or inaccessible to the person who needs it. Many households solve this tension badly in either direction. They keep health information in their heads, which is reachable but insecure in a different way—vulnerable to forgetting, confusion, and absence. Or they lock it away in a pile of papers or a forgotten folder, which is secure by obscurity but unreachable when needed. The vault offers a third way: deliberate, structured storage with appropriate access, so the right people can retrieve the right facts quickly without turning the family's private life into an open file.

Show the ordinary failure that reveals the need. A parent arrives at a new clinic or sees an unfamiliar clinician. The questions begin: medications, allergies, relevant history, previous tests, family history, recent changes. The parent answers, then corrects themselves, then finds an email with a partial note, then realises a letter is missing. The child is restless. The parent feels judged, not by the clinician necessarily but by the situation. The conversation becomes less about care and more about reconstructing information. Name the failure: recall reconstruction. Explain: when information is scattered across memory, paper, and messages, families are forced to rebuild a coherent narrative on the spot; under pressure, that reconstruction is slow and error-prone. The implication is frustration and lost attention at the very moment the family needs clarity.

A well-designed health area in the vault begins with a simple structural decision: organise by person. This is not merely tidy. It mirrors how health information is used. Clinicians and carers ask questions about an individual. Parents need to retrieve facts about an individual. Even when family-level patterns matter, they are most useful when tied to the person they affect. A person-centred structure also supports tagging, which matters because health information often intersects with school, travel, and emergencies. If a child has an allergy, that fact belongs not only in "Health" but in "School", "Trips", and "Emergency". Tags allow the same fact to be found under different pressures without duplication.

Within each person's health space, the most useful artefact is not a pile of documents but a concise summary that can be updated over time. This is not medical advice; it is information hygiene. The summary is a record of what the family knows and has been told, written in plain language, with dates when possible. It might include diagnoses as they have been communicated, allergies, current medications, significant past events, and the names of key clinicians or services. It also includes "last updated" information, not as an administrative flourish but as a marker of trust. A summary that has no update date invites doubt. Doubt creates hesitation. Hesitation wastes time. The vault's purpose is to reduce hesitation by making information both retrievable and credible.

Naming conventions matter here because health information is often retrieved during stress, and stress makes search sloppy. A name should therefore be both human and functional. The document title should include the person's name and the type of document. If a family has multiple children, a folder of files titled "Letter.pdf" is not merely annoying; it is dangerous in the sense that it increases the chance of using the wrong information. A clear naming pattern—consistent across people—reduces that risk. The visible behaviour is that any adult in the household can glance at a file list and understand what each item is without opening it. The implication is speed and fewer errors when time is short.

Tags then amplify this clarity. Person tags anchor the information. Theme tags such as "Allergy", "Medication", "Appointment", "Emergency", "School", or "Travel" make it retrievable through the questions that actually arise. A parent searching "Ava + allergy" should surface the allergy summary, any relevant letters, and any school-related notes tied to that allergy. A parent searching "Travel + medication" should surface the relevant packing notes and any documentation needed for travel. Tags are not decoration. They are retrieval handles for high-stakes moments.

Now bring in the question of sensitive details and boundaries, because the home is not a clinic and because children grow. Not every health note belongs in the shared family space. Adolescents, in particular, deserve privacy. The vault must therefore allow the family to separate "shared essentials" from "private notes". Shared essentials are the facts required for care, coordination, and emergencies: allergies, current medications, key conditions, appointment logistics, and relevant documents. Private notes might include a teenager's personal reflections, sensitive experiences, or information they do not wish to share broadly. The design principle is respect. A system that violates privacy will be resisted; resistance leads to omissions; omissions defeat the purpose. Appropriate access is thus part of reliability.

A worked scenario shows how this becomes practical without becoming clinical. A family has moved house and is attending a new surgery. The parent is asked to fill in forms and answer questions. Instead of reconstructing everything from memory, they open the vault and retrieve the child's health summary note. The summary includes allergy information and any relevant history, with dates where known. The parent can then answer questions more accurately, and if the clinician requests a document, the parent can retrieve the relevant letter or appointment note quickly because it is named clearly and stored in the child's health space. The clinician gets coherent information. The parent keeps their attention for the conversation that matters. The child experiences less adult stress, which is itself a form of care.

Name what happened: narrative availability. Explain: health care often depends on the patient's story being presented clearly; a well-organised vault allows the family to carry that story across contexts and across time, reducing the risk of omission when switching clinicians or services. The implication is not a guarantee of better care—no system can promise that—but a reduction in avoidable friction that can otherwise distort decisions.

A second named, checkable example from outside the home highlights why this matters. In 2000, the US Institute of Medicine published *To Err Is Human*, arguing that many medical errors stem from system failures rather than individual negligence. The report became influential because it shifted attention from blaming individuals to improving processes. Families can apply the same philosophy to themselves without adopting the drama. Missing a detail is rarely a sign of parental failure. It is often a sign of an information system that expects too much of memory. The vault is a process improvement for the home: it reduces dependence on perfect recall by creating a stable, shared record.

Still, a credible limitation remains. Health information changes. Medications are adjusted. Diagnoses evolve. A summary can become outdated, and outdated information can be actively harmful as an organisational artefact because it creates false confidence. The reconciliation is to treat health summaries as living documents, updated after appointments or significant changes, with a "last updated" marker. The household does not need to become meticulous record-keepers. It needs to avoid the trap of stale certainty. Stale certainty is worse than uncertainty because it stops people from checking.

Another limitation involves tool choice and security practices, which vary widely. Some families will use a notes app; others will use encrypted storage; some will rely on secure portals. The book cannot prescribe a single solution, and it should not offer security advice as if every household faces the same risks. Yet the educational principle remains: store essentials in a way that can be accessed by the people who need them, and design the vault so that sensitive information is not casually exposed. The practical implication is that families should decide, explicitly, who has access to what, and should build that decision into the vault's structure rather than leaving it to assumption.

Modern relevance makes the argument sharper. Healthcare communication is increasingly digital—portals, SMS reminders, emailed letters—yet the family's experience is often still fragmented. Documents arrive in different formats. Messages arrive in different apps. Institutional systems are not always interoperable. Families therefore carry the burden of integration. The vault is where integration happens. It is where a letter can be stored alongside an appointment note, where an allergy summary can be linked to a school form, where the family can maintain continuity despite shifting interfaces.

A quiet motif runs through all of this: the pocket card. In emergencies, many people carry a small card with essential details: allergies, key contacts, conditions. The family vault can act as a pocket card at scale—an accessible, concise, reliable set of essentials—without requiring anyone to hold everything in mind. The pocket card is not about anxiety. It is about preparedness. Preparedness is a form of calm.

The forward test is a question of trade-offs, because every system balances convenience against privacy and every household must decide where to draw lines. When the next appointment is booked, when a new medication is prescribed, when an allergy detail is confirmed, will the family capture the essentials into a secure yet reachable summary that can travel with them, or will the information remain scattered across memory and messages, forcing recall reconstruction at the worst possible moment?

Preparing For Emergencies

On 14 June 2017, in North Kensington, London, Grenfell Tower caught fire and a community experienced what emergency planners call a cascading event: one incident triggering many urgent needs at once—shelter, contact, documentation, medication, childcare, translation, decisions. In the aftermath, countless ordinary families discovered that emergencies are not only about immediate danger. They are about information. Who can be reached? Who has keys? What does a child need to feel safe? Which documents matter? Where are they? In a crisis, the mind wants to focus on people, not on paperwork. Yet paperwork, in the form of essential facts and access, can determine how quickly people are cared for.

Panic hates missing details.

That sentence is not meant to dramatise. It is meant to honour a practical truth: uncertainty amplifies fear. When a family cannot locate a contact number, cannot remember a child's allergy detail, cannot confirm where a medication is kept, cannot find a booking reference or an address, the situation feels more dangerous than it may objectively be. Emergencies compress time. They raise stakes. They reduce patience. They also tend to arrive when the household's usual organiser is unavailable—ill, travelling, stuck at work, or simply overwhelmed. This is why an "in case of" bundle is not a morbid exercise. It is a form of care that recognises the household's fragility and chooses to reduce it.

The word "emergency" can cause resistance because it pulls the mind towards worst-case imagination. Yet most families' actual emergencies are smaller and more common: a child becomes unwell at school and must be collected; a parent is called away; a relative needs to step in for a weekend; a car breaks down; a delayed train forces a change in pick-up; a sudden appointment disrupts plans. In each case, the family needs a compact set of information quickly. Not the entire vault. Not the family history. A small packet: contacts, routines, key documents, and "how we do things here". The aim is not to prepare for every conceivable disaster. The aim is to ensure continuity of care when the usual flow of life is interrupted.

Show how the failure normally unfolds. A parent is unexpectedly taken to hospital, or called away for urgent work, or simply incapacitated by illness. Another adult—perhaps a partner, perhaps a grandparent, perhaps a trusted friend—steps in. They want to help. They also lack context. Where is the school uniform? What time is pick-up? Which child has which club? Who is the teacher? What is the door code? Which neighbour has a spare key? What does the child eat when anxious? Which medication is taken, and where is it stored? Without a prepared bundle, these questions are answered through frantic phone calls, hurried text messages, and rummaging. The family is forced to improvise a handover in the least suitable conditions.

Name the problem: brittle continuity. Explain: households often rely on tacit knowledge held by one or two people; when those people are unavailable, the household lacks a usable map, and the substitute carer must reconstruct routines and contacts under pressure. The implication is not only inconvenience. It is emotional strain on children and carers at the very moment when calm, predictable routines would be most protective.

An "in case of" bundle inside the second brain is the antidote, and its defining feature is concision. It should be short enough that someone can use it quickly, yet rich enough to prevent avoidable confusion. Families sometimes make a predictable mistake here: they think preparation means collecting every possible document. The result is a sprawling archive that no one can navigate in a stressful moment. The bundle must behave like a pocket map, not an atlas. A pocket map sacrifices detail to provide orientation. That is what matters in emergencies: orientation.

Five minutes can matter.

This sentence is deliberately modest. Emergencies are rarely saved by vast plans; they are improved by small reductions in delay. Five minutes less searching for a contact number. Five minutes less arguing about where a child should be collected. Five minutes less uncertainty about allergies. Those reductions compound. They reduce stress. They reduce the risk of mistakes. They also reduce the temptation for the stepping-in relative to make assumptions that do not fit the family's needs.

Design begins with a question: what would a capable, trusted outsider need to run the household for twenty-four hours? The answer tends to cluster into a few categories: who to contact, what must happen when, how to access the home and essential accounts, and what care details matter for children (and sometimes for adults). The bundle should present these categories as clear, searchable notes rather than as a maze of files. Documents can be attached or linked, but the bundle's core should be written, because written summaries are faster to scan than PDFs and easier to understand than screenshots.

Contacts are the first category, because communication is the backbone of emergency response. A "contacts" note should include the people the stepping-in carer might need: school office, class teacher or tutor if relevant, key relatives, trusted neighbours, childcare arrangements, clubs, and any relevant professional services. The aim is not completeness. It is relevance. A contact list that includes every acquaintance becomes noisy. A contact list that includes only people who matter in a pinch becomes useful. Tags help here: person tags, "Emergency", "School", "Health". A carer searching "Emergency + school" should surface the key numbers quickly.

The second category is access: addresses, codes, keys, and the practical mechanics of the home. This is where families often rely on habit. One adult knows where the spare key is. One adult knows the alarm routine. One adult knows which cupboard holds the packed lunches. In an emergency, that knowledge becomes a bottleneck. The bundle's job is to remove the bottleneck without exposing the household unnecessarily. This is a delicate point: access details can be sensitive. The family must decide what to store and who can see it. The book's role is educational, not prescriptive, but the design principle is clear: if the stepping-in carer needs a detail to keep children safe and routines stable, the detail should be findable in the agreed place, through the agreed permissions, without a midnight phone call.

The third category is routines and non-negotiables: what must happen for the household to function. Children in particular benefit from predictability during disruptions. A short note about the morning routine, bedtime routine, school pick-up details, and any critical items (like PE days, medication routines, or comfort objects) can transform a tense day into a manageable one. These notes should be written in plain language. They should focus on observable actions rather than on psychological interpretation. The goal is to help the carer act competently, not to psychoanalyse the child. The implication is calm continuity: children feel held by familiar rhythms even when circumstances have changed.

The fourth category is health essentials. This does not mean a complete medical record. It means the key facts that matter quickly: allergies, current medications, relevant conditions, and what to do in a straightforward situation like "child has a fever at school" in terms of who to contact and what information to provide. The book cannot offer medical advice, and it should not attempt it. Yet it can insist on an organisational truth: health essentials must be easy to retrieve and easy to communicate. The stepping-in carer should not have to guess whether an allergy exists. They should not have to search through months of messages to find a medication name. A concise health summary, linked from the emergency bundle, solves this.

A scenario shows the bundle in use without theatricality. A parent is unexpectedly delayed overnight. A grandparent arrives to cover school pick-up and bedtime. They open the vault and access the "in case of" bundle. They find the school contact note, including the office number and pick-up protocol. They find the routine note, which tells them what time dinner usually happens, what the bedtime sequence is, and which items the child likes to have nearby. They find the activity note that confirms there is no club today. They find the health essentials note that flags an allergy and indicates where the relevant items are kept. They do not have to call the delayed parent repeatedly. They do not have to invent the evening. The children feel less anxious because the adult is not flustered. The grandparent feels competent rather than nervous. The household continues.

Name what happened: transferable competence. Explain: the bundle converts tacit household knowledge into an accessible form that another trusted adult can use; it reduces dependence on one person's memory and availability. The implication is not only smoother logistics. It is reduced emotional strain, because adults who feel competent transmit calm, and children read that calm accurately.

A second named example offers a broader perspective on why this matters. After Hurricane Katrina struck New Orleans in August 2005, many families were displaced and separated, and a significant part of the recovery involved reconstruction of identity and access: proving who you are, contacting who you need, finding documents, re-establishing routines. Most households will never face such a catastrophe, yet the same pattern appears at smaller scale whenever life is disrupted: documents and contact details become suddenly important, and the absence of a simple, accessible record multiplies difficulty. The family bundle is a small domestic answer to a large truth: resilience depends on information continuity.

A credible limitation deserves acknowledgement. Preparing an emergency bundle can create a false sense of control. It can also drift out of date. Phone numbers change. Schools change portals. Children's routines evolve. A bundle that is outdated can mislead. The reconciliation is to treat the bundle as a living artefact and tie it to an existing habit, such as a weekly family review or a term-start reset. The bundle does not need constant maintenance. It needs periodic refresh. The metric is simple: could a trusted person use it this week without confusion? If not, the bundle needs attention.

There is also an ethical boundary. Some information is too sensitive to share broadly, even within a family tool. Teenagers deserve increasing privacy. Adults may have health details they do not wish to place in a shared space. The emergency bundle therefore should not become a justification for oversharing. Its purpose is care continuity, not total transparency. The family must decide what belongs in the shared bundle and what belongs in private spaces, and must make those choices explicit. Respect, again, is a component of reliability because it determines whether people will participate.

The motif of the pocket map returns because it captures the bundle's real role. In an emergency, people do not need a dissertation on household life. They need orientation: who to call, what to do next, what must not be missed, where essential things are. A pocket map does not remove uncertainty. It reduces the worst kind: the uncertainty that comes from missing information. That reduction is, itself, an act of kindness to future selves and to the people who might step in.

The forward test is therefore a question about the household's relationship to dependence. Every family depends on someone—often the person who remembers. When disruption arrives, that dependence becomes vulnerability. The decision is whether to accept that vulnerability as inevitable, or to convert a small portion of household knowledge into a concise, permissioned "in case of" bundle that someone else can use without panic. The bundle's value is easiest to see in imagination. Its real value, if the day comes, will be felt in silence: fewer urgent calls, fewer frantic searches, fewer tears driven by avoidable confusion.

Chapter 7
Trips, Projects, and Kanban Boards

In 1941, in a Toyota factory in Japan, Taiichi Ohno began observing a simple, uncomfortable truth about work: when tasks are invisible, they multiply. When too much is started at once, everything slows down. His later contributions to what became the Toyota Production System were not primarily about efficiency as a moral virtue; they were about flow—how to keep work moving without drowning people in half-finished obligations. Families do not run factories, yet they live inside a constant stream of half-finished things: the holiday that is "being planned", the garden that is "to be sorted", the school application that is "on the list", the room makeover that is "happening soon", the big purchase that is "being researched". These phrases sound harmless. They are not. They are containers for untracked effort.

Most family stress is not caused by hard work. It is caused by *unseen work*.

Unseen work behaves like a low hum. It occupies attention without producing progress you can point to. It also breeds the particular resentment that comes from asymmetric awareness: one person holds the plan in their head and feels constantly "on"; others assume it will somehow resolve. A family second brain that captures information but does not help manage work-in-progress can accidentally worsen this dynamic, turning into a library of intentions rather than a mechanism for follow-through. This chapter is about the turn from storage to movement: how families take plans that drift and give them a shape that can be shared, tracked, and completed.

A quiet motif runs through these pages: the corkboard. Not the quaint craft object, but the real domestic device—the place where the family pins what must be remembered because it matters. The corkboard is visual, communal, and slightly ruthless. It forces priorities into view. It also makes absence obvious: if something is not on the board, it is not being attended to. Kanban boards are the corkboard's modern cousin, offering a way to make family projects visible without turning them into lectures or spreadsheets. Visibility is not control; it is relief. It allows the household to stop repeatedly asking, "Are we doing this?" and instead to see what is genuinely in motion.

The chapter begins with a mindset shift that seems small and changes everything: treating certain intentions as projects. A project is not a corporate artefact. It is a boundary around effort. Holidays, room makeovers, applications, and big purchases all fit this pattern because they contain multiple steps, multiple dependencies, and multiple people. When families refuse to name them as projects, they become vague background obligations that never quite start and never quite end. They live in mental space. Naming a project—"Garden reset", "Weekend in York", "Secondary school application", "Kitchen table upgrade"—gives it a home in the vault and therefore a shape the household can share. The result is a reduction in invisible mental load, because the plan no longer needs to be carried privately to exist.

This is where the most ordinary example becomes revealing. "Sort the garden" is an intention that can last for months. It remains vague because it feels overwhelming: what does "sort" even mean? Clear the shed? Buy plants? Fix the fence? Arrange a skip? The phrase holds everything and therefore moves nothing. When the same intention becomes a project outline, it begins to move because it is no longer one impossible thing. It becomes a set of concrete steps that can be assigned, sequenced, and finished. The point is not to break everything into tiny tasks for the sake of it. The point is to translate an amorphous desire into a plan the household can see, discuss, and act on without repeating the same conversation.

From there, the chapter introduces kanban boards as a family-friendly visual system for managing projects. Kanban, at its simplest, is a board with a few columns that represent the state of work: ideas waiting to be chosen, the next actions to take, and the tasks completed. It is deliberately minimal. It resists the temptation to plan an entire future in detail. It focuses on what is happening now and what should happen next. That focus matters in households because families are not short of ideas. They are short of clear, shared next steps. A board makes next steps visible. It also limits the number of things the family tries to do at once, which is where domestic plans often collapse.

The modern relevance is obvious in the way family communication has become fragmented. Projects are discussed in passing, in chats, in car rides, in late-night conversations, then forgotten or remembered differently. Boards stabilise the project's shared reality. They reduce the need for status conversations that often become disguised arguments: "I thought you were doing that." "I didn't know that was urgent." "We never decided." When the board is used well, the decision is visible and the next step is named. That is not an abstract gain. It changes the emotional atmosphere of collaboration.

This chapter also insists on a child-friendly dimension because family projects are one of the best places to teach shared responsibility without moralising. A story of siblings moving cards across a board for a party captures the point: children can see what needs doing, claim tasks, and experience progress as something they helped create. The board turns work into something tangible rather than something delivered as parental instruction. It also gives parents a way to support without hovering. The board does the reminding. The household does the doing.

Trips then become the chapter's showcase because travel planning concentrates the very problems families want to solve: scattered documents, shifting decisions, repeated lists, and the expensive consequences of forgetting. A board for a trip is not an indulgence. It is a way to bring bookings, lists, and documents into one visible flow. The chapter shows how a weekend away can be taken from idea to unpacking with fewer last-minute panics when the work is organised as cards moving through clear stages. The board does not make travel effortless. It makes travel less fragile by ensuring key items—bookings, documents, packing, money, cancellations—are visible and linked to the relevant notes and files in the vault.

Finally, the chapter confronts the quiet failure that ruins many systems: projects that never end. They linger as stale boards, half-completed lists, and abandoned notes, cluttering the vault and eroding trust. Closing a project is therefore not administrative tidying. It is part of making the second brain usable. Archiving keeps the active space clean. Capturing lessons turns experience into future templates. Converting a good checklist into a reusable template is how a family compounds calm over time. A brief review of a school application process shows how closing the loop can transform a stressful period into a resource for the future rather than a haze of forgotten effort.

The closing movement of this introduction turns on a choice families face repeatedly but rarely name. A household can treat its plans as a blur of intentions and then act surprised when nothing moves smoothly, or it can treat certain intentions as projects, make them visible, and manage work-in-progress with the kind of simple discipline that protects energy rather than draining it. The tension is not whether to have plans. Families always have plans. The tension is whether those plans will live in private mental space—breeding resentment and repeated conversations—or whether they will live on a shared board, where progress is visible, collaboration is possible, and completion is real enough to be seen.

Thinking in Family Projects

In 1969, in Copenhagen, the economist Ester Boserup published *Woman's Role in Economic Development*, arguing—against the grain of much development thinking at the time—that labour is not merely "there" as a natural resource but is shaped by structures, incentives, and visibility. Her work is often discussed in terms of agriculture and policy, yet its domestic echo is unmissable. When work is treated as background, it is taken for granted. When it is named, counted, and made visible, it can be shared, improved, and redistributed. Families live with an intimate version of that truth: the most exhausting work is frequently the work no one can see.

Say it plainly. Plans cost attention.

Most households carry a long tail of intentions: a holiday that should be booked, a bathroom that needs repainting, a school application to complete, a big purchase to research, a garden to "sort", a family photo album to curate, a cupboard to clear.

These intentions often feel like benign wishes. They are not. Each one occupies mental space, because the mind keeps trying to close loops. The unfinished plan floats in awareness like a half-heard ringtone. It returns at inconvenient moments—during meetings, at bedtime, while making dinner—and it produces a particular kind of fatigue that has nothing to do with physical effort. The fatigue comes from *holding* rather than from doing.

Show how this looks inside a home. Someone says, "We need to sort the garden." Everyone agrees. Nothing happens. The phrase returns the next weekend, and the weekend after that. When it is mentioned, it creates a small flare of tension, because everyone senses that the intention is real and the follow-through absent. The person who mentions it feels unheard. The person who hears it feels accused. The garden remains unchanged. Meanwhile, the household pays a weekly mental tax: the plan is never resolved, so it is never removed from attention. Name the phenomenon: intention debt. Explain: vague intentions accumulate like unpaid bills; each one demands periodic cognitive attention, and the total load becomes heavy even when no individual task is urgent. The implication is subtle but corrosive: people feel perpetually behind, not because they are lazy, but because they are carrying too many half-formed plans.

This is where "thinking in projects" becomes more than a productivity trope. A project is simply a plan with a boundary: a named outcome, a defined scope, and a place to live outside anyone's head. The boundary is what matters. Families often resist the word "project" because it sounds corporate, as if life is being turned into a management exercise. Yet families already manage projects. They do so informally, through conversation, memory, and occasional bursts of frantic activity. Thinking in projects is the decision to stop relying on informal management for multi-step plans, because informal management is precisely what creates intention debt.

The first step is naming, because naming turns a fog into an object. "Sort the garden" is not a name. It is a sigh disguised as a plan. It contains too much and therefore commits to nothing. A name that works is concrete enough to suggest a finish line. "Garden reset for spring" is better. "Clear the shed and set up the patio" is better still, because it implies observable completion. Naming also has a psychological effect. It reduces ambiguity. Ambiguity is the fuel of procrastination and the seed of disagreement, because different family members imagine different outcomes. A name aligns imagination. Name: shared definition. Explain: when a project is named with a clear outcome, it becomes easier to agree on what "done" means and easier to decide what to do next. The implication is less repeated conversation and more coordinated action.

Giving the project a home is the second step, and this is where the second brain does its quiet work. A project home is not a folder full of everything. It is a single page or note that acts as the project's front door: the place where the current state, key documents, decisions, and next actions can be found. The home reduces mental load because it turns the project from a floating obligation into a stable reference. Someone no longer has to remember whether the paint samples were saved or which garden centre had the right plants; the information is in the project home. Someone no longer has to ask, "Where are we with this?" because "where we are" is written down. Name: externalised state. Explain: projects drain energy when their state exists only in memory; externalising state allows the mind to release the effort of constant re-tracking. The implication is relief. Not glamour. Relief.

A worked contrast makes the point unmistakable. The vague intention: "Sort the garden." It produces weekend guilt and intermittent arguments. Now the project outline: "Garden reset: clear, repair, plant." The outline does not need to be long. It needs to identify the handful of decisions and actions that unlock progress. Clear: decide what stays and what goes; schedule a disposal run; clear the shed. Repair: check the fence panel; confirm whether tools are needed; decide who will do what. Plant: choose the two or three plants that suit the space; confirm budget; choose a date for planting. This outline is not a listicle. It is a small map. Its value is that it turns the plan into discrete commitments that can be started and finished. The project now has a beginning: "Clear the shed this Saturday." It has a visible dependency: "Buy fence panel before repair." It has a finish line: "Patio usable, plants in, shed organised." The household can now measure progress by observable changes rather than by repeated talk.

The key is that a project outline does not attempt to eliminate spontaneity. It simply relocates it. Without a project outline, spontaneity becomes chaos: decisions are made on the fly under pressure. With an outline, spontaneity becomes choice: the family can decide, calmly, whether to add a new plant or change the patio plan because the current plan is visible. Visibility creates freedom. It sounds counterintuitive. It is true. When a household cannot see what it has already committed to, it is trapped in a constant state of reactive decision-making.

This is also where trust enters, and it must be paired with behaviour rather than treated as a mood. In many families, one person becomes the "project mind" by default. They hold the details, remember the research, track the deadlines, and feel responsible. Others may help, yet the project still depends on that person's attention. The visible behaviour of a project home is that anyone can check it and understand the state. That shared visibility is a trust mechanism. It reduces the need for interrogations and reminders. It also reduces the resentment that arises when one person feels they are carrying everything. Name: distributed awareness. Explain: when project information is stored in a shared home, awareness can be shared without constant conversation; family members can participate without waiting to be briefed. The implication is a fairer emotional load, because responsibility stops being tied to who remembers most.

A second named, checkable example from outside family life clarifies why this works. In 1987, at Toyota's plants in Japan, practices associated with kanban and lean production were already well established and were being studied internationally because they reduced work-in-progress and made flow visible. The underlying principle was simple: limit what is started, make the status of work visible, and pull the next task only when capacity exists. Families can borrow that principle without importing jargon. The project home is the first step towards that visibility. It is the staging ground for later visual boards. When a family begins to treat "holiday planning" as a project with a home, it becomes possible to see what has been decided, what remains open, and what the next action is. The household stops carrying the plan as a fog and starts carrying it as a shared artefact.

A credible limitation should be faced directly. Not every intention should become a project. If families convert every small desire into a project, the vault becomes cluttered, and the household begins to feel managed by its own system. The reconciliation is to reserve "project status" for plans that meet at least two conditions: they require more than one step and they have consequences when delayed or forgotten. A one-step purchase is not a project. A purchase that involves research, timing, delivery, installation, and budget decisions is. A spontaneous day out is not a project. A holiday with bookings, documents, packing, and cancellations is. Thinking in projects is a selective discipline, not a lifestyle.

There is another limitation: projects can become a new place to hide. A family can create a project note and feel progress simply because something has been written. The garden remains untouched, but the outline looks satisfying. Name: paper progress. Explain: writing a plan can mimic action; the mind gets a small reward from "organisation" without the cost of execution. The implication is disappointment and a sense that the system is performative. The reconciliation is to ensure that every project home contains, plainly, the next visible action—something that can be done in the real world. If the next action is not clear, the project is still fog. The system should make fog obvious.

Modern relevance makes this mindset shift more urgent because families are now juggling not only domestic projects but institutional ones: applications, forms, scheduling across schools and services, multi-step admin tasks that did not exist in the same way a generation ago. These tasks arrive in fragments and are easy to postpone until they become urgent. Thinking in projects is how families prevent fragmentation from turning into panic. It is also how families protect their relationships. Projects that live in one person's head often become relationship problems, because misunderstandings pile up. Projects that live in a shared home become easier to negotiate, because the facts are visible and the next steps are clear.

A quiet motif threads through this subchapter: the labelled box. Not the deep archive box in a loft, but the box you keep near the door for things that have not found their place yet—returns, donations, repairs. A labelled box works because it creates a boundary. It says, "This belongs somewhere, and until it does, it belongs here." Projects are the same. They say, "This plan is real, and until it is finished, it lives here." The label reduces mental rummaging. The boundary reduces guilt. The home reduces confusion.

The forward test is a decision about how the household wants to carry its future. When the next multi-step intention appears—holiday, room makeover, application, big purchase, garden—will it remain a floating phrase that resurfaces as tension and guilt, or will the family name it as a project, give it a home, and make its next action visible enough that progress becomes possible without one person privately carrying the whole plan?

Using Simple Kanban Boards

In 2007, at Johns Hopkins Hospital in Baltimore, a small checklist for central line care helped drive down infections in intensive care units, and the story became widely cited not because it was glamorous but because it demonstrated a strange, powerful principle: when work is made visible and broken into clear steps, reliable outcomes become more likely. The domestic version of that principle is quieter and less measurable in lives saved, yet it is felt daily in minutes reclaimed and arguments avoided. Families do not generally fail because they lack effort. They fail because effort is scattered, started too often, and tracked privately.

Visibility changes behaviour.

A kanban board is, at heart, a way of making the state of work visible. It is a board divided into columns representing stages—ideas, next actions, in progress, done—and populated with cards representing tasks or chunks of work. The method came from manufacturing and operations, but its logic is human rather than industrial: people coordinate better when they can see what is happening, what is waiting, and what has been finished. When that visibility is missing, families resort to status conversations, which are often mislabelled as "communication problems" when they are, in fact, information-design problems. "Did you do that?" "Are we still going?" "Who's sorting the gift?" "I thought you were..." These questions are not evidence of poor relationships. They are evidence of a shared reality that is not shared enough.

Show a typical scene. A family is planning a child's birthday party. The intention is warm. The execution is muddy. One adult is thinking about the venue. Another is thinking about food. The child is thinking about friends. Siblings have ideas that appear and vanish. Messages circulate. Someone mentions balloons. Someone else assumes invitations are handled. A week passes. Then, suddenly, the party is close and the household enters a frantic phase of last-minute buying and apologetic text messages. The stress is not caused by the party. It is caused by the work being invisible until it becomes urgent. Name the problem: latent work. Explain: tasks that are not externalised do not disappear; they sit in the background until time pressure forces a burst of action. The implication is predictable: rushed decisions, duplicated effort, and a sour undertone in what should be an enjoyable event.

A simple kanban board turns latent work into visible work. The board does not need sophistication. For a family, three columns are often enough: "Ideas", "Next", "Done". Some households add "Doing" when they have multiple parallel tasks. The value of such columns is not aesthetic. It is cognitive. "Ideas" is permission to imagine without committing. "Next" is commitment: the small set of actions the household has decided to do soon. "Done" is closure: proof that effort has produced progress and a place where finished tasks can rest without haunting anyone's head.

Five words make it work.

Those five words are the names of the columns. When families build boards, they often overcomplicate them immediately, creating elaborate stages and colour codes that collapse under fatigue. A board is a tool for tired humans. It must be readable at a glance. If it requires explanation every time, it will not be used. The board should be so simple that a child can understand it. In fact, that is a good test: if a ten-year-old can look at the board and understand what is happening, the board is probably well designed.

The board also performs a subtle social function. It shifts coordination from interrogation to observation. Instead of asking, "Have you done the invitations?" a parent can see that "Send invitations" is in "Next" and, later, in "Done". Instead of a child repeatedly asking, "Are we going to have games?" they can see a card in "Ideas" and later a card in "Next". The household's emotional temperature drops because questions become less accusatory. A board makes it harder to interpret reminders as personal criticism, because the board is a neutral artefact. It holds the plan. People simply interact with it.

A story of siblings moving cards across a board makes this human. Imagine two siblings planning a party with a parent. The board is visible on a shared device or in a shared note. In "Ideas", the children add "Treasure hunt", "Music playlist",

"Cupcake decorating". The parent adds "Invitations", "Food", "Check allergies". The children argue briefly—of course they do—about which games are best. The board absorbs this energy without being offended. Then the family chooses what matters and moves a few cards into "Next". That movement is a decision made visible. It turns talk into commitment. Later, one sibling completes "Make playlist" and moves the card to "Done". The action is small, but the psychological effect is large: the child experiences completion as something they can see and claim. The parent experiences relief. Progress is no longer private.

Name what is happening: shared state. Explain: families coordinate poorly when the state of work is distributed across minds and messages; a board consolidates state in a single view that everyone can access. The implication is fewer repeated conversations and fewer misunderstandings, because the board becomes the shared memory of what has been decided and what remains.

Boards also help families manage a problem that is both common and rarely named: too much work in progress. Households start many things. They have good reasons. Someone sees a bargain and begins researching a purchase. Someone decides to redecorate and buys paint samples. Someone mentions a holiday and starts browsing accommodation. Someone volunteers for a school event and takes on responsibilities. None of these are wrong. The problem is concurrency. When too many projects are in progress, attention fragments, and tasks stall. Stalled tasks are the core of intention debt: they remain psychologically active because they are unfinished. A board makes stalled tasks visible, and visibility allows a family to decide to pause deliberately rather than to drift.

The decision to pause is not a failure. It is a form of honesty. A board allows families to distinguish "We have chosen not to do this now" from "We are failing to do this." That distinction is morally and emotionally important, because it reduces unnecessary guilt. It also reduces the corrosive dynamic where one person silently carries a task while assuming others will "get around to it". If the card remains in "Ideas", it is not a commitment. If it is in "Next", it is. This clarity is how a board protects relationships. It makes promises legible.

A second named, checkable example grounds this in a broader tradition. In 1953, in the United States, psychologist B. F. Skinner published *Science and Human Behavior*, arguing that behaviour is shaped by immediate cues and consequences. One need not accept Skinner's full framework to learn from a simple point: environments matter. A kanban board is an environmental cue. It places reminders in the line of sight. It makes completion satisfying because "Done" is visible. It makes neglect uncomfortable, not through shame, but through plain evidence. The implication is practical: boards work not by changing character but by changing what the household sees and therefore does.

Now the credible limitation. Boards can become another thing to maintain. They can become a performative surface—moving cards around without doing the work. They can also become a source of conflict if one person uses the board as a managerial weapon, assigning tasks and monitoring progress. The reconciliation begins with intent. A family board is not a performance dashboard. It is a shared aid to coordination. The board should reflect what the household actually does, not what it wishes it did. If "In progress" sits full for weeks, the problem is not the board. The problem is capacity or ambition.

The board's role is to reveal that problem so the family can adjust.

A second limitation is that some work is not easily carded. Caring labour—comforting a child, emotional support, the invisible work of noticing—is real and important, yet it does not always belong on a kanban board. If families try to put everything into cards, they risk flattening life into tasks. The reconciliation is to use boards for projects that have clear steps and clear completion: trips, parties, applications, room makeovers, purchases. Use the board as a tool for logistical coordination, not as a model of love.

The practical mechanics of creating a board can be simple without being trivial. A family can create a board in almost any tool that allows columns and movable items, or even in a basic notes space by using headings as columns and moving text blocks. The design principle matters more than the software: keep the board in a place everyone can access, keep the columns few, keep the cards small enough that they represent actions rather than vague aspirations. A card that says "Sort garden" is fog. A card that says "Book skip for Saturday" is actionable. The metric is behavioural: does the card invite a next step that can be done in a defined slice of time? If not, it will sit and poison the board with stagnation.

The motif that threads through this subchapter is the corkboard, because a corkboard is where households pin what must not be lost. A kanban board is the corkboard's disciplined sibling: it not only pins but also tracks movement. It shows what is being considered, what is being done, and what is complete. It turns a family's plans into something that can be glanced at between kettles and homework, without a meeting, without a lecture, without a flurry of messages.

The forward test is a trade-off families often avoid naming. A household can keep coordinating through conversation and memory, paying repeatedly in status questions, duplicated effort, and last-minute panic, or it can accept the small discipline of maintaining a simple board that makes work visible and limits what is started at once. The question is not whether the family will be busy. It will. The question is whether busyness will remain invisible until it becomes stressful, or whether it will be made visible early enough that the family can choose what to do next—together—before the deadline chooses for them.

Planning Trips With Boards

In May 2010, the eruption of Eyjafjallajökull in Iceland sent ash across European airspace and grounded flights on a scale that stranded millions of travellers. Families who had packed, paid, arranged childcare, and taken time off work discovered a blunt travel truth: the trip is not a single plan, but a network of dependencies. When one link breaks, everything else is pulled. The lesson is not that travel is dangerous. The lesson is that travel is a coordination problem, and coordination fails fastest when information is scattered.

Trips punish fragmentation.

A holiday can feel like a reward, yet its preparation often carries the emotional tone of a deadline. Bookings sit in inboxes. Addresses hide in confirmations. Packing lists live in heads. Someone remembers passports until they do not. Another person assumes someone else has arranged pet care, or cancelled a delivery, or checked the child's swim times. The household then experiences the classic pre-departure atmosphere: a frantic intensity that seems inevitable, as if travel itself generates chaos. In reality, much of that chaos is a design outcome. Families attempt to manage a multi-step project using informal memory and scattered messages. A travel board is a way of refusing that pattern.

A kanban board applied to trips works because travel planning is naturally staged. There is an idea stage. There is a decision stage. There is a booking stage. There is a preparation stage. There is an execution stage. There is a return stage. Families already move through these stages in a loose, improvisational way. The board makes the stages visible and, crucially, makes it obvious what is still open. That visibility reduces the number of "Have we done...?" conversations, which are not only irritating but also unreliable because they tend to happen at the worst moment—when time is short and tempers are thin.

Show a travel board in use as a domestic scene. It is a Tuesday evening. One adult is scrolling through accommodation options. Another is looking at train times. A child asks whether the hotel has a pool. Someone mentions the need for a pet sitter. Another remembers a school event that might conflict with the proposed dates. Without a shared surface, these details float, and the conversation spirals: too many threads, too many assumptions, too much hidden work. With a board, the family can capture each thread as a card, place it in the right stage, and decide what truly matters next. Name: staged visibility. Explain: a board allows the household to hold multiple travel threads without losing them, while keeping the next decision or action clear. The implication is calmer planning because the family stops trying to remember every open loop at once.

For families, the most useful travel boards often use a small set of columns that match the flow of the trip. The exact words matter less than the logic: a place for possibilities, a place for decisions, a place for preparation, and a place for completion. Many households find that "Ideas", "Decide", "Book", "Prepare", "On the trip", "Done" captures the shape. Others prefer fewer columns: "Ideas", "Next", "Done", with cards carrying their own labels. The principle is not the number of columns. It is that the board mirrors the mental model of planning and gives the family a common view.

Keep it brutally simple.

That sentence is not an aesthetic preference; it is a survival instruction. A board overloaded with columns becomes hard to maintain and quickly abandoned. Travel planning already contains enough complexity. The board should reduce it, not mirror it. The visible behaviour to aim for is a board that can be checked in under thirty seconds to answer a question like "What is the next travel task?" or "What remains unbooked?" If the board cannot do that, it is not doing its job.

The real power of a travel board comes from its ability to connect cards to the vault. A card is not merely a reminder; it is an index. A booking card should link to the confirmation note or file. A packing card should link to the trip template or packing checklist. A "Documents" card should link to passport scans where appropriate, to policy numbers, to relevant emails saved into the vault. A "Transport" card should link to tickets and addresses. This is where boards stop being decorative and become functional: they provide a visible map of action that points to the underlying information. A family no longer has to search for a booking confirmation in an inbox. The board card points directly to the stored item. Name: linked execution. Explain: when tasks are connected to their supporting documents, the family reduces search time and reduces the risk of missing critical information at the moment of use. The implication is fewer last-minute scrambles because the board acts as a hub, not a list.

A worked example follows a weekend away from idea to unpacking. Imagine a family considering a Friday-to-Sunday trip to York. The board begins with a few "Ideas" cards: "York weekend", "Train vs car", "Budget rough range", "Things we want: museum, walk, good breakfast". These cards are not commitments; they are prompts. The family discusses and moves "York weekend" into "Decide", along with "Check school calendar" and "Confirm budget". Once dates and budget are agreed, the next actions become clear: "Book accommodation" and "Book transport". Each of these becomes a card in "Book", and each links to the relevant search notes or options captured in the vault. When accommodation is booked, the card moves forward and the confirmation is stored and linked.

Then preparation begins. A "Packing" card links to the family's trip template, which already contains a checklist. A "Documents" card links to the stored confirmations and any relevant IDs. A "Food" card might link to a note of dietary needs and preferred meal ideas. A "Home" card might link to the household's leaving-the-house checklist: rubbish out, heating set, deliveries paused, neighbour notified. Each card is small enough to complete. Each is connected to reference information where needed. The board makes it difficult for the family to forget the unglamorous necessities because they are visible in the same place as the exciting parts. The trip stops being a story told in someone's head and becomes a shared artefact the family can collectively steer.

A crucial moment arrives the day before departure. In many households, this is where panic thrives: people remember everything late. With a board, the family can scan "Prepare" and see what remains. Cards not moved become visible reminders. The board's "Done" column also matters here, because it reduces anxiety. Seeing "Transport booked" and "Accommodation confirmed" in "Done" produces a specific kind of calm: the calm of evidence. Evidence is more soothing than reassurance because it is not a mood. It is a fact you can point to.

Once the trip begins, the board continues to serve without demanding attention. Some families move a few cards into "On the trip" that represent actions likely to be forgotten: "Check in time", "Parking details", "Tickets ready", "Return journey". The board becomes a small control panel. Not everything has to be carded. The board simply keeps the essentials visible. If a question arises—What's the address? What's the booking reference?—the board points to the answer. The family can then return attention to being together, which is, after all, the point of travelling.

The return phase is often neglected. Families unpack, collapse, and then leave travel artefacts scattered: receipts, photos, "lessons learned", items to wash, claims to make, thank-you messages to send. These remnants become small sources of stress that linger. A board can include a "Return" or "Wrap up" stage, making it easy to capture the last few actions: wash items, file receipts, archive documents, note what worked. This does not turn life into admin. It closes loops. Closed loops reduce mental noise.

A second named, checkable example underscores why such closure matters. In aviation, where checklists and staging are standard, the discipline includes not only take-off but post-flight procedures—because reliability includes the end of the process. Families rarely treat travel that way. They treat the end as exhaustion and scatter. The board is a way of lightly borrowing a mature process: not because family life should resemble aviation, but because the cognitive constraints are similar. People forget when tired. Systems can prevent expensive forgetting.

Still, a credible limitation must be admitted. Travel boards can become overbearing if they attempt to control every detail, turning a holiday into a project plan. Some families will find that approach draining and will rebel. The reconciliation is to use the board for what travel reliably breaks: key decisions, key bookings, essential documents, and a small set of preparation steps. Leave room for spontaneity. Leave room for the joy of unplanned moments. The board's job is to protect the trip's foundations, not to micromanage the experience.

The motif that threads through this subchapter is the itinerary pinned to a noticeboard. Many travellers have experienced the relief of having a single sheet with addresses, times, and confirmations—something you can glance at when your phone signal drops or when your mind goes blank. A travel board is that itinerary, expanded into a living map of preparation and execution, linked directly into the vault's stored notes and documents. It is a noticeboard that travels with you, not as a burden, but as a handrail.

The forward test, then, is not whether the family can plan a perfect trip. Trips will always contain surprises. The test is whether the household will choose a system that reduces avoidable surprises. When the next trip is proposed, will the family allow bookings and lists to scatter across inboxes and memories until the pre-departure panic arrives, or will they build a simple board that makes decisions, documents, and preparation visible—so that the trip's energy can be spent on being away, rather than on frantically proving that it was properly arranged?

Reviewing and Closing Projects

In January 1972, at the Massachusetts Institute of Technology, a young computer scientist named Edgar F. Codd's ideas about relational databases were already reshaping how institutions stored information: data could be organised so it remained queryable without becoming a labyrinth of bespoke structures. The promise was not merely storage. It was retrieval over time. Families do not build databases, yet they face the same long-term problem in miniature: information accumulates, projects proliferate, and without a disciplined way to *finish*, the system becomes a dump that cannot answer questions quickly. The most common failure of household organisation is not starting. It is leaving things half-alive.

Unfinished projects haunt the vault.

A family creates a board for a room makeover. They research paint colours. They capture quotes. They start a checklist. The room is eventually painted, and everyone is glad. Yet the board remains, filled with cards that are technically complete but still sitting in "Next" or "Doing". A trip plan remains populated with booking references and packing lists long after the suitcases have been unpacked. A school application board is left open with forms attached, deadlines passed, and messages saved, and it sits there like an open tab in the mind. Months later, someone searches the vault and finds a thicket of old boards and notes. Trust erodes. People stop believing the system reflects reality. The second brain begins to feel like an attic.

Show the domestic moment when this costs real time. A parent needs a document for something straightforward—perhaps a copy of a confirmation or the details of an application that was submitted. They search and find three boards with similar names, two conflicting versions of a checklist, and a "final" PDF that is not final. The parent opens one file, then another, trying to work out which artefact reflects what actually happened. Ten minutes later, they have learned something depressing: the vault contains the past, but it does not contain closure. Name the failure: open-loop residue. Explain: when projects are not formally closed, they leave behind artefacts that look active; these artefacts create confusion during later retrieval and add cognitive friction to new work. The implication is that the system becomes less useful over time, precisely when it should become more valuable.

Closing a project has two aims that are easy to state and surprisingly easy to neglect. The first is to remove active clutter: move what is no longer needed out of the working space so the current view remains clean. The second is to extract future value: capture what was learned and turn the most effective elements—checklists, templates, decisions—into reusable assets. Closure is not tidying for its own sake. It is how the household compounds knowledge rather than repeatedly paying for the same mistakes.

The psychology behind closure matters. A board filled with half-finished cards creates a subtle sense of failure, even when the project is actually complete. Humans read "unfinished" as "still owed". That sense can make the vault feel heavy. Conversely, a board moved to an archive with a clear "completed" marker creates a different feeling: completion. Completion is an emotional state as much as a factual one. It signals that effort has been contained and that the mind can release it. The system should support that release, because family life contains too many obligations to carry them indefinitely.

Close it. Then learn from it.

Those seven words are the discipline. Closure without learning is mere tidying. Learning without closure is a romantic fantasy about reflection that never quite happens. The household needs both. The first act—archiving—keeps the second brain reliable. The second act—capturing lessons—keeps it intelligent.

Archiving is often misunderstood as deletion. It is not. Archiving is relocation: moving a completed project into a space designed for history, not for action. This protects search and daily visibility. When a family opens its project board space, it should see what is truly active. When it searches, it should be able to find past projects, but those projects should clearly read as past. This is not only an aesthetic preference. It is a trust requirement. People will only use a system they trust, and trust is built when the system behaves predictably: active looks active; archived looks archived.

Naming conventions play a crucial role here, because once projects become archived, they become part of a family's long-term memory. A project titled "Trip" tells future-you nothing. A project titled "York weekend" tells a bit more. A project titled "York weekend – Feb 2026" tells enough to be retrieved quickly without confusion. Dates are particularly valuable in archives because they prevent accidental reuse of obsolete details. The visible behaviour to aim for is that any archived project can be identified by name alone, without opening it. The implication is faster retrieval and fewer mistakes, especially when the family repeats similar projects: another holiday, another application, another party.

Capturing lessons is where the second brain earns its name. Families often repeat the same errors not because they do not learn, but because their learning remains trapped in experience and fades under pressure. A simple post-project review extracts that learning into a durable form. The review does not have to be long. It needs to be honest and specific. What worked? What surprised us? What would we do differently next time? Which checklist item saved us? Which missing step caused a scramble? This is not self-improvement theatre. It is operational memory.

Pair abstractions with visible behaviours. If the lesson is "start earlier", that is a sentiment, not a lesson. A usable lesson is "book accommodation before booking activities" or "save confirmations into the vault the same day" or "create a packing list that includes chargers and swim kit". If the lesson is "communication", translate it into a behaviour: "make one place where decisions are recorded" or "move cards into 'Next' only when agreed". The metric is practical: can someone act differently next time because of what was written? If not, the review has become vague comfort rather than useful memory.

Turning good checklists into templates is the final step in making closure productive. A checklist that worked once is a fragile success if it remains attached only to that one project. A template is how a family captures a good pattern and makes it easy to repeat without reinventing. The template should not be treated as sacred. It should remain editable, because families change. Yet it should exist, because starting from zero each time wastes attention. A family that has a "weekend trip" template, an "application" template, and a "party" template will feel a quiet compounding over time: less panic, fewer missed steps, faster start-up.

Now show this through the promised example: a school application process. A family undertakes an application that involves deadlines, documents, references, and decisions.

They create a project home and perhaps a board. Cards represent actions: gather required documents, request references, draft statements, submit forms, confirm receipt, track outcomes. The family gets through it. Relief arrives. Then comes the question: what happens to the project artefacts? If nothing happens, the board remains, and the vault becomes a graveyard of applications. If closure is practised, the family archives the board into "Completed projects", labels it with the year and child's name, and ensures the final submitted documents and key correspondence are stored in the child's school records space with clear names. Then they write a short review note: which documents were hardest to locate, which steps took longer than expected, what the family would do earlier next time, what information would have made the process calmer. Finally, they extract the checklist that proved useful—perhaps the sequence of steps and the list of required documents—and convert it into an "Application template", stored where future projects can copy it.

Name what is happening: compound calm. Explain: closure converts one stressful experience into reusable structure; the family reduces future effort by preserving what worked and clarifying what did not. The implication is that each major project, even when difficult, can leave the household better equipped rather than merely exhausted.

A second named, checkable example adds depth and shows that this is not a purely domestic obsession. In 1986, after the Space Shuttle Challenger disaster, the Rogers Commission's report examined organisational failures, including communication and decision-making under schedule pressure. The lesson, again, is not that families resemble aerospace programmes. The lesson is that systems degrade when schedules and commitments accumulate without feedback loops. Reviewing and closing a project is a feedback loop. It is how the household protects itself from repeating avoidable failures. Without such loops, families rely on hope: hope that next time will be smoother. With loops, they rely on memory made durable.

A credible limitation must be acknowledged. Some projects end messily. A family might abandon a room makeover halfway through. A holiday might be cancelled. An application might not succeed. In such cases, "closing" can feel emotionally loaded, as if it requires declaring failure. The reconciliation is to treat closure as a factual act rather than a moral verdict. A cancelled trip still has artefacts—refund correspondence, policy documents, lessons about booking terms—that might matter later. An abandoned project still produces knowledge: what made it too much, what resources were missing, what the household's capacity actually was. Closure here is not a celebration. It is clarity. Clarity prevents the same disappointment from recurring under a different name.

Another limitation is the temptation to over-review. Families are busy. The review must respect that. It should be light enough to do. The best reviews are often small: a handful of sentences written while the experience is still fresh. The vault does not need memoirs of every project. It needs practical memory: the pieces that will save time and reduce friction next time.

The motif threading this subchapter is the closed drawer. An open drawer invites snagging; it catches clothes, scrapes hips, signals unfinished tidying. A closed drawer is not perfection; it is simply an environment that supports movement. Projects left open in the vault are open drawers. They catch the mind. They snag searches. They make the system feel messy. Closing projects is the act of shutting drawers, not to impress anyone, but to make the household easier to live in.

The forward test is a choice between two futures. In one future, the family's second brain slowly fills with half-finished boards and stale checklists until it becomes another place where Important Things go to get lost. In the other future, projects leave behind clean archives and distilled templates, so the vault becomes sharper with time rather than duller. The question is whether the household will treat completion as an afterthought, or whether it will make closing the loop part of what it means to finish—so that the next project starts not from scratch, but from the best of what the family already learned.

Chapter 8
Recipes, Routines, and Home Reference

In March 2020, in the United Kingdom, supermarket shelves briefly emptied in ways that made many households rethink what "ordinary life" depends on: not grand plans, but repeatable competence. The drama was never really about pasta. It was about the sudden exposure of hidden systems—how meals are planned, how supplies are tracked, how routines hold when stress rises. In calmer times, families can muddle through with improvisation. Under pressure, improvisation becomes exhausting. The home reveals itself as an intricate machine run largely by memory, habit, and unspoken knowledge.

Most domestic life is repetition.

That sounds dull until one notices what repetition does to the mind. Repeated tasks become automatic when they are supported by structure; they become draining when they are re-decided each time. Cooking is a daily decision factory: what to make, what is in the fridge, what the children will eat, what time allows, what energy permits. Mornings are a choreography: bags, clothes, lunches, permissions, schedules. Bedtimes are a negotiation: one more story, one more glass of water, one more delay. Cleaning is a perpetual return. The household's "how we do things" is, in practice, a network of micro-protocols. When those protocols are held only in one person's head, the home becomes dependent on that person's attention. When they are externalised into shared reference, the home becomes more resilient and, quietly, more humane.

This chapter turns the second brain towards the most underestimated category of family knowledge: the stuff that is not dramatic enough to be documented until it becomes a problem. A missing recipe is a small inconvenience until it becomes the reason you order takeaways yet again. A poorly defined bedtime routine is a minor friction until it becomes the nightly argument that drains everyone. A forgotten "how to" is irrelevant until the router drops out during a school deadline or a work call. Seasonal tasks are easy to ignore until winter arrives and you cannot remember where the grit is, or the school term starts and you realise you have missed a form. The home does not fail because families are careless. It fails because families rely on private memory for public life.

A quiet motif runs through this chapter: the laminated sheet on the fridge. Not because the solution is to laminate everything, but because it captures a truth about domestic competence. The best household knowledge is usable at a glance. It is short. It is findable. It survives tiredness. It does not demand a meeting. A family second brain is, among other things, a digital version of that laminated sheet—searchable, shareable, updateable—without the clutter of paper stuck to magnets.

The chapter begins with recipes because food is where time, energy, and decision fatigue collide. Many families already "have recipes", yet they have them in the least useful form: scattered across cookbooks, browser tabs, screenshots, and half-remembered ingredients. The result is repeated searching and repeated decision-making. A recipe library inside the vault is not a culinary hobby. It is a way of reducing daily cognitive load. The difference between a recipe saved properly and a recipe saved vaguely is the difference between a calm weeknight and another round of "What should we have?" that ends with low-grade irritability. The chapter explores the practical judgement behind building such a library: when to copy a recipe into your system, when to link out, and how to tag in ways that reflect real constraints—season, effort, dietary needs, and the household's shifting appetite. The point is not maximal collection. It is fast retrieval under ordinary fatigue.

Modern relevance shows up here in a quietly brutal fact of family life: the average weekday is not designed for creativity. People come home tired. Children are hungry. Time is short. Under those conditions, "having options" is not comforting; it is paralysing unless options are filtered. Tags become a domestic technology. A family that can filter recipes by "15 minutes", "batch cook", "freezer-friendly", "vegetarian", or "cold-weather" is not being precious. It is being realistic about what can be done when everyone's patience is thin. A simple example—planning a week's meals by filtering tags—reveals how the vault can convert culinary chaos into a set of choices shaped by reality rather than aspiration.

From food, the chapter moves into routines, because routines are the home's operating system. A routine is not a moral statement. It is a repeated sequence of actions that either reduces friction or generates it, depending on whether it is clear and shared. Many families treat routines as unspoken, which makes them brittle. When routines are unspoken, children do not know what "get ready" means; partners interpret "help" differently; everyone assumes someone else has noticed what needs doing. The result is predictable conflict. Documenting routines—mornings, bedtimes, cleaning—does not remove human variability. It makes expectations visible. It also makes routines negotiable in a healthier way: instead of arguing in the moment, families can co-create a routine when calm, then rely on it when tired. The chapter emphasises co-creation with children because ownership changes everything. A routine imposed feels like control; a routine co-written feels like competence.

A bedtime routine is the most revealing example because it sits at the intersection of tired bodies and emotional need. When children are overtired, they resist. When adults are overtired, they snap. A bedtime routine that exists as a shared checklist shifts the dynamic. The checklist becomes the neutral script: teeth, pyjamas, bag ready, story, lights out. It does not have to be rigid. It has to be visible. The result is not perfect peace, but reduced bargaining and fewer forgotten steps. In the language of the second brain, a checklist is a memory prosthetic; in the language of family life, it is a way of being kinder when you have fewer emotional resources available.

Then come household "how to" guides, the most neglected treasure in domestic organisation. Every household contains expertise that is rarely written down: how to reset the router, how to work the heating, where the fuse box is, how to run the washing machine on a particular cycle, how to lock up, how to handle the bins, how to make the coffee, how to find the spare keys. This knowledge tends to concentrate in one person, not because they are superior, but because they happened to learn it first. The household then becomes dependent on them. Dependence shows up in small questions that interrupt work, and it shows up in bigger moments when that person is away or ill. A mini-guide—short, standardised, stored in the vault—turns dependence into shared capability. The story of a teenager successfully doing laundry because a note existed is not quaint. It is the future of a resilient home: children learning competence, adults regaining time, the household becoming less fragile.

The final section of the chapter widens time. Seasonal and annual checklists are where families stop being surprised by recurring events. School term starts. Holidays approach. Winter arrives. Tax time appears. Birthdays repeat. The sensation of "I am sure I am forgetting something" is not a personal failing; it is a system signal. It means the household is trying to run annual cycles on ad hoc memory. A seasonal checklist captures the repeated tasks that are easy to miss precisely because they are not daily: update uniforms, check shoes, refresh emergency contacts, service the car, prepare for cold weather, renew subscriptions, schedule appointments. The chapter follows a start-of-term checklist over several cycles to show what compounding looks like in domestic life: the first time is messy, the second time is quicker, the third time feels almost calm. The family does not become perfect. It becomes prepared.

This chapter's deeper through-line is about dignity. Domestic work is often dismissed as trivial, yet it is the infrastructure that makes education, employment, and wellbeing possible. When that infrastructure depends on one person's memory, it becomes a source of inequity and resentment. When it is externalised into shared reference, it becomes a shared asset. The home stops being a place where one person holds the invisible map. It becomes a place where the map is on the wall—digitally, quietly, reliably.

The closing tension sits in a choice families face without quite naming it. A household can keep re-deciding daily life—re-finding recipes, re-explaining routines, re-answering "how do you...?", re-inventing term-start logistics—or it can invest in a small body of shared reference that makes repetition lighter. The question is not whether life will repeat. It will. The question is whether repetition will remain a drain, or become a kind of calm competence that frees energy for the things families actually want more of: conversation, play, rest, and the ordinary pleasure of an evening that does not feel like a minor emergency.

Building a Recipe Library

In October 2017, at the University of Bath in England, researchers published a paper in *Appetite* examining what they called "decision fatigue" in food choice, and the idea travelled quickly because it matched a familiar household sensation: the more choices people make, the worse their later choices tend to become. Weeknight cooking is not merely a matter of ingredients. It is a repeated sequence of micro-decisions made when attention is already spent. The kitchen smells of onions or the sharp tang of a just-opened jar, a pan clicks onto a hob, and someone—often the same someone—stands with the fridge door open trying to answer the most ordinary question with the least ordinary cognitive load: what are we having?

Dinner happens every day.

The burden is not the act of cooking. Many people like cooking, at least sometimes. The burden is the constant re-deciding, the endless search for "something that works": something quick but decent, familiar but not boring, suitable for whoever is present, aligned with whatever constraints the day has imposed. That burden is intensified by the modern ecology of recipes. The household's culinary knowledge is scattered across cookbooks, loose pages, bookmarked websites, social media posts, screenshots, and half-remembered improvisations. The result is a paradox: families have more access to recipes than any generation before them, yet dinner can still feel like a daily emergency. Abundance without retrieval is not abundance. It is noise.

A recipe library inside the vault is an attempt to convert that noise into a small, trustworthy set of options that can be found under pressure. This is not about becoming a "meal prep person" or building a curated brand of domestic perfection. It is about building a system that answers the questions families actually ask at 6.15 p.m.: What can we make quickly? What uses what we already have? What works in winter? What can we batch-cook? What meets a dietary constraint without turning dinner into a separate meal for everyone? The library's measure of success is not how many recipes it contains. It is whether it makes the next decision easier.

The first design principle is brutally pragmatic: store recipes in the form you will use. Families often save recipes in ways that look tidy but fail in practice. A link saved without context is a promise to your future self that future self will have time to click, scroll, and interpret. A photo of a cookbook page is a promise that future self will remember which book it came from, and will be able to read it in poor light with flour on their hands. A screenshot of a social post is a promise that future self will decode the missing quantities and guess the method. These promises are usually broken. A good recipe library replaces promises with retrieval.

That leads to the useful question: when should a recipe be copied into the vault, and when should it merely be linked? Copying is work. Linking is easy. The temptation is to link everything and call it a library. The reality is that some recipes do not survive linking. Websites change. Pages disappear. Paywalls appear. Food blogs bury the method under a long narrative, which is charming until you are hungry. The recipes that are most valuable to a family—reliable weeknight staples, special dishes repeated at celebrations, the "everyone actually eats this" meals—deserve durability. Those are the ones worth copying into the vault in a clean, readable format. The recipes that are occasional experiments, or that require a specialist technique you rarely use, may be perfectly fine as links. Name the distinction: durability threshold. Explain: recipes that are used repeatedly and under time pressure should be stored in a durable, frictionless form; occasional recipes can remain external references without undermining daily reliability. The implication is a library that stays lean and useful rather than becoming an archive of aspirational cooking.

A second principle follows: optimise for search, not for browsing. Many families imagine a recipe collection like a cookbook: something you flip through. In practice, a digital library earns its keep when it can be queried. Search is not merely typing a title. It is asking the system for "winter, quick, vegetarian" or "batch cook, freezer-friendly" or "dairy-free, child-approved". That requires tags, and tags must reflect household reality. The most elegant culinary taxonomy in the world is useless if it does not map to the way the family actually thinks and eats.

Tags in a family recipe library tend to cluster into a few categories because family life has predictable constraints. One category is time and effort: "10–15 minutes", "30 minutes", "slow cooker", "one pan", "weekday", "weekend". Another is season and mood: "winter", "summer", "comfort", "light", "picnic". Another is dietary and preference: "vegetarian", "vegan", "gluten-free", "dairy-free", "nut-free", "spicy", "mild". Another is structure: "batch cook", "freezer", "leftovers", "lunchbox". A final category is social function: "guests", "birthday", "school night", "sick day". The point is not to tag obsessively. It is to tag in a way that reduces decision fatigue by narrowing choices quickly. Name: constraint-based retrieval. Explain: when tags reflect constraints, the family can filter options rather than generate them from scratch; fewer options reduces cognitive load and reduces the risk of defaulting to the easiest, least satisfying choice. The implication is not gourmet living. It is steadier, calmer feeding.

Still, tags can be overdone. A library with thirty tags used inconsistently becomes a new kind of clutter. The reconciliation is to accept a small shared vocabulary and use it consistently. Families do not need a taxonomy. They need a handful of words everyone understands. The practical marker of good tagging is that another adult—or an older child—can apply the tags correctly without being taught. If only one person knows the system, the library becomes another private burden.

Now consider the shape of a recipe note itself, because the note is the unit of use. A family recipe note must respect the conditions of cooking: hands are messy, attention is intermittent, interruptions are constant. The note should therefore be readable at a glance. It should begin with the ingredients and quantities in plain measures the household actually uses. It should separate the method into short steps. It should include the cooking time and the key constraint ("needs marinating", "best if prepped earlier") if relevant. It should also include family-specific metadata: who likes it, what substitutions worked, what to double, what to avoid. This is not culinary pedantry. It is the difference between a recipe that survives contact with real life and one that looks nice in a folder.

A small but profound addition is the "next time" line: a single sentence capturing what the household learned. "Use less chilli." "Double the sauce." "Add frozen peas at the end." "Works with chickpeas." "Kids prefer it with rice." These notes convert experience into reliable future action. Without them, families repeat the same micro-mistakes and then blame themselves for being disorganised. With them, the library becomes an evolving record of what actually works for that particular household.

At this point a credible counter-example should be admitted. Some people cook primarily by feel. They rarely follow recipes, and they find written instructions constraining. For such households, a library might seem unnecessary or even insulting to the cook's craft. That is a fair concern. The reconciliation is to distinguish between culinary creativity and household coordination. A recipe library is not a demand that everyone cook by script. It is a shared reference that allows other people to cook adequately when the primary cook is busy, tired, or absent. It is also a way of preserving the household's favourites in a form that can be shared across generations. If a family has one confident cook and several less confident ones, the library becomes a bridge. The primary cook keeps their freedom. The others gain competence. The home becomes less dependent on one person's memory.

A second named, checkable example clarifies why preserving favourites matters. In 2004, the British chef and writer Elizabeth David's influence on home cooking was being reassessed in biographies and essays that noted how recipes can function as cultural memory—stories preserved through method and taste. Families enact a smaller version of that phenomenon. A recipe is often attached to a person: a grandparent's stew, a parent's Sunday roast variation, a dish learned at university, a sauce that became "our thing". When such recipes live only in someone's head, they are fragile.

When they are captured in a family library, they become shareable memory.

The library's most visible payoff arrives when planning a week's meals stops feeling like a trial. Imagine a household on a Sunday afternoon. The week ahead is crowded: late meetings, a club night, a school event. Without a system, meal planning becomes a negotiation between aspiration and exhaustion, often resolved by repeating the same two meals or defaulting to takeaways. With a tagged library, the household can choose constraints first and recipes second. They filter for "weekday" and "30 minutes" and "child-approved". They see a handful of candidates, not hundreds. They choose two that rely on cupboard staples, one batch cook to create leftovers, one lighter meal for a busy night, and one "comfort" dish for the evening everyone returns tired. The plan emerges not from inspiration but from structured choice.

The tags do the thinking.

That sentence captures the quiet genius of a well-built library. The tags embody decisions the family has already made about what counts as "quick", what counts as "winter food", what counts as "safe for everyone". Those decisions are then reused. The household is no longer re-litigating the meaning of "easy" each night. It is using the library's accumulated logic. The board or list for the week can then link directly to the recipe notes, which link to any necessary documents or shopping lists. The week becomes a chain of small, predictable actions rather than a series of nightly improvisations.

Linking, again, is where the vault becomes more than a collection. A recipe note can link to a shopping list template, to a pantry inventory note if the family keeps one, to a substitution note ("what to do when we're out of eggs"), to an allergy summary if relevant, to a list of "packed lunches that work". The point is not to create an encyclopaedia. The point is to create a small, interconnected system that reflects how cooking actually happens: decisions leading to ingredients, ingredients leading to actions, actions leading to repeated learning.

Modern life introduces an extra friction that makes the library even more valuable: devices and distractions. Recipes are often consumed in the same feed as entertainment, which encourages impulsive saving and forgetful retrieval. The family library functions as a deliberate boundary. It says: if a recipe is good enough to cook, it is good enough to store properly. That boundary reduces the endless "I saw a recipe somewhere" problem that haunts many households. It also reduces the tendency to plan meals around novelty rather than around what time and energy allow.

There is a subtle ethical dimension here too, because food labour is frequently unevenly distributed in families. A recipe library, when shared, can redistribute that labour. It makes it easier for a partner to cook without asking for instructions. It makes it possible for older children to take responsibility for one meal a week, because the information is clear and the options are visible. The library becomes a tool of independence. Independence is not only about doing chores. It is about having access to the knowledge that makes doing possible.

The motif of the laminated sheet returns because the best recipes, like the best household routines, are designed for use. They are legible. They are findable. They survive tiredness. They are not written to impress. They are written to feed people on a Tuesday.

The forward test sits in a choice between two kinds of freedom. One kind of freedom is the freedom of spontaneity: deciding each night based on impulse and mood. The other is the freedom that comes from preparation: a small library that reduces decision fatigue and makes cooking less draining. Families often assume these freedoms are opposites. They are not. A good recipe library does not eliminate spontaneity. It gives spontaneity a foundation. The question, then, is whether the household wants to keep paying the nightly tax of re-deciding, or whether it wants to build a searchable, tagged collection of meals that actually work—so that the next time the fridge door opens and the day's patience is already spent, the answer to "What are we having?" can be found quickly, calmly, and together.

Documenting Daily Routines

In December 2018, in Chicago, the researcher Daniel L. Carlson and colleagues published work in *American Sociological Review* on the division of household labour and the tensions that arise when expectations are misaligned. The details vary by household, yet the pattern is stubborn: conflict often flares not because anyone refuses to help, but because people carry different internal scripts for what "help" means. The hallway smells faintly of detergent, a school bag thuds onto the floorboards, and a parent says, "We need to get moving," as if that sentence were a plan rather than a mood.

Routines are invisible scripts.

They govern mornings, bedtimes, cleaning, getting out of the door, and returning home. They are not merely sequences of actions; they are agreements—often implicit—about who does what, when, and how. When these scripts remain unspoken, they produce a familiar domestic phenomenon:

everyone is "busy" and yet nothing feels coordinated. One person feels they are carrying everything. Another feels they are being criticised for not reading minds. Children learn, quickly, that adults will repeat themselves and that rules are negotiable when fatigue hits. The household becomes a place where minor transitions—shoes on, teeth brushed, lunch packed—trigger disproportionate friction.

Documenting routines inside the vault is a way of making these scripts visible enough to share. It is not a bid for control. It is a bid for clarity. Clarity is the opposite of nagging. Nagging is what happens when a routine exists only in one person's head and must be repeatedly transmitted through speech. A documented routine shifts the burden from constant verbal prompting to a stable reference that anyone can consult. That shift matters because family life is an environment of interruptions. Speech is fragile. Notes persist.

The case for documented routines begins with a simple observation about human cognition: we are bad at repeated coordination through memory alone. Even highly competent people struggle to execute sequences reliably when tired, distracted, or stressed. Families live in those conditions more often than they admit. A morning routine is executed under time pressure. A bedtime routine is executed under low emotional bandwidth. Cleaning routines are executed when everyone would rather do something else. If a household relies on each person's internal memory of "how we do this", then the routine becomes dependent on mood and on whoever happens to be most assertive in the moment. Name the problem: mood-driven execution. Explain: when routines are not externalised, they are enacted inconsistently and require repeated negotiation; inconsistency invites bargaining and increases friction. The implication is predictable fatigue, because the household spends emotional energy re-deciding what should already be settled.

The second brain offers a different model: the routine as shared reference. A routine note is a small artefact that describes the sequence in plain language, with a level of detail appropriate to the household's age and temperament. It answers questions before they become arguments. It allows delegation without micromanagement. It also allows the family to improve the routine over time, because once something is written down, it can be edited. Oral routines do not evolve well; they just produce more reminders.

Still, a routine note can become a weapon if it is imposed rather than agreed. Families are not businesses. People do not respond well to a checklist used as a moral judgement. The difference between empowerment and control is not the existence of a routine, but the way it is created and used. A routine co-created feels like shared competence. A routine dictated feels like surveillance. The distinction is crucial, especially with children and teenagers whose autonomy is developing and whose cooperation depends on dignity.

Co-creation is not sentimental. It is strategic. When children help shape a routine, they learn the logic behind it. They also gain ownership: the routine becomes "ours", not "yours". Ownership changes behaviour because people defend what they helped build. The visible behaviour of co-creation is that the routine includes the child's language and priorities, not only the adult's. A child may care about choosing clothes the night before because it reduces morning stress. A teenager may care about having a predictable shower slot. These preferences are not obstacles; they are design inputs.

Consider the morning routine as a show of how small changes alter a household's emotional climate. In many families, mornings collapse into a set of shouted prompts: "Have you got your blazer?" "Where's your water bottle?" "Brush your teeth!" "Shoes!" The child hears noise, not guidance. The adult hears resistance, not confusion. Meanwhile, the same missing items recur because nothing in the system changes. A documented morning routine can include a simple sequence: wake, wash, dress, breakfast, bag check, out. The crucial addition is the "bag check", externalised as a shared checklist. The checklist lists what matters in that household: lunch, water bottle, PE kit day, homework folder, instrument, keys. This is not a moral document. It is a memory aid. Name: external prompt. Explain: when the routine includes a shared prompt, responsibility shifts from adult memory to the system; the child can self-check and the adult can step back. The implication is reduced shouting and increased independence, because the routine becomes something the child can follow rather than something that is done to them.

Now turn to bedtime, where routines are often most emotionally charged because everyone's reserves are low. A bedtime routine is also the ideal example because the conflict is rarely about the steps themselves; it is about the negotiation of those steps. "One more story" is not a request for literature. It is often a request for connection, control, or delay. When the routine is unclear, every step becomes a bargaining point. The adult responds with escalation. The child responds with creativity. The house becomes tense.

A documented bedtime routine does not eliminate the child's desire for connection. It creates a predictable frame for it. Imagine a family where bedtime has become a nightly battle. The child resists. The adult repeats themselves. Tears appear.

Voices rise. The next day, everyone is tired and the cycle repeats. The family decides to externalise the routine into a shared checklist stored in the vault and displayed in a way the child can see—on a device, printed, or otherwise accessible. The routine is short, written in the child's words where possible, and includes a small "choice" point that preserves autonomy: choose pyjamas, choose story, choose a quiet activity for five minutes. The routine also includes a single, explicit end: lights out. The child can see the pathway. The adult can refer to the checklist rather than issuing commands. The atmosphere shifts from argument to sequence.

Five minutes. Then teeth.

That kind of sentence—short, concrete—matters. It pairs a time boundary with a step. It reduces ambiguity, which reduces bargaining. It also gives the child a sense that time is being respected. The checklist becomes a neutral third object in the room: it is not the adult's mood, and it is not the child's will. It is the shared plan. Name: neutral mediator. Explain: a shared routine artefact reduces interpersonal conflict by relocating the "rule" from the adult to the agreed system; the adult becomes a supporter of the plan rather than its enforcer. The implication is a calmer bedtime not because anyone became more virtuous, but because the household reduced ambiguity and repeated negotiation.

The routine's success depends on what it does not do. It does not attempt to contain every possible exception. Children get ill. Nights vary. Guests arrive. The routine should be stable but not brittle. It should include a phrase that signals flexibility without reopening negotiation: "If you're poorly, we adjust." That sentence acknowledges reality while preserving the idea that the routine exists. Families abandon routines when routines feel like a lie. The remedy is honesty: the routine is what we aim for on ordinary nights. Ordinary nights are frequent enough to justify structure.

Cleaning routines offer a different kind of friction: not emotional bargaining, but avoidance and resentment. Many households experience cleaning as a recurring moral drama: someone notices mess, someone else does not; someone feels taken for granted, someone else feels criticised. Documenting cleaning routines can prevent this drama by clarifying scope and cadence. The goal is not a spotless house. The goal is predictable maintenance that stops small messes becoming big conflicts. A routine might specify a small daily reset and a weekly deeper clean, with tasks visible and distributed. The key is that the routine must be realistic enough to be followed without heroic effort. If it demands too much, it becomes a source of failure and shame. Name: sustainable cadence. Explain: routines that match capacity are more likely to be enacted consistently; consistency reduces the need for emotional enforcement. The implication is reduced resentment because expectations align with reality.

A credible limitation must be faced: documenting routines can feel like turning home into a rulebook. Some families will find written routines oppressive or infantilising, especially for older children. The reconciliation is to document routines at the level of friction. If a routine is working well, it may not need documentation. If a routine reliably causes conflict, the household benefits from making it visible. Documentation is a response to friction, not an ideology. It is also not permanent. A routine can be documented for six weeks, refined, and then removed from prominent view once it becomes habitual. The vault is not obliged to display everything all the time. It needs to store what can be retrieved when needed.

There is also a counter-example that deserves respect: some families thrive on spontaneity and minimal structure. Their routines are flexible, and conflict is low. For them, heavy documentation may add unnecessary weight. The second brain is not a universal prescription. It is a tool for households where the cost of repeated negotiation is high. The reconciliation is to adopt the smallest amount of documentation that reduces real friction. If a family only needs a leaving-the-house checklist and a bedtime script, that may be enough. Excess structure is not sophistication. It is clutter.

The motif of the laminated sheet returns because it captures the desired qualities of routine documentation: concise, visible, and tolerant of tiredness. A routine should be able to survive a bad day. It should work when people are not at their best. That is the entire point. Families often design systems for their ideal selves. Routines should be designed for their tired selves.

The deeper philosophical thread is about autonomy. Documented routines can liberate children rather than control them when they are framed as tools for self-management. A child who can follow a routine without constant prompting experiences competence. A teenager who can consult a household "how we do mornings" note without asking for instructions experiences respect. Adults who are not forced into constant reminding experience relief. The home becomes less dependent on one person acting as the household's living alarm clock.

The forward test rests on a trade-off most families encounter daily. A household can keep relying on verbal prompting and improvisation, accepting the daily friction as inevitable, or it can treat its most conflict-prone routines as shared knowledge worthy of a place in the vault. The question is not whether routines will exist. They already do, in the form of invisible scripts and repeated arguments. The question is whether the family will choose to make those scripts visible enough to share—so that on the nights and mornings when patience is scarce, the household can follow a plan it agreed to when it was calm, rather than fighting about the same steps yet again.

Household How To Guides

On 4 October 2021, Facebook's services went dark for hours, taking WhatsApp with them and leaving households everywhere briefly cut off from the place they had been using as an improvised instruction manual. In London, commuters stared at phones that would not deliver messages; at home, people discovered how many domestic questions had been quietly routed through a chat thread. The broadband might still have been working, the kettle still boiling, the hallway still smelling faintly of wet coats—but the household's "How do I...?" line to the person who usually knows had snapped. The outage was global. The panic was local.

The note did the thinking.

That is the strange power of a household "how to" guide: it replaces urgent messaging with calm retrieval. Most homes have an internal map of procedures that is rarely acknowledged until it fails. How to reset the router when the video call freezes. How to run the washing machine on the cycle that does not ruin school shirts. How to lock up so the back door actually latches. How to bleed a radiator, change a fuse, silence the smoke alarm, find the stopcock, locate the spare key. These are not glamorous competencies, and that is precisely why they are left undocumented. They seem too basic to write down—until they become too stressful to remember.

A household how-to guide is a short, stored, searchable instruction that captures one practical procedure in the simplest usable form. It is not a philosophy of domesticity. It is a reliability device. In a family second brain, such guides do a particular job: they take knowledge that has accumulated in one person's head and make it shareable without friction. This matters for fairness, for resilience, and for dignity. A home that depends on a single memory is a home that becomes brittle as soon as that person is tired, away, or simply fed up with being interrupted.

Show the common pattern. A teenager wants to wash their football kit. They are willing, even proud to do it. They stand in front of the machine, confronted by symbols, buttons, and choices that might as well be an exam paper. They call for help. The parent shouts instructions from another room, half-listening to a work call. The teen mishears "thirty" as "thirteen" or confuses "quick wash" with "delicates". The kit emerges damp, smelly, or shrunk. Everyone is irritated. Name what happened: tacit procedure. Explain: the household relies on knowledge that exists only as informal expertise; transferring it verbally under pressure introduces error and resentment. The implication is that willing help becomes discouraging, and the household defaults back to the same person doing everything because "it's easier".

A mini-guide changes the transfer mechanism. Instead of transmitting a procedure through shouted fragments, the household stores it once in a stable form. The teen follows it independently. The parent is not interrupted. The outcome improves. That improvement is not merely practical; it changes the social contract. The child experiences competence rather than correction. The adult experiences relief rather than dependence. The home becomes a place where knowledge is not hoarded, but shared.

The strongest argument for how-to guides is not that they save time—though they often do. It is that they reduce the number of moments where someone's attention is treated as the default infrastructure of the home. Attention is finite. In families, it is usually the scarcest resource. Every "How do I...?" shouted up the stairs is a claim on that resource. In healthy households, those claims are welcomed in moderation. In stressed households, they become sparks. A guide absorbs the spark.

A useful way to see these guides is as domestic "standard operating procedures", without the stiff language. Institutions have long understood that repeated actions require stable instructions. In 1911, Frederick Winslow Taylor published *The Principles of Scientific Management*, arguing—controversially, and often crudely—that work could be made more efficient through standardisation. Homes are not factories, and it would be grotesque to treat family life as an assembly line. Yet Taylor's era grasped a basic truth that applies gently in domestic space: when tasks repeat, people benefit from a shared method that does not have to be re-invented each time. The difference is that in a family, the purpose is not productivity for profit. It is reliability for peace.

Still, there is an immediate objection. Isn't writing instructions overkill? Doesn't it make home feel bureaucratic? It can, if done badly. The reconciliation is to write only what the household keeps stumbling over, and to write it in a form that respects the reader's patience. A household how-to guide should be shorter than the interruption it prevents. It should be clear enough to be followed without asking questions. It should avoid being precious. If it becomes a manifesto, it has failed.

The format that works best is almost boring in its simplicity. Start with a title that matches the question people actually ask—"Reset the router", "Run the washing machine for school uniforms", "Lock up at night", "Where the stopcock is". Add a one-sentence purpose so the reader knows they are in the right place. Then give the steps as short, sequential actions written in plain verbs, with any crucial settings or locations named precisely as they exist in that home. If there is a "do not do this" warning, keep it specific and minimal, not dramatic. If there is a troubleshooting note, keep it to the most likely failure. Finish with what "done" looks like, because people relax when they know how to tell they have succeeded. This is not literature; it is a handrail.

Precision matters because families run on quick glances. "Press the small button" is not helpful when there are three small buttons. "Turn it off and on" is ambiguous when "off" could mean a switch, a plug, or a button. A guide should name the physical reality: "the white socket behind the bookcase", "the blue dial on the left", "the second shelf in the hall cupboard". The guide becomes a tiny map of the household. That map is especially valuable for people who did not set things up: teenagers, partners, visiting relatives, babysitters. A home that relies on undocumented familiarity quietly excludes those people from competence.

Consider the router, the modern household's most resented box. When it fails, everything fails at once: school portals, streaming, work calls, messaging, even the smart doorbell that insists on being clever. The procedure for fixing it is usually simple, yet it is rarely written down. One person knows where the router lives, which cable goes where, which lights should blink, and what sequence of actions tends to restore service. Everyone else holds a vague belief that "it's complicated". The result is dependence. A router guide punctures that myth. It gives the household a shared ritual: locate, check, restart, wait, confirm. The reward is not merely restored internet. It is restored agency.

The same logic applies to locking up, a task often loaded with unspoken anxiety. Was the door checked? Are the windows shut? Is the back gate secured? Who set the alarm? In many homes, locking up is one person's private routine, so when someone else does it they feel uncertain, and uncertainty breeds either repeated checking or avoidance. A guide externalises the routine. It makes "locked up" a verifiable state rather than a personal reassurance. The emotional payoff is quiet: fewer midnight doubts, fewer passive-aggressive questions in the morning, fewer moments where someone feels they must redo someone else's work "just in case".

Laundry is where the human story lands because it is a task children can genuinely take on, and because failure is tangible. Imagine a teenager—call her Leila—who wants to be treated as capable but keeps getting stuck on domestic details that adults treat as obvious. One afternoon she decides to wash her own clothes before a school trip. The parent who usually does laundry is out. In the vault, Leila finds a short note titled "Laundry: school kit and everyday clothes". It tells her where the detergent pods are, which drawer they live in, which cycle name corresponds to "normal", which temperature works in that house, and what to do if the machine refuses to start because the door is not properly latched. She follows it. The machine hums. The smell of detergent spreads through the kitchen. Later, she hangs the clothes and realises she did not need to ask anyone. This is not a triumphant coming-of-age scene. It is better: it is ordinary competence becoming accessible.

Name what is happening: transfer of capability. Explain: a written guide allows knowledge to move from the expert to the learner without requiring the expert's presence; the learner gains independence and the household gains redundancy. The implication is profound for family dynamics. When capability is shared, help stops being a favour and becomes a norm. Children are more likely to contribute when they can succeed without being coached through every step. Adults are less likely to burn out when they are not the single point of failure for every domestic system.

A second named, checkable example underlines why this matters beyond convenience. In 2010, psychologist Roy Baumeister and journalist John Tierney's book *Willpower* popularised research on self-control and depletion, reinforcing an observation many families recognise: when people are tired, they make worse decisions and have less patience for friction. Domestic life produces tiredness by default. A how-to guide is a friction reducer. It does not ask people to be more disciplined. It removes the need for discipline in moments where discipline is least available. If a teen can follow a note rather than interrupt a parent, the household has spared itself a small conflict that might otherwise cascade into a larger one.

Yet guides can fail. They can become outdated when the household changes a device or when a procedure evolves. They can become too long, too clever, too full of edge cases. They can also become a subtle form of gatekeeping if only one person writes them in language others do not use. The reconciliation is to treat guides as living notes with a clear expectation of revision. A guide should be dated quietly in its metadata or title if needed, and edited when someone discovers a missing step. The best guides are improved by use. They invite small corrections. They are not sacred texts.

Another limitation is social: some people would rather ask than read, especially children. That is not laziness; it is often a bid for connection. The trick is not to replace all asking with documentation. It is to reserve asking for what deserves human attention—comfort, judgement, conversation—and to shift routine procedural questions to the vault. A guide is not meant to banish interaction. It is meant to stop procedural interruptions masquerading as relationship.

The motif to thread through this work is the label inside the cupboard door. Many households already do a primitive version of documentation: a handwritten note saying which switch controls which light, or which day the bins go out. That label is powerful because it is local, visible, and humble. A household how-to guide is the digital extension of that label: still humble, still practical, but searchable, shareable, and less likely to be thrown away. It lives in the vault like a set of labels for the entire home's functioning, not as decoration, but as infrastructure.

The deeper value of these guides is that they make the home less person-dependent. Person-dependence is a hidden risk. It shows up when one parent travels for work and the other suddenly realises they do not know the password for the heating controls. It shows up when a child is old enough to help but cannot, because the knowledge has never been shared. It shows up when a relative steps in during a family emergency and cannot work the alarm. A home that has documented its basic procedures is not merely organised. It is resilient.

The forward test is a decision most families avoid because it sounds silly until it is suddenly urgent. Will the household keep treating practical knowledge as something that "just lives" in one person's head, accepting the interruptions and the resentment as the price of getting things done, or will it capture a small set of mini-guides—router, laundry, lock-up, and the other repeat offenders—so that competence can be shared without drama? The question is not whether the home needs experts. It does. The question is whether expertise will remain private property, or become a family asset that anyone can retrieve when the lights blink, the washing machine beeps, and the person who usually knows is not there to answer.

Seasonal and Annual Checklists

In September 2009, in New York City, Captain Chesley "Sully" Sullenberger and First Officer Jeffrey Skiles brought US Airways Flight 1549 down on the Hudson River and got everyone out alive. The incident became famous for skill under pressure, yet one mundane detail mattered as much as heroism: disciplined procedure. In emergencies, people do not rise to the occasion so much as they fall back on what has been rehearsed. At home, the stakes are usually smaller, but the cognitive pattern is the same. When September arrives and the school term begins, when winter closes in, when holidays approach, families do not suddenly become more organised. They fall back on whatever preparation ritual exists—or they improvise, again, with the familiar metallic taste of stress.

The calendar repeats. We forget anyway.

That is not a character flaw. It is a system reality. Annual events feel predictable in theory, yet they arrive amid changing schedules, shifting needs, and cumulative fatigue. Each season carries its own cluster of tasks: school forms, uniform checks, new timetables, updated logins, and the sudden discovery that a child has grown out of shoes over the summer. Winter brings heating quirks, darker afternoons, damp coats, and a new intensity of illness and indoor living. Holidays bring travel documents, gifts, packing, house preparations. Tax time brings paperwork and deadlines, and with it the quiet fear of having missed a document that now matters. In all of these, the household experiences the same emotional texture: a low hum of "I am sure I am forgetting something" that can sharpen into panic if a deadline appears.

Seasonal and annual checklists are a way of interrupting that cycle. They are not life-hacks. They are a gentle acknowledgement of how memory actually works. Humans are poor at infrequent, multi-step tasks, particularly when those tasks are distributed across weeks and involve multiple people. Families are even worse at them because family life is not a single project; it is many projects running in parallel. A seasonal checklist externalises the recurring tasks into a shared reference that can be reused, lightly updated, and trusted. It converts "I think we did that" into "It's on the list and it's ticked".

The case for these checklists begins with the distinction between daily routines and cyclical routines. Daily routines—mornings, bedtimes—become habits through repetition. Seasonal routines do not. They are too infrequent to lodge reliably in habit memory, and they are too context-dependent to be effortless. A child's uniform needs change. School requirements change. The household's work patterns shift. Even the weather feels different year to year. If the household relies on habit for cyclical routines, it will repeatedly fail, and then interpret that failure as personal inadequacy. Name the problem: low-frequency complexity. Explain: tasks that recur annually contain enough steps and variability that they are not reliably automated by habit; without external support they are prone to omission. The implication is predictable stress spikes, which families mistakenly accept as "just how it is".

A seasonal checklist, properly designed, has three properties. It is specific enough to be actionable. It is short enough to be used. It is stable enough to be reused. Many families miss one of these. They write checklists so vague they are useless ("Get ready for school"), or so detailed they are unreadable, or so customised to one year that they cannot be reused without rework. The art is to write at the level that prevents the common failures in that household. If the family repeatedly forgets to check shoe sizes, shoes belong on the list. If the family never forgets to buy stationery, stationery does not need to be there. A checklist is not a catalogue of everything that could possibly matter; it is a tool aimed at preventing the failures that actually happen.

The second brain makes this easier because it allows checklists to live as reusable templates. A checklist can be duplicated each year, named with the year, and then adjusted. The original remains as a base. The new version reflects the current reality. The family gains continuity without rigidity. In practice, this means the list becomes more accurate over time, because each cycle teaches the household what it truly needs to remember. This is where annual checklists stop being mere reminders and become a learning system. Name: compounding preparedness. Explain: each cycle produces small improvements to the checklist, reducing future omissions and friction; the household's system becomes sharper through use. The implication is that seasonal transitions become calmer, not because the household has more time, but because it stops paying the same attention-tax every year.

A start-of-term checklist is the clearest example because school is a recurring institutional rhythm that interacts with every part of family life: schedules, transport, meals, clothes, activities, devices, and emotional regulation. The checklist begins as a modest attempt to prevent a predictable September scramble. In Year One, the family creates a list in the vault a week or two before term starts. It includes the tasks that are usually forgotten until the last minute: confirm term dates and inset days, check uniform and shoes, locate the PE kit, ensure lunch arrangements are set, confirm club schedules, update emergency contacts, check whether any medical forms or permissions are required, test logins for school portals, locate travel cards or transport details. These are not glamorous tasks. They are the ones that ruin mornings when missed.

Imagine the first run. The family checks the list the weekend before term. They find that one child's jumper is too small. They order a new one. They discover that the school portal password has expired. They reset it while they have time. They find that the PE day has changed, and they adjust. On the first morning, there is still rush—there always is—but the rush has a different quality. It is about getting out of the door, not about crisis-solving. The household has moved some decisions out of the morning and into the calmer weekend. That is the checklist at work: shifting effort to where it costs less.

Then Year Two arrives. This is where compounding begins. The family duplicates last year's checklist, renames it, and reviews it briefly. They notice what was missing last time. Perhaps they forgot to update the child's allergy information on a form. Perhaps they forgot to label new uniform items.

Perhaps they underestimated how long it takes to break in new shoes. These are not abstract insights; they are small, practical facts. The family adds two items and deletes one that was unnecessary. The list becomes better tailored. The family also now has last year's completed checklist to refer to, which creates a subtle psychological shift: evidence of competence. The system no longer feels like a hopeful plan. It feels like something the family has already done.

Year Three arrives and the checklist now has history. The children are older; perhaps one is now capable of taking ownership of part of the list. The checklist becomes a shared artefact rather than a parent's private reminder. The child checks their own kit and ticks it. Another child looks up the timetable and confirms it. The adult handles the portal login and contact updates. This distribution matters because it turns preparation into a shared project, not a silent burden. The household is not merely organised; it is educating its members in how to be organised. The second brain becomes a training ground for independence.

The motif here is the tide mark.

Seasonal tasks are like tide marks: they show where the water reaches each year, and if you ignore them you are surprised again when the water returns. A family checklist is a way of marking that line deliberately, so the household is not repeatedly startled by predictable surges. When the list is reused, the tide mark becomes clearer. When the list is ignored, the tide behaves as it always has, and the family experiences it as chaos rather than rhythm.

Winter preparation offers a second way to see the logic. Winter is not an emergency; it is an annual shift in conditions that changes what the household needs. Homes become damper. Clothes take longer to dry. Dark mornings make departures harder. Heating systems are tested. Illness and indoor living change the household's routines. A winter checklist might include checking the boiler service date, locating spare blankets, ensuring outdoor gear still fits, checking torches, refreshing basic supplies, confirming car preparedness if relevant, and reviewing routines that become harder in the dark. Again, the list should reflect the household's reality, not an imaginary ideal. A winter checklist that assumes an organised garage and a well-stocked shed will irritate a family that has neither. A useful list begins with the home as it is.

A credible limitation must be faced: seasonal checklists can become another form of nagging, another source of guilt, another document that feels like a failing grade when not completed. This happens when families treat checklists as moral scorecards. The reconciliation is to treat the checklist as a support, not a verdict. The list exists to reduce friction, not to prove virtue. It should be short enough that partial completion still creates value. If a family only manages to check shoes and portal logins, that may prevent the worst failures. The checklist should be designed to deliver disproportionate benefit early, not to demand total compliance.

Another limitation is variability. Some years are calm; some are chaotic. A new job, a move, illness, a newborn, a bereavement—life events can make a routine season impossible. In those years, the checklist should not be abandoned in shame. It should be simplified. The system must honour reality. A "minimum viable" seasonal checklist is often the most important version because it keeps the household functional through difficult periods. It also preserves trust in the vault: the checklist remains a tool, not an accusation.

There is also the question of what belongs on an annual checklist and what should remain elsewhere. The checklist should not swallow the calendar or the vault. A checklist is a trigger, a set of prompts that point to other stored information. "Update school contacts" might link to the contacts note. "Check timetable" might link to the term's schedule. "Review emergency info" might link to the "in case of" bundle. The checklist is not a dumping ground for details; it is a map of key actions, connected to the vault's deeper information.

The power of these lists becomes obvious when a family compares two Septembers. In one, the household discovers missing items on the first morning, scrambles for replacements, argues about blame, and starts term depleted. In the other, the household uses a start-of-term checklist to move key tasks earlier, distribute preparation, and begin the term with less emotional debt. The difference is not perfection. It is margin. Margin is what families lack.

A final named example clarifies why margins matter. In 1935, the psychologist Frederic Bartlett published *Remembering*, arguing that memory is reconstructive: people do not retrieve the past like a file; they rebuild it using fragments and assumptions. That is why "I thought we did that" is so common. The family is not lying. The family is reconstructing. Seasonal checklists are a response to Bartlett's insight without the academic language: stop relying on reconstruction for tasks that matter. Write it down. Tick it. Leave less to assumption.

The forward test is deceptively simple, and it arrives every year with the turning of the seasons. When the next recurring transition approaches—term start, winter, holidays, or any annual obligation—will the household treat the familiar unease of "we're probably forgetting something" as background noise, or will it build and reuse a checklist that converts that unease into concrete prompts, shared action, and visible completion? The question is not whether life will interrupt. It will. The question is whether the family wants to face the interruption with a system that already remembers what matters, or with the hope that memory will be kind this time.

Chapter 9
Photos, Memories, and Milestones

In January 2019, in California, the company behind Google Photos quietly changed the way it presented personal archives to users, leaning harder into automated "memories" and algorithmic resurfacing. The technical details were less interesting than the social fact: for the first time in human history, a large proportion of families were carrying a near-total visual record of their children's lives in their pockets, and yet were increasingly unable to *use* it. A phone vibrates on the kitchen counter, a thumbnail flashes—last year, five years ago—and the image arrives without context, like a postcard with the address torn off. It is strangely moving. It is also strangely empty.

We are drowning in souvenirs.

This chapter is about that contradiction: the more we record, the less we remember in the ways that matter. Families once had a few albums, a tin of prints, perhaps a shoebox of letters. The limitations of film and storage forced selection. Now selection is optional, and so it often never happens. Photos accumulate by default. Screenshots pile up. Short videos multiply. Keepsakes are photographed and then also kept. Cloud storage makes it feel safe to defer decisions indefinitely, yet deferral has a cost: meaning dissolves into volume, and the archive becomes a warehouse that nobody visits. The family ends up with a vast collection of images that cannot be navigated, searched, or shared without effort, and effort is exactly what family life lacks.

The second brain, in its earlier chapters, has been building a shared vault for practical knowledge and plans. Here the vault becomes something else as well: a family memory system that is not merely an accidental by-product of device ownership. Memory is not the same as data. Data is what gets saved. Memory is what can be returned to, interpreted, and told. The difference is not sentimental. It is structural. An image without context becomes a fragment. An image linked to a story becomes a thread.

The work begins with a difficult question many families avoid because it feels emotionally charged: what is worth keeping? The problem is not that people love their children too much. The problem is that digital abundance turns love into hoarding. Ten near-identical photos of a child scoring a goal feel like proof of presence, proof of attention, proof that the moment mattered. Deleting nine can feel like betrayal, even when the tenth is better. Families rarely admit how much anxiety sits under their archive: the fear of forgetting, the fear of losing, the fear that if the photo disappears, the love disappears with it. This chapter refuses that false equation. Keeping is not caring. Curating is caring.

Deciding what to keep is therefore not a technical task; it is a meaning task. It requires criteria that respect both emotion and reality. The criteria must be simple enough to apply when tired, and honest enough to prevent the archive becoming a digital attic. The chapter approaches selection with a steady hand: keep what is representative, what is distinctive, what carries story; discard what is repetitive, blurry, accidental, or only significant because it exists. It also introduces a third option often neglected: defer consciously. Some decisions are too charged to make quickly. A family can create a small "decide later" holding space without turning the whole archive into one. The point is not ruthless minimalism. It is an archive that can be used without dread.

From selection, the chapter moves to the neglected craft of curation. Many people imagine curation as an artistic project requiring time they do not have. The reality is that a lightweight, consistent workflow outperforms heroic bursts of sorting once a year. A small monthly ritual—or a short session after major events—can keep the archive human-scale. The workflow is not about perfection; it is about cadence. A family that can reliably review, select, and tag a handful of photos each month will, over time, build an archive that is searchable and shareable. A family that waits for a free weekend to "sort the photos" will likely never do it, because the archive grows faster than the motivation.

Modern life offers an unexpected opportunity here: curation can become a family activity rather than a solitary chore. A Sunday session can turn into reminiscing, laughter, and the kind of storytelling that children secretly crave even when they pretend they do not. That shift matters because it reframes curation as relational. It is not "admin". It is narrative. When children help select photos, they reveal what they found meaningful, which is often different from what adults assume. One child will choose the blurry photo of the dog because it reminds them of a joke. Another will choose the quiet photo of a car journey because it reminds them of feeling safe. The archive becomes a mirror, and families learn themselves.

Then comes the move that turns photos into history: linking images to stories. Most family photo libraries are silent. They contain faces and places but not meaning. Years later, someone finds a photo and cannot remember why it mattered. The remedy is not to write essays under every picture. It is to attach a few words of context—who, where, why, and what was felt. A short note, a voice recording, a child's own description: these are small additions with disproportionate impact. They restore the address on the postcard. They also protect against a particular cruelty of digital memory: the way it can resurface an image without warning, stripped of context, and therefore stripped of care.

The chapter treats this linking as an act of generosity to future selves and to children. A first-day-of-school photo is a classic example precisely because it is so common. Without context, it becomes one more uniformed face among many. With a child's own description—what they were nervous about, what they were excited about—it becomes a time capsule. The child grows up and hears their younger voice, and the family archive becomes more than nostalgia; it becomes continuity. This is how the second brain shifts from storage to meaning: by connecting artefacts to interpretation.

Finally, the chapter considers sharing—especially with children—and the complicated ethics of visibility in a networked age. Families are encouraged culturally to document and broadcast, yet children grow into autonomy, and a childhood archive is not the parent's public property. The chapter holds that tension without moral panic. It asks how families can share richly at home while being cautious in public. It explores age-appropriate ways to look back together: curated albums, "year in review" notes, themed collections, small rituals such as a birthday tradition of revisiting the past year. These practices do not require performance. They require attention. They teach children that their lives are not merely content, but story.

A subtle motif runs through this chapter: the shoebox. Not the romantic shoebox of old letters only, but the shoebox as a metaphor for undigested accumulation. Digital archives often become shoeboxes by default—vast, unlabelled, rarely opened. The second brain offers a different fate for the shoebox: not a storage container, but a curated collection where each item earns its place, and where opening it feels like recognition rather than overwhelm. The aim is not to keep everything. The aim is to keep what can be *returned to*.

This matters now because the scale of modern documentation has outpaced the human capacity to interpret it. Families create thousands of photos each year without meaning to. The result is an archive that feels both precious and oppressive. It is precious because it contains lives. It is oppressive because it cannot be navigated. The chapter does not romanticise the past, when many moments were never recorded. It recognises a new problem created by a new abundance: the problem of turning documentation into memory without turning family life into curatorial labour.

The closing movement of this chapter lands on a forward tension that is both practical and philosophical. Every family must decide what kind of archive it is building. Is it a warehouse of proof—evidence that moments occurred—or a library of meaning—moments chosen, named, and connected to story? The difference is not merely aesthetic. It determines whether children will inherit a digital pile or a usable history. It determines whether looking back becomes a pleasure or an exhaustion. The second brain can hold either. The question is which one the family is willing to create, and what small rituals of selection and storytelling it is willing to repeat until the shoebox becomes, quietly, an archive worth opening.

Deciding What To Keep

On 2 June 2014 at Apple's Worldwide Developers Conference in San Francisco, the company announced iCloud Photo Library, a feature designed to make a person's photos appear everywhere, almost automatically. The Moscone Center was cool with air-conditioning; the light from the stage screens washed the audience in blue, and the promise sounded like relief: no more losing pictures, no more hunting across devices. A decade later, many families can feel the unintended aftertaste of that promise. When storage becomes frictionless, keeping becomes mindless. The archive grows. The meaning thins.

Choice is a kind of care.

The modern family photograph is born into a strange economy. Capturing has become effortless, sometimes compulsive, while deciding has become emotionally expensive. A parent takes ten near-identical photos of a child playing sport, not because ten are needed, but because the moment feels important and the device invites repetition. The child's face is a blur in three, perfect in one, and identical in the rest except for the angle of the ball and the parent's tremor of excitement. Later, the parent scrolls and hesitates. Deleting feels like erasing. Keeping feels like drowning. The archive becomes a place where love and anxiety quietly share a folder.

This tension is not solved by pretending the problem is trivial. For many families, photographs are not merely images. They are evidence of a life, proof of attention, proof that someone was there. Keepsakes carry the same charge: a crumpled drawing, a birthday card with misspelt affection, a wristband from a hospital visit, a medal from a race. The emotional weight comes from what these items stand for, not from their material form. That is why digital hoarding is so seductive. A family tells itself it can keep everything and decide later, and the sentence has the soothing tone of kindness. Yet "later" rarely arrives with time and clarity. It arrives with more images, more folders, and less patience.

The second brain changes the frame. It asks the family to treat memory as something that can be designed, not merely accumulated. Designing memory begins with the uncomfortable move of selection, because selection forces a distinction between what mattered and what merely happened to be recorded. That distinction feels harsh until it is seen clearly: recording is not remembering. Recording is producing raw material. Remembering is shaping it into something retrievable, shareable, and coherent.

A useful archive is not the biggest one.

One way to see the problem is through the older technology of the contact sheet. In the era of film, photographers would review a grid of tiny images and mark the few that deserved enlargement. The contact sheet was not a sentimental ritual; it was a constraint. It demanded comparison. It demanded judgement. Digital cameras removed that constraint, and so families rarely practise the art of marking "the one". Yet the need remains. The archive still asks, quietly: which image will stand for this day when the rest has faded?

The first criterion, then, is representativeness. A family does not need every frame of a child's tennis serve; it needs the frame that represents the moment most truthfully—emotionally and visually. This criterion feels almost offensive at first, because it sounds like reduction. In practice, it is liberation. A single representative image carries the story more powerfully than ten versions that blur into each other. Representativeness does not mean selecting only posed smiles. It often means selecting the image that contains the texture of the moment: the child's concentration, the mud on the knee, the glance towards a friend, the parent's laughter in the background. It is the image that can be looked at later and still *feel* like that day.

The second criterion is distinctiveness. Many images are functionally identical: same location, same expression, same composition, taken seconds apart. Distinctiveness asks a simple question: does this image add information? Not information in the technical sense, but narrative information. Does it show something different—another person, another angle, a different emotion, a different stage in the event? If not, it may be redundant. Redundancy is the silent killer of archives. It fills storage, but more importantly it fills attention. When everything is kept, nothing is special, and the archive becomes exhausting to browse. Distinctiveness restores hierarchy. It lets the archive breathe.

The third criterion is story potential. Some photos are beautiful but inert; others are imperfect but alive with narrative. A blurry image of a child in mid-laugh can carry more future meaning than a crisp, ordinary portrait. Story potential is a criterion that respects the way family memory actually works. Families remember through narrative: "That was the day we got lost", "That was the trip where it rained all week", "That was when she insisted on wearing the cape". A photo with story potential acts as a hook for those memories. A photo without story potential is often just a record of faces.

The fourth criterion is future utility, used carefully and without turning family life into a compliance exercise. Some images have practical value: a photo of a child's passport when travelling, a picture of a serial number, an image of a school notice pinned to the fridge. These images are not keepsakes in the emotional sense; they are working documents. The danger is that practical images often get mixed into sentimental archives, creating noise. When families separate practical capture from memory capture, they reduce the chaos. The practical images can live in the vault's reference spaces. The sentimental images can live where they will be revisited. The criterion is not "keep for ever". It is "store where it will be found when needed".

A fifth criterion, increasingly important, is consent and privacy. Children grow. Their relationship to their own past changes. An image that feels adorable to an adult may feel exposing to a teenager. A keepsake that feels harmless to a parent may feel intimate to the child who created it. Selection is therefore also a moral act: deciding not only what the family keeps, but who gets access, and in what form. The vault can hold private memory without turning it into a public performance. This is not prudishness. It is respect for personhood.

These criteria sound abstract until they are put against the real scene of the sports photos. Picture a parent returning from a Saturday match. They have ten shots of the same moment: the child running, the ball in the frame, a goal. The parent compares them. One image is sharp and shows the child's face, not merely the back of their head. Another captures the teammate's reaction, turning the moment into a social story rather than a solitary one. The rest are near-duplicates. The parent keeps two. They discard eight. The result is not loss. The result is clarity. Two images are now findable, shareable, and meaningful. Eight are now no longer a burden of indecision.

Delete the near-duplicates.

That sentence feels brutal on the page, yet it becomes surprisingly gentle in practice when it is paired with a clear logic: duplication is not devotion. A family can keep one representative photo and still honour the moment fully. The mind tends to treat deletion as erasure because the images are treated as the moment itself. The moment, of course, is not in the file. The moment is in lived experience and in the stories the family tells. The image is a cue, not the memory.

Now consider keepsakes, where the emotional charge is often stronger because the items are physical. Families tend to accumulate children's artwork, certificates, and small objects because each one feels like a fragment of a child's becoming. The problem appears years later, when boxes multiply and nobody knows what is in them. The same criteria apply, with slight translation. Representativeness becomes "does this piece stand for that phase?" Distinctiveness becomes "is this different from the other twenty drawings of the same character?" Story potential becomes "does this connect to a memory worth preserving?" Consent becomes "would the child want this kept?" Utility becomes "does this document matter for reference?" The act remains the same: compare, choose, store intentionally.

A second, checkable example helps because it shows how selection can become a cultural practice rather than a private struggle. In 2011, in Tokyo, Marie Kondo published *Jinsei ga Tokimeku Katazuke no Mahō* (later translated as *The Life-Changing Magic of Tidying Up*), bringing a Japanese approach to decluttering into global popular culture. Many people latched onto her language of joy because it gave emotional permission to let go. The book's influence has been widely documented, yet its most useful contribution to family archives is not the slogan. It is the insistence that objects should serve a life, not burden it. A family photo archive, too, should serve a life. If it becomes a source of guilt, it has stopped serving.

Still, there is a credible counter-example: some families should be cautious about aggressive discarding. In grief, for instance, a person's relationship to images can change rapidly. A photo that feels meaningless today can become precious later, because it is one of the few remaining traces of someone's presence. Families also differ in their tolerance for loss. For some, keeping more is genuinely comforting. The reconciliation is the third option that competent archivists use and families often ignore: deferral with boundaries. Deferral is not avoidance when it is structured. A family can create a small, time-boxed holding place for emotionally difficult decisions, separate from the main archive, and revisit it later with more steadiness. The archive remains usable without demanding that every decision be made immediately.

The discipline here is not deletion. It is containment. A "decide later" space, kept deliberately small, prevents the entire vault becoming a limbo. It also changes the emotional experience of curation. People become more willing to discard near-duplicates when they know that the genuinely hard items have a safe temporary home. The contact sheet motif returns: the marked selections go forward into the album; the uncertain frames do not get promoted, but they are not destroyed in haste either. The family retains agency.

The fear underlying digital hoarding is often the fear of forgetting. Psychology has long shown that memory is reconstructive rather than photographic; Frederic Bartlett made that argument forcefully in *Remembering* (1932) in Cambridge, and later research has built on the idea that context and narrative shape what we recall. Families sometimes respond to that fragility by trying to store everything, as if total capture could defeat forgetting. Yet total capture often produces the opposite: it makes retrieval harder, and so remembering happens less. A smaller, curated archive is more likely to be revisited, and revisiting is what reinforces memory. Volume is not the ally people imagine.

The vault's role is therefore not to become infinite storage. It is to become a trustworthy home for what the family truly wants to carry forward. Trust depends on findability, and findability depends on restraint. When families commit to meaning over volume, they create an archive that can be used in ordinary life: to share with grandparents, to show a child their earlier self, to build a "year in review", to anchor a story at a birthday. Those uses are the point. An archive that cannot be used is not an archive; it is a digital attic.

The shoebox returns here as a quiet warning. A shoebox is comforting because it hides mess. A digital shoebox does the same. It offers the relief of keeping without choosing. Yet the shoebox becomes heavy. It moves house after house. It gathers guilt. A family second brain can hold a shoebox, but it can also do better: it can turn the shoebox into a curated set of stories, marked like a contact sheet, chosen with care.

The forward test is not a demand for minimalism; it is a question about identity. When a family looks at its swelling archive, does it want to be the kind of household that keeps everything because deciding feels too sharp, or the kind that chooses a few representative, distinctive, story-rich artefacts and allows the rest to fall away without shame? The decision is not merely about storage. It is about whether memory will remain an accidental pile, or become an intentional inheritance that someone can actually open, search, and recognise.

Simple Photo Curation Workflows

In March 2023, the British Library in London reported it was dealing with a major cyber incident that disrupted services for months, a public reminder that digital collections—however venerable—survive through maintenance, not hope. Libraries do not merely store; they curate, catalogue, and back up, because without those disciplines a collection becomes unusable or lost. The domestic photo archive is not a national library, yet it shares one hard truth: preservation is not a single act. It is a rhythm. When the rhythm stops, the archive does not freeze. It decays into noise.

Small habits beat grand intentions.

Families tend to approach photos with the psychology of a loft clear-out. They imagine a heroic day when everything will be sorted, duplicates deleted, albums made, captions written. That day rarely arrives, because the archive grows while the family waits. A workable workflow accepts a less romantic reality: curation must be light, frequent, and slightly boring. It must fit the tired edges of life. It must also reward itself quickly, otherwise it will be abandoned like every overly ambitious organising project. The aim is not to create an art book. The aim is to keep the visual history usable—findable, shareable, meaningful—without becoming a curator by profession.

Begin with a scene that many parents recognise. A child asks to see "the photos from that trip". The parent opens the phone and begins to scroll. The trip is somewhere between a month of screenshots, a burst of school events, and three versions of the same sunset. The child loses interest before the parent finds the moment. The parent feels a particular kind of defeat: not the failure to have taken photos, but the failure to have access to them. Name what happened: retrieval collapse. Explain: when capture is effortless and organisation is absent, the cost shifts from taking to finding, and the finding cost arrives precisely when the family wants to share. The implication is that the archive becomes private, even when it is technically "saved", because it cannot be used socially in the moments that matter.

A simple photo curation workflow is therefore a retrieval system. It is designed backwards from the moment of wanting to revisit. It assumes the archive will grow and that attention will remain scarce. It focuses on three actions that families can realistically repeat: review, select, and label—lightly. The work lives in the vault not as an endless stream, but as a set of curated slices, each small enough to hold in the mind.

The first move is to set a cadence that matches how memory accumulates. Monthly works for many families because it captures ordinary life without becoming constant admin. "After major events" works for families who prefer fewer sessions: birthdays, holidays, school plays, sports tournaments. What matters is not the calendar choice but the repeatability. A workflow that is technically perfect but psychologically unlikely is a fantasy. A workflow that is slightly imperfect but repeated becomes a quiet force. The evidence here is behavioural rather than statistical: families keep what they can do when tired. They abandon what requires an idealised weekend.

Once cadence exists, review must be contained. Reviewing everything is the trap. It produces overwhelm and procrastination. Review should therefore operate with a boundary: a single month, a single event, a single folder, a single camera roll segment. Boundary turns curation from an existential task into a finite one. The mind relaxes when it knows the edges. This is why professional archives work in batches. A family can do the same, without adopting professional language.

Selection then becomes easier because it is local. Families do not need to decide the worth of their entire photographic life; they need to choose the representative images for the last month or the last event. The criteria from the previous section—representativeness, distinctiveness, story potential—become practical because they are applied to a small set. Selection can be brisk. Keep a handful. Discard the near-duplicates. The aim is to leave behind a set that can be browsed without fatigue.

Tagging, finally, should be minimal and consistent. Most families fail here because they treat tags as a tax. The trick is to make tags answer the questions the household actually asks. Who is this about? Where is this? What is this event? Sometimes, what theme does it represent—"firsts", "holiday", "school", "sport", "grandparents". A tag is a handle. Handles are not decoration; they are how an archive is carried. A small number of handles, used consistently, makes photos retrievable years later without relying on memory or scrolling.

The quiet motif running through this workflow is the contact sheet. In photography, the contact sheet is the place where abundance is tamed into selection: a grid of possibilities and a few decisive marks. A family's monthly review is a modern contact sheet ritual. It says: we see the abundance, and we choose what represents us. The act of choosing is the mark. The mark turns a stream into a story.

A Sunday session illustrates how this can become human rather than managerial. Imagine a family on a wet Sunday afternoon. The kitchen smells of toast. Rain taps the window. Someone suggests looking at photos from the past month. They cast the images to a television or gather around a tablet. At first it feels like a chore disguised as nostalgia. Then a child laughs at a picture of the dog wearing a ridiculous cone after a vet visit. A parent remembers the exact phrase the child used that day. A sibling points out a small detail an adult missed: "That was when we found the secret path." The selection happens almost incidentally, because the family is already discussing meaning. They choose five or ten photos that capture the month. They add a couple of tags—"March 2026", "school play", "park", "Nan". The session ends not with exhaustion but with a gentle warmth. The archive has been reduced and enriched at the same time.

Name what happened: social curation. Explain: when curation is shared, it becomes both memory-making and memory-preserving; the family does not merely store images but re-encounters them, strengthening recall and increasing the chance those images will be revisited. The implication is that the workflow sustains itself through reward. It is not "one more task". It becomes a form of family attention.

A second named, checkable example helps anchor why light workflows work better than heavy ones. In 1932, Frederic Bartlett published *Remembering* in Cambridge, arguing that memory is reconstructive: people build memories through repeated telling and contextual cues, not by pulling perfect records from storage. A monthly curation ritual aligns with that insight. It is not merely about organising files. It is about creating recurring cues for reconstruction—selected images, named events, small labels that make future retrieval possible. The archive becomes more human as it becomes more organised.

Yet the workflow has a credible limitation. Some families will find monthly review unrealistic, and some periods of life—new babies, illness, moves—will make any cadence collapse. The reconciliation is to design the workflow to degrade gracefully. A workflow that requires the same effort every month is brittle. A workflow that can be scaled down to a minimal session is resilient. Minimal might mean selecting only three photos from the month and tagging them with the month and the primary event. That is enough to keep the archive anchored. The family can return later when life calms. The key is that the workflow remains a habit of small selection rather than an all-or-nothing performance.

Another limitation is technological drift. Phones change. Cloud services change. Families split across devices and platforms. The reconciliation is to keep the workflow tool-agnostic in its logic. Review happens in batches. Selection produces a small set. Labels are simple. The curated output is stored in the vault in a way that is independent of any single photo app's interface. This is less about paranoia than about preserving effort. If the family has put time into selecting and tagging, that value should not be trapped in a fragile system.

The workflow also needs a boundary around perfectionism. Many intelligent people, especially those with strong professional habits, attempt to build a taxonomy of their entire life: detailed tags, nested albums, year-by-year structures. It looks impressive and fails quickly, because the cognitive overhead is too high for domestic life. The better approach is to measure friction. If tagging feels heavy, reduce tags. If selection takes too long, reduce the target number. If review feels tedious, shorten the session. The workflow should be engineered for follow-through, not theoretical elegance. A family archive is not a research database. It is a living collection meant to be revisited.

Consider the practical pay-offs in visible behaviours. When a parent can find "holiday 2024" in seconds, they share stories more often. When a child can browse "first day of school" images without scrolling for ten minutes, they ask to look back again. When grandparents receive a small monthly set rather than an overwhelming dump, they respond with attention rather than polite silence. These are measurable outcomes in the only currency that matters here: use. An archive that is used stays alive. An archive that is ignored becomes dead weight.

A subtle but important benefit follows: curation reduces the emotional volatility of algorithmic resurfacing. When a device decides what to show, it can produce delightful surprises and painful ambushes. A curated vault allows the family to choose what it revisits and when. This is not a rejection of convenience; it is an assertion of agency. The workflow ensures the family's own selected "best of" exists, rather than relying on whatever a system chooses to resurrect.

The contact sheet motif returns at the end because it clarifies the trade-off. A contact sheet contains many frames; a marked contact sheet contains a handful of chosen ones. The family cannot escape abundance. Phones will keep capturing. Children will keep being photographed. The decision is whether abundance remains unmarked—an endless shoebox—or whether the family will mark it, month by month, event by event, with small acts of selection and naming.

The forward test is simple and uncomfortable. When the next month ends, or the next birthday passes, will the family trust the fantasy of later—believing it will one day have the time and energy to sort thousands of images—or will it commit to a small, repeatable curation session that produces a curated set the family can actually find, share, and enjoy? The archive will grow either way. The question is whether it will grow into noise, or into a usable history marked, like a contact sheet, by deliberate choice.

Linking Photos To Stories

In 1988, at the University of California, Berkeley, the computer scientist Randall Munroe's future colleague—though unknown then—was already living in a world where digital files multiplied faster than meaning. That same year, the Xerox Palo Alto Research Center had a phrase for the problem they were studying in offices and homes alike: people could *store* far more than they could *retrieve*. The technological outcome was predictable—more storage, better search—but the human outcome was subtler. A file without context is a husk. A photo without a story is the same.

Words give pictures a home.

Families notice this most sharply when they stumble upon an image that should matter and yet feels oddly distant. A photograph appears: a child in a borrowed costume, a kitchen table covered in glitter, a hospital wristband, a blurred seaside horizon. The image proves that something happened, but it does not tell you what it *was*. The mind strains. Was that before the move or after? Was that the year the grandparents visited? Why was the child crying? The photograph offers a surface, and the family wants depth. This is the moment when a second brain can do what a camera cannot: restore context.

A photo is a powerful cue, but cues require labels to work across time. The human brain retrieves memories through association—place, people, emotion, narrative sequence. When those associations fade, the image becomes less of a doorway and more of a locked door with a familiar handle. Name the problem: context decay. Explain: as time passes, the associative links that make an image meaningful weaken; without a small anchor of words, the family's ability to reconstruct the story becomes patchy and biased towards whatever happens to be remembered most vividly. The implication is not merely forgetting. It is misremembering, or remembering only the broad outline without the texture that makes the memory human.

A few words can prevent that. Not many. A sentence, sometimes a phrase. A short voice note that captures the cadence of a child's excitement or the dry humour of an adult. Families often overestimate the burden of annotation because they imagine captions as mini-essays. They are not. A good annotation behaves more like a museum label than a diary entry: enough to locate the artefact in time, place, and meaning, while leaving space for interpretation.

Consider a first-day-of-school photo, the modern family's most overproduced image. The child stands at the doorway, uniform crisp, bag absurdly large, expression caught between pride and dread. The parent takes several frames. Later, those frames become part of the archive, mingling with other first days, other uniforms, other doorways. A decade on, the family looks back and struggles to separate one from another. The face is older now; the details blur. The photo becomes generic, even though the day was not.

Now add one small thing: the child's own description. It could be spoken into a phone as a ten-second voice note, or typed with help, or dictated and transcribed. "I was scared about the big playground. I liked my teacher's green earrings." That is enough. The earrings are a pin in the map. The playground fear is the emotional weather. Suddenly the photo is not merely a record of appearance. It is a record of experience. The child, older, hears their younger self and recognises a continuity of feeling: the same nervousness before new rooms, the same attention to small details. The parent hears it too and remembers what they had forgotten.

Five words can change everything.

The act of linking photos to stories is therefore an act of making memory legible. It is also an act of handing back authorship. Family archives often default to the adult's perspective because adults control devices and storage. When children contribute words, the archive becomes less like a parent's scrapbook and more like a shared history. This matters ethically as well as emotionally. Children deserve to be more than subjects of photography. They deserve to be narrators.

A named, checkable example from cultural history makes the point without sentimentality. In 1915, in New York, the photographer Lewis Hine produced images documenting child labour for the National Child Labor Committee. The photographs are powerful, but what makes them historically decisive is that they are accompanied by names, ages, locations, and brief notes. Without those words, they would still be affecting. With those words, they become evidence and story, impossible to dismiss as mere atmosphere. The family archive is not political reportage, yet it shares the same structural truth: the image alone is ambiguous; context makes it interpretable.

At home, ambiguity is not only about facts. It is also about meaning. A photo of a birthday cake might be joyful or bittersweet, depending on what happened that day. A photo of a packed car might be a holiday beginning or a move away from a beloved home. A photo of a child in a hospital corridor might represent recovery, fear, boredom, or all three. Words do not sterilise the image; they honour its complexity. They prevent the future viewer—often the child grown older—from imposing a simplistic interpretation onto a complicated moment.

The second brain makes linking practical because it supports relationships between artefacts. A photo can sit beside a note. A note can contain a link to an album. A voice recording can be attached to a date. This is not mere technical convenience; it is a philosophical shift. It treats family history as a network, not a pile. The family does not need to label everything. It needs to label the moments that will matter later, and it cannot always predict which those will be. That uncertainty is not a problem. It is a guide. It suggests a principle: annotate at moments of transition, emotion, and change.

This principle becomes visible in simple behaviours. After a first day, a family captures a child's description. After a trip, the family writes a short note: "Rained all week. Discovered the bakery on Rue des Martyrs. Dad lost the keys; we laughed for an hour." After a grandparent visit, someone records a voice note about a story the grandparent told. The annotation is not a performance for social media. It is a private act of preservation. It protects details that would otherwise be sanded down by time into a generic "we went" or "we did".

The motif here is the postcard. A photograph is like a postcard image: it shows the scene. The story is the writing on the back. Without the writing, you still have a view, but you lose why it was sent, who sent it, and what it meant. Families, in the rush of capture, often keep only the front of the postcard. Linking photos to stories restores the back. It also restores the voice, which is often the first thing to fade from memory. A child's phrasing, a parent's dry aside, a grandparent's repeated expression—these are the textures that make family history feel inhabited.

A credible limitation should be faced honestly: annotation can become another burden, another reason families feel behind. The reconciliation is to keep the unit of effort tiny and to treat annotation as selective. A family does not need to caption every meal and every playground visit. It needs to attach words to a few images that carry disproportionate future value. The selection criteria from earlier—representativeness and story potential—apply here too. A representative photo of a month, with a single sentence, can anchor dozens of unlabelled images. The archive gains structure without demanding completeness.

Another limitation is privacy. Words add sensitivity. A photo of a child in tears is one thing; a caption explaining why they were in tears can expose intimate family dynamics. A voice note can capture a child's vulnerability. The reconciliation is not to avoid stories, but to manage where they live and who can access them. The vault's shared-versus-private boundaries matter here. Some stories are for the family's inner circle. Some are for parents only. Some can be offered to the child first and shared only with their consent. This is not overcaution. It is the recognition that stories endure longer than moods, and what feels shareable in the moment may feel invasive later.

The payoff of linking is measurable in use. When a family can search for "first day" and not only see pictures but also read or hear the child's own words, the archive becomes something people return to. When a teenager can revisit a younger version of themselves and hear their voice, the archive becomes less about parental nostalgia and more about identity. When adults, in a difficult year, can find a note attached to a photo that reminds them they have survived hard transitions before, the archive becomes a support, not just a record.

There is also a quieter payoff: linking resists the flattening effect of time. Without stories, many childhood images blur into a single impression: "They were small. They smiled. Time passed." With stories, the past becomes differentiated. The child was not merely small; they were specifically worried about the playground, thrilled by a teacher's earrings, proud of a new spelling book, furious about an itchy jumper. The difference is dignity. A person deserves to be remembered in detail.

Linking also changes the present. When families know they will capture a few words, they pay attention differently. They listen for the phrase that sums up the day. They notice what the child notices. They become slightly more present, not because they are chasing mindfulness as a lifestyle, but because the act of recording context requires noticing context. The second brain, used well, does not replace attention; it trains attention.

The postcard motif returns because it keeps the practice grounded. The family does not need to build a perfect chronicle. It needs to write the back of the postcard often enough that the images remain addressable. A few words, attached consistently to selected photos, can turn a digital pile into a living archive—one that can be searched, shared, and inhabited.

The forward test is uncomfortable precisely because it is small. The next time a family takes a photograph it knows it will want to see again—a first day, a birthday, a departure, a return—will it leave the image as a silent front, trusting that future memory will supply the missing back, or will it add a sentence or a voice note while the context is still warm? The decision is not about productivity. It is about whether the family wants its archive to be a gallery of surfaces, or a collection of postcards with something written on the back.

Sharing Memories With Children

In May 2018, under the European Union's General Data Protection Regulation, a set of ideas long discussed by privacy lawyers acquired a sharp practical edge: data about a child is not merely "family business", but information with rights attached to it. The law's details can be arcane, yet its cultural message is plain enough to hear even at a kitchen table in Manchester or a flat in Glasgow. A child's image is not just a cute moment. It is a trace. It can travel. It can persist. Families began to feel, often without naming it, that the old habit of sharing everything was no longer harmless.

Children remember differently.

When adults talk about "memories", they often mean nostalgia: a soft looking-back, warm and vaguely curated by sentiment. Children, however, use memories as building material. Looking back helps them understand who they are, what they have survived, what they are capable of, and where they belong. That is why sharing memories with children is not an indulgence. It is part of how families transmit identity. It teaches continuity: you were loved then, you are loved now; you changed, and you remained yourself; you had hard moments, and you got through them.

The second brain makes this possible in a more deliberate way than the casual scroll on a phone. A casual scroll is governed by accident: whatever appears first, whatever a device chooses to resurface, whatever someone happens to remember. Deliberate sharing is governed by intention. It selects, frames, and offers context. Name the difference: intentional recall. Explain: when families choose what to revisit and how to present it, they shape the meaning children draw from the past, reducing randomness and increasing coherence. The implication is profound: the family's archive becomes not merely a store of images but a teaching tool—quiet, non-didactic, embedded in ordinary life.

One of the simplest age-appropriate forms is the curated album. Curated does not mean elaborate. It means bounded. A bounded album answers a child's question without exhausting them. Young children, especially, do not want to wade through 400 photos. They want a handful that tell the story. The child's attention works in scenes, not in data streams. A curated album for "holiday", "first days", "grandparents", "our pets", "snow", "birthday parties" gives them a set of familiar doors they can open. Each door leads somewhere comprehensible.

There is a parallel here with the way oral cultures preserved history. In many societies, story is stored not in total chronology but in memorable sequences: origin stories, seasonal rituals, family legends. The second brain can support a modern version of this without pretending to be anthropological reenactment. A themed collection functions like a family legend: "the year we moved", "the winter the boiler broke", "the summer we camped in the rain". The theme gives structure. Structure makes recall possible. Without it, a child's early years become an undifferentiated blur.

A second approach, particularly useful as children grow older, is the "year in review" note—short, concrete, and written in a style that invites recognition rather than performance. Adults often assume children do not care about such things, and then are surprised when a teenager reads it quietly and keeps it. The key is the tone. It should not sound like a press release. It should sound like a family voice. A year in review works when it combines a few photographs with a few sentences that capture what mattered: a new friend, a new school, a hobby that took over the living room, a difficult patch, a small triumph that adults might otherwise forget. Name what this produces: narrative scaffolding. Explain: children use narratives to make sense of their lives; a yearly note provides a stable frame that helps them connect events across time. The implication is that the child inherits a story of themselves that is not solely reactive—"you were always difficult" or "you were always brilliant"—but textured and fair.

The third approach is the shared ritual, and this is where the second brain becomes a living practice rather than a repository. A birthday tradition is an ideal example because it is already a cultural moment of reflection: the year turns, the child grows, the family marks time. Picture a simple ritual. On the evening before a child's birthday, or on the morning itself, the family opens a curated set from the past year. It might be twelve photos, one per month, or a small selection around a few key events. They look together. The child is invited to choose favourites and to say why. An adult adds context sparingly: "That was when you learned to ride without stabilisers," "That was the day you insisted on baking alone," "That was when we got lost and you kept calm." The child hears themselves described in terms of choices and capacities rather than mere outcomes.

The point is not to manufacture sentiment. It is to make time legible. Children live forward. They experience time as a sequence of immediate days. Ritualised looking back helps them see pattern. It also offers a rare form of attention: attention to the child as a person across time, not merely as a set of needs in the present. The second brain supports this by holding the curated set and the associated notes in a stable place, so the ritual does not depend on adult memory or the luck of an algorithmic resurfacing.

Keep it private.

That sentence is not puritanical. It is protective. The most important memories are often not the ones suited to public sharing. Families sometimes confuse sharing with valuing, as if a moment becomes real only when posted. Yet public sharing introduces a different audience and a different set of incentives: performance, approval, comparison. Children sense that shift even when adults pretend they do not. An archive designed for family intimacy has a different character. It can include awkwardness, vulnerability, and small unglamorous truths that matter deeply but do not belong in public space.

Privacy, in this context, is not merely about strangers. It is about the child's future self. A child grows into a person with preferences, boundaries, and a social life. Images and stories that feel benign to adults can become sources of embarrassment or harm later. The second brain's shared-versus-private structure becomes essential here. Some albums are for the whole family. Some are for parents. Some are for the child alone as they mature. The decision is not fixed; it evolves. The vault allows it to evolve without losing material or turning it into public content by default.

A named, checkable example clarifies why this is more than moral hand-wringing. In 2008, Facebook launched a "People You May Know" feature that accelerated the discoverability of social connections, and over time similar recommendation systems have made it easier for content—photos, tags, comments—to reach unintended audiences. The technical details shift year by year, but the pattern is stable: sharing is rarely fully controllable once it leaves the home. The implication for family memory is simple. Private sharing retains agency. Public sharing trades agency for reach.

Still, there is a credible counter-example. Some families are geographically dispersed, and public or semi-public platforms are how grandparents, aunts, and cousins stay connected. For those families, the choice is not between sharing and not sharing, but between different degrees of risk and control. The reconciliation is to separate two acts that are often entangled: sharing and archiving. A family can share selected images with relatives while keeping the richer, more contextual archive inside the vault. Sharing becomes an extract, not the source. The second brain becomes the authoritative record. What goes out is chosen and limited. What stays in is fuller and safer.

This separation matters because children need different kinds of memory at different ages. For younger children, looking back is often about sensory delight and reassurance: "That was you in the puddles." For middle childhood, it becomes about competence and belonging: "That was when you joined the club." For adolescence, it becomes about identity and autonomy: "That was when you started to change." If the archive is public-first, it is shaped by adult choices and external audiences. If the archive is home-first, it can be shaped with the child's participation, increasingly so as they grow.

Participation is the key word. When children help curate, they learn that memory is made, not merely stored. They also learn a subtle ethical lesson: images have power and should be handled thoughtfully. A child who is invited to choose which photos appear in a family album begins to understand consent as a lived practice, not an abstract rule. They learn that their preferences matter. They also learn how to respect others' preferences, because siblings quickly discover they do not always like the same images of themselves.

The second brain supports participation through design choices that make contribution easy. A child can record a short voice note about a day. A child can select a "best of" photo from an event and attach a caption. The action is concrete. It has a visible outcome: the photo appears in the curated collection, the voice note sits beside it. Name what this creates: co-authored memory. Explain: when children contribute to the archive, they experience themselves as agents in their own story, and the family gains access to the child's perspective, which is often surprising and emotionally precise. The implication is that the archive becomes truer. It captures not just what adults saw, but what children felt.

The motif in this section is the hearth. Not in a nostalgic, storybook sense, but as a practical image of where families gather to make meaning. A phone camera captures a thousand fragments scattered through the week. The hearth is where fragments become story. The second brain can act as a digital hearth: a place where the family returns, warms itself on shared recollection, and then goes back out into ordinary life. A curated album is a log on the fire. A year in review is a slow-burning piece of wood that lasts. A birthday ritual is the moment everyone gathers close.

The benefits are not merely emotional. They show up in behaviour and language. Children who have access to a usable archive ask fewer anxious questions about the past because the past is accessible. They argue less about what "really happened" because there is context and shared reference. They develop a richer vocabulary for describing their own experiences because they have practised doing so in captions and voice notes. Families become better witnesses to each other's lives.

Yet there is always a tension: the archive can become a tool of control if adults use it to police the child's narrative. "Look, you were happy then," an adult might imply, as if an image refutes a feeling. A photograph can be weaponised. The reconciliation is to treat the archive as invitation rather than evidence. Memories are offered, not used to win arguments. The second brain, for all its structure, should not become a courtroom. It should remain a hearth.

The forward test arrives quietly, and it is not about technology. The next time a family considers sharing a child's image outside the home, will it pause long enough to weigh the trade-off—reach versus agency, performance versus intimacy—and will it also offer the child a say in how they are remembered inside the home? The archive will exist regardless. The question is whether it will be a public stream shaped by default, or a private hearth where children learn, year by year, to tell their own story.

Chapter 10
Weekly Sync, Permissions, and Backups

In June 2017, A.P. Møller–Mærsk found itself rebuilding core systems after the NotPetya cyberattack, an episode that became famous not because it was dramatic—although it was—but because of a quieter detail. Reports later described how recovery hinged, in part, on an unexpected remnant: an intact piece of infrastructure in a remote office, the corporate equivalent of a spare key discovered in the bottom of an old drawer. In Copenhagen, where decisions had to be made fast, the technology story was inseparable from a human one: clarity is not what you own, it is what you can recover. The room would have sounded like urgency—phones, footsteps, the staccato of keyboards—and smelled faintly of warm plastic and overworked machines. The crisis did not create the need for a system. It revealed whether one had been maintained.

Family life rarely arrives with a headline, but it does arrive with the same physics. Plans drift. Passwords change. A child's timetable quietly shifts mid-term. A portal stops recognising a login. A phone is lost. A relative needs information on a day when nobody can think straight. A second brain can hold knowledge, memories, and intentions; it can also, if neglected, become a museum: impressive, silent, and slightly useless in the moment you actually need it. The difference between a living system and a frozen archive is not intelligence, nor even effort. It is maintenance—small, regular acts that keep the vault aligned with reality.

A weekly family sync sounds, at first, like the sort of thing competent people do in glossy productivity books. Families are right to distrust anything that smells of corporate ritual. Yet households already hold meetings; they are simply disguised as arguments in the hallway, last-minute negotiations in the car, or the exhausted exchange of information over the sink. The question is not whether families coordinate. They must. The question is whether they coordinate *deliberately*, using a shared reference, or whether they coordinate through friction and repetition, burning attention on re-deciding what was already decided.

Picture a Tuesday morning where nothing goes catastrophically wrong, but everything drags. Somebody assumed PE kit was needed. Somebody else assumed it was not. A permission slip is remembered at the moment shoes are on, which is to say too late for calm. The day begins with a tiny tax on goodwill. Multiply that by weeks and it becomes atmosphere: a household where people feel they are always "reminding", always "chasing", always slightly alone with responsibility. Name the dynamic: invisible coordination cost. Explain: when plans and reference information live in scattered heads and scattered apps, the household pays repeatedly in interruptions, micro-conflicts, and avoidable urgency. The implication is not merely inefficiency; it is erosion of trust, because repeated surprises feel, psychologically, like repeated neglect—even when nobody intended neglect at all.

A weekly sync is an attempt to move that cost out of the weekday bloodstream and into a bounded moment. Not a long moment. Not a grand summit. A short one that says: we look together, we decide together, we update the shared system together. It is the household version of checking the map before setting off, rather than arguing at every junction. When it works, it does not feel like administration. It feels like relief.

The content of such a sync matters less than its structure. Families do not need elaborate agendas; they need a predictable arc that matches how life actually unfolds. Looking back briefly prevents the week becoming a blur of half-finished threads. Looking forward surfaces constraints before they harden into emergencies. Updating boards and lists turns the second brain from one person's private coping mechanism into a shared artefact. The artefact is crucial. A family cannot "communicate better" into the void; it can only coordinate through something stable enough to point at. Without the stable thing, the most diligent communication becomes chatter.

There is, however, a moral hazard in any family review: it can become a trial. When somebody forgets, the temptation is to litigate character. Why are you always like this? Why can't you remember? Why am I the only one who cares? Those questions are understandable and corrosive. A strong system refuses them. It treats errors as signals about friction, not evidence of moral failure. If a form was missed, what in the capture flow allowed it to vanish? If a task languished, what about the checklist made it invisible or too long? If the week felt chaotic, what information was not surfaced early enough? The review is not a place to be righteous; it is a place to be accurate.

Accuracy changes tone.

A useful review identifies stale items with the cold eye of a librarian, not the hot anger of a disappointed manager. Stale does not mean shameful. It means the system contains claims about reality that are no longer true. A plan has changed. A commitment is no longer relevant. A project has drifted from "next" to "someday" without being named as such. When the vault contains too many stale promises, it becomes distrusted.

People stop checking it because it lies to them. That is how a second brain dies: not through a single failure, but through the slow accumulation of uncorrected mismatches between the system and the household's actual life.

The best families—meaning the most sustainable ones—do something unfashionable. They downgrade. They simplify. They choose fewer priorities for a week than their ambition would like, because they respect the actual bandwidth of tired humans. A weekly refresh is where that respect becomes concrete. It is where the family decides what genuinely matters in the next seven days and what can wait without guilt. The emotional payoff is subtle but real: fewer weekday surprises, fewer emergency conversations, fewer resentful reminders. The cognitive payoff is obvious: people stop carrying as much in their heads.

Then there is the other half of maintenance, the half that feels less cosy and more like plumbing: permissions, passwords, boundaries. Every family system runs, whether acknowledged or not, on access. Who can see what. Who can edit what. Who can delete what. Which information is shared by default and which is private by design. These questions become sharper as children grow. A five-year-old does not need access to everything. A fifteen-year-old who is expected to manage their own commitments, however, cannot be treated like a guest in their own household's information system.

This is where the second brain quietly becomes a training ground for autonomy. Giving a teenager access to more of the family vault is not merely a technical step; it is a relational one. It says: we trust you with shared reality. Yet trust is not the same as exposure. A family can grant access while maintaining privacy, but only if boundaries are explicit and technically supported. Otherwise, privacy becomes a constant negotiation, and negotiation becomes conflict. Families deserve better than that.

The spare key motif returns here, because access is a form of key management. A household that runs on a single person's logins—one parent who "knows where everything is"—has not built resilience; it has built a bottleneck. Bottlenecks feel efficient until the bottleneck is unavailable. Illness, travel, a dead phone, a forgotten password: the smallest disruptions can suddenly make the household helpless. A shared vault exists to reduce dependence on heroic remembering; it must not recreate the same dependence in the form of heroic access.

Still, too much sharing creates a different fragility: the fragility of blurred boundaries. Children, especially adolescents, need private space to think and to become. Adults need private space too. The aim is not a household panopticon. The aim is a shared core of reference and plans, with respectful compartments around it. The second brain supports this by allowing "parents-only" areas for sensitive documents, "child spaces" for commitments and school materials, and agreed lines about what is shared and what is not. The agreement matters as much as the tool. Without agreement, the system becomes a source of suspicion. With agreement, it becomes a source of calm.

And then, beneath everything, sits the question most families avoid until they are forced to face it: what happens when the tool breaks? A second brain is a repository of reliance. The more a family uses it, the more it becomes a single point of comfort—and, if neglected, a single point of failure. Digital resilience is not a hobby for anxious technologists. It is a basic form of care for a household that has decided to keep its important knowledge in one place.

Backups have a reputation for being boring and slightly paranoid. In truth, they are the opposite. A good backup is an expression of optimism: it assumes the family will still want these records later. It assumes the future exists and will be lived. It also recognises a reality that is neither dramatic nor rare: devices are lost, accounts are locked, services change, and human beings make mistakes. When families do not back up, they are not being carefree. They are being dependent on luck.

A story makes this concrete without melodrama. A phone slips from a pocket on a rainy day. The screen goes black. The immediate loss is inconvenience; the deeper loss arrives later, when someone realises that the photograph of a passport, the scan of a school certificate, the note with emergency contact details, the carefully curated album from a grandparent's last birthday—these were not merely "on the phone". They were the phone. The family did not just lose a device. It lost a slice of its shared memory and shared administration. Recovery, when possible, feels like a second chance. When it is not possible, the feeling is sharper than annoyance. It is bereavement for a version of the past that now cannot be retrieved.

What makes this chapter's themes urgent is not technology's novelty but technology's normality. Families now live through systems: school portals, messaging threads, cloud storage, shared calendars, authentication prompts that demand attention at the worst moments. The second brain was introduced earlier as a refuge from scatter. This chapter is the argument that refuge must be maintained. Without a weekly practice, the vault becomes stale. Without permissions and boundaries, it becomes either unsafe or unusable. Without backups, it becomes brittle. These are not separate concerns;

they are three faces of the same question: can a family build a system it can rely on without turning someone into the household's unpaid systems administrator?

The answer is not perfection. The answer is proportion. The weekly sync is proportionate because it is short and regular, rather than heroic and rare. The review is proportionate because it focuses on alignment, not blame. Permissions are proportionate because they evolve with the child, rather than being fixed by habit. Backups are proportionate because they aim for recovery, not technical elegance. A family does not need to think like an IT department. It needs to think like a family that values continuity.

The emotional centre of all of this is shared reality. Shared reality is the opposite of nagging. It is the opposite of guessing. It is the opposite of one person carrying the mental load while others remain vaguely informed. When a household has shared reality, it can disagree without chaos because it disagrees on top of a common map. When it lacks shared reality, even agreement becomes fragile because it is based on assumptions that drift unnoticed.

The hearth motif from the previous chapter has a stern cousin here: the fire drill. Not in the sense of panic, but in the sense of rehearsed competence. A weekly sync is a gentle rehearsal of coordination. A permissions check is a rehearsal of trust with boundaries. A backup is a rehearsal of recovery. Families that rehearse do not eliminate crises; they reduce the damage crises can do. They also reduce the everyday friction that makes normal life feel harder than it needs to be.

The chapter closes, not with a tidy lesson, but with a choice that sits at the heart of any shared system. Will the second brain remain a private coping strategy—something one adult maintains in the margins, resented by others as "another thing"—or will it become a shared practice with shared access, shared refresh, and a plan for recovery when reality does what reality always does? The spare key can exist. The question is whether the family will decide where it lives, who can use it, and how often they check that it still turns the lock.

Running a Weekly Family Sync

In February 2001, a small group of software developers gathered at Snowbird, Utah, and produced what became the Agile Manifesto: a short statement that helped reshape how complex work gets done under uncertainty. The conference-room details are less famous than the outcome, yet the scene is easy to imagine—paper cups, the dry hum of heating, laptops clicking as someone tries to turn half-formed frustrations into sentences that will hold. The manifesto's lasting contribution was not a new tool. It was a cadence: work reviewed regularly, plans made visible, assumptions tested before they harden into failure.

Small meetings change whole weeks.

Families are not software teams, and domestic life does not need corporate theatre. Yet the structural problem is oddly similar. A household is a small organisation that runs on invisible coordination: who is where, when; what needs doing; what must not be forgotten; what has changed since last time; what matters most *this* week rather than in some imagined ideal one. The family second brain can hold plans and reference information, but it cannot, by itself, force anyone to look. A vault becomes real only when it is *visited together*.

A weekly family sync is the moment when a household converts stored information into shared situational awareness. Picture the alternative. A parent sees a message in a school app on Tuesday lunchtime and assumes everyone else has also seen it. A teenager notices the message and assumes the adults already know. A partner is copied into an email but does not open it because the subject line looks like noise. By Friday morning, nobody can quite explain why the PE kit is missing, why a form is unsigned, why a lift was never arranged. The day is not ruined; it is merely jagged. Jaggedness has a cost. It shows up as sharp words, rushed exits, and the peculiar resentment of feeling "ambushed" by a life that is entirely predictable in retrospect.

Show a simple scene. Sunday evening, the kitchen smells faintly of washing-up liquid and warm toast; a phone vibrates on the worktop. Someone says, "What's on this week?" and, without a shared system, the room fills with guesses. Name the pattern: coordination by interrogation. Explain: when families lack a regular forum for aligning plans, they fall back on ad hoc questioning, which is cognitively expensive and emotionally charged, because questions often arrive when someone is already busy, tired, or defensive. The implication is that the second brain, even when built carefully, risks becoming one person's private coping strategy—the organised adult's hobby—rather than a household asset.

The weekly sync changes the social meaning of the system. It says, quietly, that the vault is not an archive maintained by a single conscientious keeper. It is a shared map. Shared maps reduce conflict not by making everyone agreeable, but by reducing the number of surprises that masquerade as disagreements. When people argue, they argue about priorities; that can be healthy. When they argue because their mental pictures of the week are incompatible, they are not debating priorities at all. They are colliding in fog.

The most effective syncs are short because their purpose is not exhaustive discussion. Their purpose is *alignment*. Alignment is a technical-sounding word, but in family life it has visible behaviours. People stop asking the same question twice. People stop hedging with "I thought you said..." because the system records what was decided. People stop relying on memory for information that should be externalised: times, addresses, dates, what must be brought, who has already agreed to what. The metric is not perfection. The metric is fewer weekday ambushes.

A workable agenda tends to follow the shape of human attention. First, a brief look back, not to dwell, but to notice. What actually happened last week? What slipped? What did the family underestimate—time, energy, travel? Looking back is not nostalgia here; it is calibration. Name the concept: feedback loop. Explain: feedback loops reduce error because they force a system to compare expectation with reality, then adjust. The implication is plain: without some form of weekly feedback, a family's planning becomes a fantasy in which every week is equally spacious and nobody ever gets ill, overwhelmed, or distracted.

Then, a look forward. The coming week is scanned for fixed points: school events, appointments, travel, deadlines. Not in order to control everything, but to see constraints early enough to act without panic. Constraints are not the enemy; late-noticed constraints are. A family that sees Thursday's conflict on Sunday can decide calmly whether to swap responsibilities, change a commitment, or accept a trade-off. A family that discovers it on Thursday at 7.40 a.m. is forced into improvisation, and improvisation is where resentment breeds.

Finally, the sync updates the shared system so that it remains trustworthy. Boards and lists are not decorations; they are promises. When a list contains stale items, the system starts lying. People learn not to rely on it. Trust erodes with an almost mechanical predictability. Once trust is lost, the household returns to memory and message-scrolling, and the second brain becomes another abandoned app on someone's phone.

A short example shows how this works without fanfare. A family is planning a midweek school trip that requires a packed lunch, a consent form, and a specific drop-off time. In the absence of a sync, each requirement arrives as a separate interruption: a message here, a paper slip there, a last-minute reminder shouted from the stairs. With a sync, the requirements are extracted once and placed where everyone can see them. The child knows what they must bring. The adults know who will sign, who will pack, and who will drop off. The "system" is not the technology; it is the shared agreement made visible.

The deeper point is philosophical. Families often treat organisation as a private virtue: a trait some people possess and others lack. The weekly sync reframes it as a collective practice. That matters because it shifts the moral tone. If the system lives in one person's head, every failure feels personal—someone forgot, someone didn't care, someone is unreliable. If the system is shared and reviewed, failures become diagnostic—something was not captured, not surfaced, or not made clear enough. Diagnosis invites adjustment. Blame invites defensiveness.

The history of communal practices supports this more than modern productivity culture does. In June 1935, in Akron, Ohio, Alcoholics Anonymous began with the radical premise that regular meetings—people returning to the same room to tell the truth about their week—could change lives. The movement's goals are not a template for family logistics, but its structure is instructive: complex human behaviour changes through repeated, social acts, not through lone bursts of willpower. The family sync is a domestic version of that insight, scaled down and stripped of ideology. It is not about confession. It is about reality-checking together.

And yet a credible limitation must be faced. Not every household can hold a weekly meeting at the same time, every week, in peace. Shift work breaks rhythms. Co-parenting across homes complicates shared calendars. Neurodiversity can make "meetings" feel oppressive or exhausting. Some families carry unresolved conflict that will not be cured by sitting at a table with a device between them. The reconciliation is to treat the sync as a form, not a script. The form is simple: a bounded moment of shared looking, shared deciding, shared updating. It can happen on a walk. It can happen in the car before a regular activity. It can be split into two shorter check-ins. Its success is not measured by serenity; it is measured by whether it reduces surprises and distributes knowledge more fairly.

The motif here is the forecast. A weekly sync is the household's weather report. It does not control the weather. It reduces the shock of it. When a family checks the week's forecast, it sees storms early: the double-booked evening, the tight turnaround between school and a clinic, the day when someone must work late. It also sees clear skies: the pockets of time that can hold something restorative. Forecasting changes behaviour. People pack umbrellas. They leave earlier. They do not curse the rain as if it were a moral failing.

The forecast motif also protects the sync from becoming a trial. Weather is impersonal. A forecast is not an accusation. When the family notices that Wednesday looks brutal, the tone can remain practical: "We should simplify." When someone missed a task last week, the tone can remain analytical: "What made that easy to miss?" The second brain becomes a meteorological instrument rather than a disciplinary system.

The practical shape of a sync can remain remarkably consistent across ages, while its content evolves. With young children, the week is translated into concrete anchors: which days are school days, which days include an activity, which day someone will be picked up by a friend's parent. With teenagers, the sync shifts towards negotiation and autonomy. A teenager's commitments are real constraints, not optional add-ons. Giving those commitments a place in the shared review respects them. It also makes it harder for adults to pretend they did not know—an underrated source of adolescent anger. Meanwhile, adults retain what they need to manage the household's shared obligations without creeping into surveillance.

Notice what happens when the sync is skipped for a few weeks. The forecast stops being checked. The system drifts. Small surprises return. People revert to private coping: one person starts carrying everything again, another starts disengaging, the children return to "just tell me" rather than "I'll check". Nothing catastrophic occurs. That is precisely why the drift is dangerous. Catastrophe is rare; erosion is common. The weekly sync is not an emergency measure. It is an anti-erosion practice.

The sync also produces a subtle redistribution of mental load. When the whole household participates in looking and updating, the act of remembering becomes communal. A child learns to consult the system rather than ask a parent as a default. A partner stops relying on the other partner as the human calendar. The second brain fulfils its promise: not to make life tidy, but to make shared life fairer.

There is an emotional dividend too, and it is worth naming without sentimentality. A family that can see its week together tends to argue less about logistics and more about values. That is healthier. Logistics arguments are often proxy wars in which one person feels unseen and another feels controlled. When logistics are handled in a shared, bounded ritual, the room for those proxy wars shrinks. People still disagree. They simply disagree on clearer ground.

The forecast returns one last time as a forward test. When the next week begins, will the household meet it as a series of ambushes—each message and form arriving like a gust through an open door—or will it treat the week as weather that can be read in advance, prepared for, and occasionally accepted with a shrug? The second brain can hold the map; the weekly sync decides whether anyone uses it, together, before the first raindrops hit.

Reviewing and Refreshing Plans

In January 1986, after the Challenger disaster, the Rogers Commission produced findings that were uncomfortable precisely because they were not mysterious. Richard Feynman, serving on the commission, demonstrated the effect of low temperature on the shuttle's O-ring seals with a simple, physical test—an object in a glass of ice water, a material that did not rebound as expected. The scene is almost domestic in its clarity: cold, a small experiment, a result you can see with your own eyes. The implication was brutal. Catastrophe often emerges not from one dramatic mistake but from a system that keeps accepting small mismatches between what it believes and what is true.

Families do not launch spacecraft. Yet they do run systems.

A family plan is a set of assumptions: who will do what, when, with which resources, under which constraints. The second brain holds those assumptions in visible form. Reviewing and refreshing plans is the practice of checking whether the assumptions still rebound—whether the system still behaves as expected when pressed by the reality of a new week. When that check does not happen, staleness accumulates. Staleness is not merely untidiness. It is misinformation.

A stale item is a plan that has silently expired. A list entry that no longer matters. A "next action" that nobody believes in. A project that is not dead enough to be archived yet not alive enough to be moved. Each stale element feels minor. The problem is additive. A second brain can endure a handful of stale notes; it cannot endure a culture of staleness. Trust goes first. People stop checking. Then the whole system reverts to memory, scrolling, and last-minute negotiation. The vault becomes a decorative cupboard: tidy shelves, useless keys.

A five-word sentence belongs here. Trust dies by degrees.

Reviewing and refreshing plans is therefore not an aesthetic preference; it is the maintenance of reliability. Reliability shows up in behaviour. People consult the system before asking a human. People accept its prompts. People stop keeping private duplicate lists "just in case". A family's second brain, when reliable, reduces the number of conversations required to keep life moving. That reduction is measurable, even if families do not count it. Fewer interruptions. Fewer repeated questions. Fewer frantic searches through chat threads. A calmer start to Monday.

The review begins with a deceptively simple act: clearing. Clearing means removing claims that are no longer true. A school event that has passed without being marked as done. A recurring chore list that no longer reflects who is actually home on which day. A shopping list full of items nobody wants now. Show the scene. Someone opens the family board and sees "Book dentist appointment" sitting there for six weeks, glowing with the false urgency of an overdue task. Nobody booked it. Nobody even tried. The card is not helping; it is accusing. Name the concept: cognitive noise. Explain: when the system displays unresolved items that have lost their context, it produces noise—signals that prompt guilt rather than action. The implication is predictable: people avoid the system to avoid the feeling.

Clearing is not punishment. It is the restoration of signal. When a stale item is deleted, postponed, or archived, the system becomes more honest. Honesty is the foundation of trust. The moral twist is that families often treat deletion as failure: "We didn't do it, so we shouldn't remove it." That is backwards. Keeping an untrue item is not virtuous; it is a kind of lying to the future. Better to name it accurately: "Not this week." Or "Not happening." Or "Waiting for a reply." Those labels are not mere words; they are decisions, and decisions reduce mental load.

A refresh continues with updating projects. Projects are living things. They change shape as information arrives. A holiday plan becomes a budget conversation. A school application becomes a series of document requests. A home repair becomes a chain of trade-offs between money, time, and tolerable inconvenience. The second brain can hold the moving parts, but only if someone periodically re-stitches them into a coherent picture. Without updating, projects sprawl. They become a scatter of notes—one in email, one in messages, one as a vague intention that floats between adults like a damp cloud.

Show a concrete example. A family wants to "sort the garden". The phrase sits in the system as a single task for months. It never happens. Why? Because it is not a task. It is a project disguised as a task. It contains sub-decisions: what counts as "sorted", what budget exists, who has time, which tools are needed, whether to prioritise safety, aesthetics, or low maintenance. During the refresh, the family turns the vague phrase into a smaller truth: "Book a green waste collection", "Measure space for a shed", "Agree planting plan". Name the move: decomposition. Explain: decomposing a project turns ambiguous work into specific actions that can be completed, and completed actions restore a sense of momentum. The implication is psychological as much as practical: families stop interpreting non-progress as laziness and start interpreting it as a clarity problem.

The most delicate part of a refresh is deciding what truly matters this week. Not what matters in a perfect life. Not what matters in a version of the household that sleeps eight hours and never gets ill. What matters in the week that is actually coming, with its known constraints and likely fatigue. This is where the review either becomes a calm calibration or a scolding session. A scolding session happens when someone uses the review to perform moral superiority: "You didn't do this." "You always forget." "I'm the only one who cares." It feels satisfying in the moment and poisonous afterwards. The antidote is to focus on the system.

Systems can be changed without humiliating anyone.

Consider a missed task: packing a child's swimming kit for Monday. Show the two versions. In the scolding version, the adult says, "You forgot again," and the conversation collapses into identity: one person defending, one person prosecuting, the child absorbing tension. In the systems version, the adult says, "Our leaving-the-house checklist didn't include swimming, and Monday mornings are too rushed for memory." The difference is not politeness; it is causality. The systems version points to an adjust-able object: a checklist, a routine, a reminder placed where it will be seen. Name what changes: attribution. Explain: when families attribute failure to personal traits, they trigger defensiveness and shame; when they attribute failure to friction in the system, they trigger problem-solving. The implication is a more resilient household, because resilience depends on adaptation rather than blame.

This is not naïve. Personal responsibility remains real. People still choose. Yet systems shape choices by shaping the environment in which choices are made. A household that pretends systems do not matter ends up relying on willpower. Willpower is a scarce resource, particularly at 7.15 a.m. on a wet Monday. A household that accepts systems matter uses design instead: checklists, shared notes, visible boards, clear ownership, and small routines that reduce decision fatigue.

A second named, checkable example strengthens the argument. In aviation, the routine use of checklists became famously associated with safety after the 1935 crash of the Boeing Model 299 during a U.S. Army evaluation flight at Wright Field in Dayton, Ohio; the aircraft was too complex for one pilot to reliably manage from memory, and the response was not to demand superhuman pilots but to formalise procedure. The family context is smaller, but the principle holds. Complexity outgrows memory. Procedure is not bureaucracy; it is protection. The implication for a weekly refresh is direct: the aim is not to become "more disciplined". The aim is to move critical steps out of fragile memory and into reliable prompts.

Still, there is a counter-example worth respecting. Some families fear that too much planning and reviewing will sterilise spontaneity, turning life into a spreadsheet. This fear is not silly. A hyper-managed household can become joyless, especially for children who already feel monitored by school and technology. The reconciliation is to notice that staleness and chaos are also anti-spontaneity. When a household is constantly firefighting, it has little room for unplanned pleasures. A well-run refresh does not fill the week; it clears space within it. It removes avoidable friction so that spontaneity becomes possible without collateral damage.

The refresh also has an ethical dimension as children mature. Who gets to decide what matters this week? In many families, adults assume that children's needs are self-evident, and children assume adults' plans are arbitrary impositions. A shared review can surface both sides without turning the conversation into a debate club. The child's school project has a deadline; that is a constraint. The adult's work travel matters; that is a constraint. The family's desire for a quiet evening matters too. The review is where constraints are seen early and trade-offs are made deliberately. Deliberate trade-offs feel fairer, even when nobody gets everything they want.

The motif for this subchapter is the compass. A compass does not tell you how fast to walk or whether it will rain. It tells you whether you are drifting. Plans drift in subtle ways. A single added commitment nudges bedtime later. A broken appliance steals an evening. A forgotten form triggers a morning scramble. Each drift is small. Over weeks, drift becomes a new normal that nobody chose. The weekly refresh is the moment the family checks its compass: are we heading where we intended, or have we been carried off-course by accumulated small events?

Checking the compass requires choosing what not to carry. This is where families often hesitate, because removing items can feel like lowering standards. Yet standards are not measured by the length of a task list. They are measured by the proportion of commitments that are honoured. A short list completed is a higher standard than a long list abandoned. A refresh that cuts the list is not giving up; it is restoring credibility. Credibility is a gift to the future week. When Tuesday arrives and the system shows only a handful of priorities, those priorities carry weight. When it shows twenty, it carries none.

A refresh also tests the balance between planning and reality. Some weeks are simply too full. The system's job is to make that visible early enough to choose an approach: simplify meals, reduce optional commitments, accept a messier house, outsource a task if possible, or postpone a project. None of this is advice in the sense of prescribing decisions; it is an observation about how families sustain themselves: they survive by making trade-offs explicit rather than pretending they are not needed.

The most common reason refreshes fail is emotional, not technical. People associate review with judgement. They enter the conversation braced for blame. That brace makes even neutral comments feel like criticism. A wise family sync therefore protects tone by making the review about objects in the system, not about the people in the room. The language matters. "This task didn't get done" is different from "you didn't do this". "Our checklist didn't catch that" is different from "you forgot". The first set invites adjustment. The second invites defence.

There is also a subtle point about memory and identity. Adults sometimes cling to forgotten tasks as evidence of their own virtue: "Look how much I'm trying." Children sometimes cling to unfinished tasks as evidence of unfairness: "You always expect too much." A refresh that calmly removes stale items denies both performances. It insists on a harder standard: reality. Reality can feel unsentimental. It is also freeing. It allows the family to stop auditioning for moral roles—martyr, rebel, perfectionist—and start acting like collaborators navigating a shared life.

The compass returns as a forward test. When the next week begins, and the inevitable surprise arrives—a changed school schedule, a forgotten message, a burst of tiredness that makes everything slower—will the family treat the second brain as a trustworthy compass and adjust course together, or will it treat the system as an ornament and return to the old method: improvisation, accusation, and private resentment? The refresh is not the week. It is the moment that decides whether the week will be steered or merely survived.

Managing Permissions and Boundaries

On 25 May 2018, the European Union's General Data Protection Regulation (GDPR) took effect, and inboxes across London filled with privacy notices from organisations suddenly keen to announce what they knew, what they kept, and what they claimed to control. The morning had an oddly domestic texture: the ping of new emails, the blue light of a phone on a kitchen counter, the faint smell of coffee turning bitter as it cooled. A law designed for states and corporations arrived, as such things do, in ordinary homes—where most people were not thinking about "data governance" at all, but about school messages, family photos, passwords nobody could remember, and the uneasy sense that too much of life now sat behind a login.

Access is a kind of power.

In a family second brain, permissions and boundaries are where power becomes visible. The vault works because it is trusted, and trust is not a warm feeling; it is a practical judgement about what will happen when someone opens the door. Who can see the emergency contacts? Who can edit the travel plan? Who can delete a document that matters? Who can browse old notes that were never intended as family reading? These questions are not technical footnotes. They decide whether the system feels safe enough to use, and safe enough to share.

A familiar scene shows why this gets tense as children grow. A teenager asks for access to the family vault because they are tired of being told "It's in the notes somewhere." They are also, quietly, tired of being treated like a guest in their own life. A parent hesitates, not because they relish control, but because the vault contains more than logistics: saved scans, sensitive correspondence, perhaps a note written in a private moment that was never meant to become communal artefact. The teenager hears hesitation as mistrust. The parent hears the request as a demand for full disclosure. A week later, the teenager starts their own system—screenshots, private lists, a separate calendar—because they need autonomy. Name the concept: shadow systems. Explain: when access is unclear or feels unfair, people build parallel systems outside the shared one, which increases confusion and erodes the very clarity the second brain exists to provide. The implication is paradoxical:

over-protection of the vault can make the household less safe and less organised, because information fragments into places nobody can reliably search.

Permissions are easiest to think about as doors. Doors are not insults. They are architecture. A front door does not mean the household distrusts its neighbours; it means the household recognises that some spaces are shared and some are not. In digital systems, the same principle applies, but the materials are strange. A child can copy a document in seconds. A partner can forward a screenshot without malice, just convenience. A mis-tap can delete something important. The door metaphor matters because it forces an uncomfortable clarity: boundaries exist even in loving homes, and pretending otherwise does not remove them—it merely leaves them to be enforced through awkward confrontations.

Show the practical behaviour that "boundary" becomes. A family uses a shared login for a notes app because it is simple. Everything appears everywhere. The parent who set it up feels relief: one password, one place. Then a phone is lost, or a child signs into a school computer and forgets to log out. The shared account becomes a single point of exposure. Name the concept: risk concentration. Explain: when multiple people share one identity, access cannot be limited or audited, and any compromise affects everyone at once; convenience is purchased by bundling risk. The implication is not panic but design pressure: a mature shared system cannot rely indefinitely on the shortcuts that work when children are small and the vault is thin.

This is where families benefit from thinking like librarians rather than like referees. A referee watches for wrongdoing. A librarian designs access so that most people can do what they need without needing special permission each time. In practice, that means distinguishing between kinds of material. Some information is truly communal: schedules, lists, home reference notes, family projects. Some is semi-communal: things one adult needs but others occasionally reference, such as insurance documents or appliance warranties. Some is private: journals, personal correspondence, notes written to think rather than to share. The boundary problem is not solved by pretending everything is either "secret" or "public". It is solved by creating gradations that match how the household actually lives.

A second checkable example helps anchor why gradations matter beyond the home. In March 2018, the Cambridge Analytica scandal broke into public view, centred on how data gathered through Facebook was used in political advertising, with major reporting in the United Kingdom and the United States. The details were debated, but the structural lesson was plain enough to verify: when data moves across boundaries without clear consent, trust collapses, and the people affected often discover it late. The household version is smaller, but the moral mechanics are recognisable. When a teenager discovers that parents have been reading notes they assumed were theirs, the injury is not only privacy; it is betrayal. The implication is sharp: a family vault that ignores consent will eventually destroy the conditions for sharing, even if nobody intends harm.

At this point, a credible limitation deserves respect. Some families hear "permissions" and imagine bureaucracy: endless configuration, fragile rules, constant policing. They are not wrong to worry. Over-complicated access control can make the system unusable, especially for tired adults and younger children. If using the vault starts to feel like applying for a licence, people will stop. And when people stop, the system fails in silence. Reconcile it honestly. Boundaries are not meant to add friction everywhere; they are meant to remove friction where it hurts. The aim is not maximal security. The aim is *appropriate* security—enough to protect dignity and reduce avoidable risk, without making daily life heavier.

A useful way to keep "appropriate" from becoming vague is to pair it with visible decisions. Who can view? Who can edit? Who can delete? Those are not theoretical questions. They can be answered by choosing simple roles that match real behaviour: some spaces are read-only for most people because accidental edits create mess; some spaces are editable because shared plans must evolve; some spaces are hidden because privacy is not negotiable. Even without naming any particular software, these roles exist as patterns. The family is designing not only a vault, but a set of social expectations.

This is why passwords belong in the conversation, even if nobody enjoys talking about them. Passwords are not merely technical strings; they are permission tokens. When everyone uses the same password, the household is effectively saying, "We are one person." That may feel cosy when children are young. It becomes distorted as children become individuals with legitimate private lives. Conversely, when everyone uses separate accounts with no shared access, the household is saying, "We are strangers." That is equally distorted. A functioning family vault sits between those extremes: a shared space whose access is intentional, surrounded by private spaces whose privacy is respected.

Consider the teenager again, now older—fourteen or fifteen, old enough to travel independently to school, old enough to manage their own commitments, old enough to feel humiliation sharply. They ask for access to the "in case of" bundle, the travel planning area, and their own school notes, because those things affect them directly. They do not ask for access to a parent's private notes. The parent's first impulse might be to grant access broadly, as a sign of trust, or to restrict access tightly, as a sign of caution. Both impulses can misfire. Show the better scene. The parent treats access as a staged handover, like giving someone a key to the house and explaining which doors it opens. The teenager gains access to the shared areas that support autonomy: their timetable, activity commitments, travel documents, and family plans that require their participation. The teenager also gains a space of their own within the system—an area that is theirs to organise, not as a toy, but as a genuine workspace. Name the concept: graduated autonomy. Explain: autonomy is learned through meaningful responsibility, and responsibility requires access; granting access in stages acknowledges growth while preserving boundaries that protect everyone. The implication is cultural: the vault becomes a training ground for adulthood, not a mechanism of parental oversight.

The word "oversight" is loaded, and rightly. Families often confuse two different acts: enabling and monitoring. Enabling means giving someone what they need to act competently. Monitoring means watching them to control behaviour. A second brain can serve enabling beautifully; it can also become a monitoring trap if parents use it as a window into children's private lives. The difference is not in the tool. It is in the agreement. Agreement must be explicit, because implicit agreements are where betrayal breeds. A teenager's privacy is not a reward for obedience; it is part of their emerging personhood. A parent's need for visibility into certain shared obligations is not tyranny; it is part of keeping the household running. The vault can hold both truths, but only if boundaries are treated as mutual, not unilateral.

The motif returns. Keys can be copied. That is the peculiarity of digital life: a key is not a piece of metal that stays in one pocket; it is information that can be duplicated, forwarded, guessed, or stolen. This changes the ethics of access. In a physical home, a child borrowing a key is obvious. In a digital home, access can expand invisibly. This is why clarity matters more than cleverness. Families do not need intricate rules. They need a shared understanding of what belongs where and who is meant to be able to see it.

That understanding shows up in small habits. A parent writes a note for themselves about a difficult conversation with a school, and places it in a private area rather than in the general school folder. That is not secrecy; it is respect for context. A teenager saves a personal reflection in their own space and does not worry that it will become family reading. That is not rebellion; it is safety. A partner stores a copy of a passport scan in the travel area so that anyone can access it when packing, rather than keeping it in a private folder that becomes a bottleneck. That is not oversharing; it is collaboration. Each choice is a boundary act. Each boundary act protects the system's trust.

Trust, again, is measurable through behaviour. When trust exists, people stop asking, "Do you have that?" and start asking, "Is it in the vault?" When trust exists, children check for themselves. When trust exists, adults stop keeping redundant private backups out of fear. When trust exists, mistakes become rare and recoverable rather than frequent and corrosive. The permission model is not a technical subchapter; it is the operating system of trust.

There is also a long-term question hidden inside permissions: what happens when a child leaves home? The family vault may contain the child's medical history, educational records, and a decade of photos. Some of that will remain relevant to the family as a whole; some of it properly belongs to the emerging adult. Families who treat the vault as parental property stumble here. Families who treat the vault as shared heritage handle it with more grace. The difference is philosophical: is the second brain a tool of household management, or a shared archive of a shared life? The answer affects how permissions are designed from the start.

A final tension sharpens the whole topic. Too much openness can feel unsafe; too much restriction can feel infantilising. Both can push people into shadow systems, secrecy, or conflict. The vault is meant to reduce those outcomes, not provoke them. The forward test is therefore a diagnostic one. When someone in the household hesitates to use the system—when they choose a screenshot, a private note, a whispered reminder instead—what are they protecting? Is it privacy that deserves a boundary, or is it mistrust created by unclear boundaries? The family second brain cannot answer that question alone. But it can make the question visible, and it can hold the agreements that turn keys and doors from sources of anxiety into quiet architecture for a life shared, and a life respected.

Backups and Digital Resilience

On 1 July 2013, Google shut down Google Reader, ending a service that had quietly organised the reading lives of millions from its home in Mountain View, California. The outcome was not merely annoyance; it was amputation. People discovered, in a single morning, that a well-loved tool could vanish on a corporate timetable, and that "my information" often means "my information as long as someone else's business model continues to support it". That lesson has not aged out. It has matured. A family second brain is more intimate than an RSS reader, but it is built on the same modern bargain: continuity depends on technologies and organisations whose priorities are not the household's priorities.

Resilience matters.

A second brain earns trust by being there when needed: the school letter, the travel document, the address, the password hint that stops an evening collapsing into irritation. That trust can be destroyed quickly if the system becomes fragile—if one lost phone, one locked account, one discontinued app turns a shared vault into a sealed box. The aim of backups is not perfection. The aim is continuity under ordinary misfortune. It is the difference between a system that supports family life and a system that becomes another source of stress.

Start with a scene that families recognise. A parent realises, at the end of a long day, that their phone is missing. Perhaps it slipped between car seats. Perhaps it fell from a coat pocket at the supermarket. The first emotional wave is not philosophical. It is practical: photos, messages, school apps, the note with the swimming timetable, the login that was never written down because "it's saved on the phone". The second wave is sharper: the second brain lives in that device, or at least the pathway to it does. The household's carefully built clarity suddenly feels like it was written on a single piece of paper in the rain. Name the concept: single point of failure. Explain: when a system depends on one device, one account, or one person's memory, it can collapse under a predictable, common mishap. The implication is simple and slightly unsettling: organisation without resilience is an illusion.

Backups are often misunderstood as a purely technical chore, something performed by enthusiasts with spare weekends and colour-coded cables. In reality, backups are a social promise. They say: "This matters enough to protect." The family vault contains two kinds of material, and they demand different kinds of protection. Some items are irreplaceable: photographs, recordings, letters, notes that capture family history. Some items are replaceable but costly: scans of documents, appliance manuals, school policies, receipts, booking confirmations. Both can be lost, and the cost of loss is not equal. A resilient system begins by noticing that difference, because resilience is not about copying everything everywhere; it is about protecting what cannot be reconstructed, and making the reconstructable easy to reconstruct.

A five-word sentence belongs early. Copy what you cannot replace.

This is where the metaphor of the lifeboat earns its keep. A lifeboat is not the ship. It is not comfortable. It is not where anyone wants to live. It exists for the moment when the ship is compromised and there is still a future worth reaching. Backups are the lifeboat of the second brain. They are not meant to be beautiful. They are meant to be dependable. If the vault is the place everyone consults, the backup is the place nobody wants to consult—until the day it is needed, when it must work without drama.

The best-known lifeboat principle in computing is the "3-2-1" idea: multiple copies, stored on different media, with at least one copy off-site. The virtue of the principle is not the arithmetic; it is the insistence on independence. Copies that share a failure mode are not truly copies. If everything lives in one cloud account, a locked account can take everything at once. If everything lives on one laptop, a stolen bag can remove everything at once. Independence is what turns "I saved it" into "I can recover it".

Show how this plays out in ordinary family decisions. A household keeps its second brain in a notes tool that syncs across phones and laptops. That feels like safety because the information appears in multiple places. Yet "sync" is not the same as "backup". Sync is a mirror. A mirror faithfully reflects mistakes. Delete the wrong folder, and the deletion can propagate. Corrupt a file, and the corruption can propagate. Lose access to the account, and every device becomes a locked door. Name the concept: propagation risk. Explain: systems designed for convenience can spread errors quickly across all connected devices, which means redundancy without independence does not guarantee recovery. The implication is uncomfortable but empowering: resilience requires at least one copy that does not automatically follow every change.

The word "export" becomes important here, because export is one of the few actions that makes data portable. Export turns the living, interactive system into a snapshot that can be stored elsewhere. It is the family's equivalent of printing out a passport copy before travel—except the "paper" is a file that can be read later, ideally without needing the original service. A household second brain typically includes notes, attachments, images, and links. Exporting must therefore be judged not only by whether the content is captured, but by whether its meaning survives outside the tool. A note may export as plain text, losing tags and links. A task board may export as a table, losing its visual flow. A photo library may export images but lose albums. Each loss is not catastrophic, but each shapes what recovery will feel like under stress.

A second checkable example helps because it shows that loss of meaning through obsolescence is not theoretical. The BBC Domesday Project, created in 1986 in the United Kingdom to mark nine hundred years since the original Domesday Book, stored contributions from schools and communities on LaserDisc, a format that became difficult to access within a couple of decades as hardware and software changed. The project is now famous not because it failed artistically, but because it revealed a hard truth: digital information can become unreadable long before it is forgotten. Name the concept: format fragility. Explain: digital preservation depends on formats and readers; when formats fall out of use, the effort required to retrieve information can become disproportionate. The implication for families is direct: the second brain should, when possible, keep at least some crucial material in widely readable forms—text that can be opened by many programmes, images in common formats, documents that do not depend on a single proprietary viewer.

And yet, the family second brain is not a museum. It is a working system. The question is not whether to preserve everything forever in some archival purity, but how to design a reasonable path back to functionality after a disruption. That path has layers. The first layer is account resilience: passwords that are recoverable, recovery email addresses that still exist, second-factor authentication methods that are not tied to a single lost device. The second layer is device resilience: information accessible from more than one device, not just cached on one phone. The third layer is data resilience: exports or copies stored somewhere independent. Each layer reduces the probability that a mishap becomes a crisis.

The story of recovery makes the value legible. After the lost phone, a parent sits at a laptop late at night, not in heroic mode but in a quiet, anxious concentration. They log into the shared vault from a browser. They cannot remember one of the passwords because the phone used to fill it in. The password manager, thankfully, is accessible from the laptop—because it was not only on the phone. They reset the password using a recovery email that is still monitored, rather than an old address abandoned years ago. They download a recent export of key documents—the "in case of" bundle, travel scans, school contacts—from a cloud folder that is not the same account as the notes tool. They breathe again. The household's clarity survives not because the parent is clever, but because the system had a lifeboat and the lifeboat was reachable.

Name what is often missed: the distinction between backing up "data" and backing up "capability". Data is the content. Capability is the ability to act: to log in, to find, to recover, to continue. Families sometimes copy files obsessively while ignoring capability. They save documents but forget where the passwords live. They export notes but do not test whether they can be opened. They store a backup on an external drive that nobody can locate when needed. The implication is blunt. A backup that cannot be used is theatre.

This is where modest discipline has outsized returns, and it need not become a second job. In professional IT, resilience is often discussed through "recovery time" and "recovery point": how long it takes to restore, and how much recent information can be lost without serious harm. Families can think in the same way without adopting professional jargon as a lifestyle. How long can the household tolerate being without the vault? An hour, perhaps. A day. A week would be painful. How much recent information can be lost? Losing a month of curated photos might feel like grief. Losing a week of shopping lists is trivial. These are not moral judgements; they are prioritisation. They guide which parts of the second brain merit frequent snapshots and which can rely on the tool's built-in sync.

A credible limitation deserves a full, honest paragraph because resilience has trade-offs. Backups increase the number of copies of sensitive information. More copies can mean more exposure if storage is careless. A family that exports medical summaries, identity documents, or personal notes without thinking about where those exports sit may reduce one risk while increasing another. Name the concept: risk transfer. Explain: resilience mechanisms can move risk from one domain to another—availability becomes stronger while confidentiality becomes weaker if backups are poorly protected. The implication is not fear but sobriety: families should treat backups as part of their privacy boundary design, not separate from it. A lifeboat should not be left unlocked on the dock.

Another limitation is structural. Some tools do not export cleanly. Some export formats are awkward. Some vendors offer only partial extraction, making the household dependent on continued access. And sometimes the family's system is a messy blend of services: photos in one place, documents in another, tasks in a third. Digital life is rarely neat. The reconciliation is to accept that resilience will also be imperfect. The goal is not a single elegant backup solution. The goal is a reasonable safety net for the materials that matter most, and a tested path back to access.

Testing is the quiet hero here. A lifeboat that has never touched water is a prop. A family that occasionally tries to open an export, tries to log in from a second device, tries to locate the "in case of" folder without the usual phone, is not being paranoid. It is being realistic. These are small, controlled rehearsals that prevent a real emergency from becoming an information disaster. The second brain's promise is reduced friction; resilience rehearsals protect that promise.

Resilience also includes the possibility that a tool disappears without warning, or changes in ways that make it less suitable. This is not cynicism; it is observing how software evolves. Pricing shifts. Features move behind paywalls. Companies merge. Services sunset. The point is not to distrust every provider, but to design for eventual change. Portability is the household's insurance policy. When the vault's structure is clear—consistent naming, sensible tags, documents stored in common formats—migration becomes possible. When the vault is a tangle of proprietary features, migration becomes an ordeal. The hidden implication is almost philosophical: good organisation is not only about present-day retrieval; it is also about future freedom.

The lifeboat motif returns for the last time with a forward-facing test. The family second brain will grow. It will contain more memories, more plans, more evidence of a life lived with attention. That growth increases both its value and its vulnerability. A resilient system does not ask, "How do we stop bad things happening?" It asks, "When something ordinary goes wrong, do we still have continuity?" The diagnostic question is therefore simple enough to sit in the mind without ceremony: if the primary tool vanished tomorrow, could the household recover what matters—photos that cannot be retaken, documents that take hours to replace, the small strands of context that stop a stressful week from unravelling—or would the second brain reveal itself as a single ship with no lifeboat at all?

About the Author

Arian Velkor cares deeply about how ordinary families live with technology. For years he has listened to parents, carers, and partners describe the quiet chaos of forms, passwords, photos, and plans that never quite make it out of one person's head. His work grows from those conversations and from his own experience juggling work, parenting, and caring responsibilities across generations.

Raised in a home where a single kitchen drawer held everything from recipes to birth certificates, Arian learned early how much a household depends on shared memory. He now translates that very human, paper-based instinct into the digital age, favouring simple, durable systems over flashy tools. His writing is practical, warm, and firmly on the side of tired adults who want things to work without needing a new personality.

Drawing on ideas from information design, behaviour change, and family systems, Arian specialises in making invisible work visible and shareable. He believes children deserve to grow up in homes where they can find what they need, contribute to shared plans, and learn healthy digital habits by example. This book is his invitation to families everywhere to replace heroic remembering with gentle, shared clarity.

9 789376 551866

Printed at Repro India Ltd.